SOCIAL PORTRAIT

OF EUROPE

DÉPÔT
DEPOSIT

September 1998

eurostat

A great deal of additional information on the European Union is available on the Internet.
It can be accessed through the Europa server (http://europa.eu.int).

Cataloguing data can be found at the end of this publication.

Luxembourg: Office for Official Publications of the European Communities, 1998

ISBN 92-827-9093-2

Printed in Belgium

Symbols and abbreviations

*	provisional or estimated data
:	not available
-	nil
.	not applicable or data not statistically significant
0	less than half the unit used

EU-15	European Union of Fifteen
EU-12	European Community of Twelve (without A, FIN, S)
EUR-11	Participating countries in the EURO (B, D, E, F, IRL, I, L, NL, A, P, FIN)
B	Belgium
DK	Denmark
D	Germany
EL	Greece
E	Spain
F	France
IRL	Ireland
I	Italy
L	Luxembourg
NL	Netherlands
A	Austria
P	Portugal
FIN	Finland
S	Sweden
UK	United Kingdom

SOCIAL PORTRAIT OF EUROPE

eurostat

Contents

Page

EUROSTAT

Directorate E - Director Lidia Barreiros

Editors: Catherine Blum and Peter Whitten
Tel: 4301 33274 / 33012
Internet: peter.whitten@eurostat.cec.be

Foreword

The European Union is currently undergoing profound change in numerous economic and financial spheres. This comes at a time when the provisions of the Treaty of Amsterdam and the outcome of the special Employment Summit are strengthening EU social policy. The essence of the policy challenge is to combine the individual's need for security with society's demands for mobility and adaptability. This third edition of the Social Portrait of Europe is therefore a welcome and timely addition to the development of the awareness of Social Europe.

Almost all Member States experienced economic recession in the early 1990s. Thus, the economic and social background to the Portrait is one of stagnant or falling employment levels and increasing unemployment rates in some countries. Simultaneously, a more flexible Labour Market is developing. With respect to GDP per head, gaps between EU-15 countries have narrowed between 1990 and 1996.

Education and training are well recognised as key elements in the fight against unemployment. Participation rates in post-compulsory education and training have increased significantly over the past 2 decades. Furthermore, the concept of life-long learning, particularly prevalent in the Nordic countries, is becoming increasingly common throughout the EU-15.

Equal opportunities for women and men remain an important issue in the Union. Although the gender gap in education participation has largely disappeared in most countries, unemployment rates for women are in general higher than those for males. Women also predominate in part-time work and hold low-status positions.

The increase in life expectancy reflects the relatively high welfare standards reached throughout the Union. This phenomenon coupled with the drop in fertility over the last thirty years means that European societies are ageing: less children, more elderly people with all the resulting implications for as health care, pension funding and the Welfare State in general.

The modernisation of the Welfare State is under way in almost all countries. The sources of social contributions still vary greatly between Member States with some basing their contributions primarily on wages while others finance their welfare systems mainly through taxes levied on overall incomes.

With one or two exceptions, salaries and incomes tend to be more evenly distributed among the population in the more prosperous Member States. In those countries where income lags behind the Community average, inequality in income distribution is generally more evident.

The ten chapters of this Social Portrait of Europe follow a common format. Each begins with a general outline of the content. Where relevant, major initiatives undertaken at Community level as well as definitions, sources, methodological explanations and other relevant points are outlined in boxes.

This book is very much the product of the collective work of Eurostat's Population and Social Statistics Directorate and I would like to thank all those individuals and teams that assisted in its production and particularly Catherine Blum who was responsible for the project.

Yves Franchet

Lídia Barreiros

Economic background

Recession in the early 90s

Recession, deterioration of the labour market and slowdown of house-hold consumption affected almost all Member States in the early 90s and employment has become a common concern (see box p. 4). Today, growth is back in a non-inflationary context.

At the same time, social protection expenditure as a percentage of total EU GDP has continued on an upward trend because of an increase in health care expenditure, unemployment benefits and retirement pensions. However, the slowdown of GDP growth is at the root of the sharp rise of the ratio during the first years of this decade.

During this period, the share of revenue from employers' social contributions decreased nearly everywhere. Furthermore, there is evidence of some shift in the funding of social expenditure, from contributions based on employees' wages and salaries to other sources more closely related to total income.

With respect to GDP and private consumption per head, gaps between EU-15 countries have narrowed between 1990 and 1996. However regional disparities have globally remained the same.

This is in brief the macro economic background of the Social Portrait of Europe.

— For EU-15 the GDP growth rate in real terms was 1.5% per year between 1991 and 1995 compared with 3.3% between 1986 and 1990.
— The employment (full-time equivalent) rate decreased from 57.6% of people aged 15-64 in 1990 to 55% in 1996 in EU-15 as a whole.
— The ratio social protection / GDP reached 28.4% in 1995, 4 percentage points more than in 1980. It ranged from 20% in Ireland to 35.6% in Sweden in 1995; United Kingdom and Germany were close to the EU average.
— In most Member States, old age/survivor benefits made up the largest share of social benefits in 1995: 44% on average for EU-15. In Ireland, the Netherlands, Portugal and Finland, on the other hand, sickness/disability benefits accounted for the major part of total social bene-

fits. Unemployment benefits and family/child allowances came third and fourth respectively with 8.4% and 7.6% in EU-15 as a whole.

The renewal of European social policy : a solid foundation on which to build

In 1993, the Commission launched a wide-ranging consultation on the future of European social policy. The purpose of this exercise – which was driven forward by the Green and White Papers on Social Policy in 1993 and 1994 – was to develop a blueprint for the renewal of social policy in a period of dynamic change. This in turn led to the medium-term Social Action Programme 1995-1997, which sought to develop a more broadly-based, innovative and forward-looking approach to European social policy.

This approach has evolved further over the past few years and has borne fruit.

Employment policy has moved decisively to the top of the European agenda. The new employment title in the Treaty of Amsterdam makes employment a matter of common concern. The Luxembourg Jobs Summit followed by the adoption of the 1998 Employment Guidelines and the submission of national employment action plans has brought forward the co-ordination of Member States' employment policies through the development of an integrated employment strategy.

A number of key legislative proposals have been adopted by the Council, helping to complete and consolidate the framework of minimum social standards needed to underpin the Single Market.

A set of detailed and ambitious work programmes has been adopted by the Commission. These policy initiatives – for example the Action Plan for free movement of workers and the Green Paper on work organisation – provide the building blocks for the ongoing renewal of social policy.

The social policy debate has been extended to areas of mutual concern – such as demographic trends, modernising social protection and the fight against racism.

Dialogue with the social partners has produced significant results, helping to reinforce the legitimacy and effectiveness of European- level activity.

The links between social policy and other Community policies have been strengthened, reflecting the conviction that social progress must be promoted across the board. Examples of this are the commitment in mainstreaming equality of opportunities between women and men, the integration of health protection requirements into other community policies, and the 1997 Communication on environment and employment.
Source: Abstract from "Social Action Programme 1998 — 2000". Communication from the Commission — Brussels, 29/4/1998 COM(1998) — 259 final

Sources

This chapter is based on the following documents:
- "The economic accounts of the European Union 1996" European Commission — Eurostat — Statistics Europe
- "EC Economic data Pocket Book" — n° 314/98 – European Commission — Eurostat — DG II.
- Spring 1998 — Economic Forecasts" — Commission services.
- Social Protection expenditure and receipts , 1980 — 1995". — Eurostat — Directorate E — Unit E 2. ,

Recession affected living conditions in the early 1990s

....

It is agreed that rapid growth of Gross Domestic Product (GDP) brings with it an improvement in employment, in services and more generally in households' living conditions. At the same time, it is recognised that, by reason of its construction, the GDP indicator (national or regional) does not reflect on the well-being of a population such as the quality of life at work, the strength of community spirit, the nature of the environment, etc.

The expected recovery is confirmed

....

In comparison with the annual rates in real-terms of GDP growth recorded in the sixties and late eighties, current rates represent a distinct slow-down. For 1997 and 1998, the forecasts are respectively 2.7% and 2.8% for EU-15 as a whole, compared with an average 3.3% from 1986 to 1990. The years 1991-1993 were particularly mediocre, and some countries recorded negative GDP growth (in real terms). Even so, Ireland did better and so, to a lesser extent, did the Netherlands, Austria, Portugal and Denmark. Finland and Sweden, on the other hand, saw their GDP shrink for three years running.

The 1994 recovery was particularly marked in the United Kingdom, but Finland and Denmark ran out of steam in 1995; 1996 did not live up to expectations. 1997 will be better, and forecasts for 1998 are relatively high. The exception of Ireland needs to be stressed: here not only has growth been uninterrupted over the past six years, but the rate has been almost consistently three times the European average (Table 1).

Table 1 - Variations in GDP - EU-15, 1961 - 1998

(GDP at constant prices - annual % change)

	1961 1973	1974 1985	1986 1990	1991 1995	1995	1996	Estimates 1997	Forecasts[2] 1998
B	4.9	1.8	3.0	1.2	2.1	1.5	2.7	2.8
DK	4.3	2.0	1.4	2.0	2.6	2.7	2.9	2.7
D[1]	4.3	1.7	3.4	2.1	1.8	1.4	2.2	2.6
EL	7.7	2.5	1.9	1.1	1.8	2.6	3.5	3.8
E	7.2	1.9	4.5	1.3	2.8	2.3	3.4	3.6
F	5.4	2.2	3.2	1.1	2.1	1.5	2.4	3.0
IRL	4.4	3.8	4.7	5.9	11.1	8.6	10.0	8.7
I	5.3	2.7	3.0	1.1	2.9	0.7	1.5	2.4
L	4.0	1.8	6.4	5.4	3.8	3.0	4.1	4.4
NL	4.9	1.9	3.1	2.1	2.3	3.3	3.3	3.7
A	4.9	2.3	3.2	2.0	2.1	1.6	2.5	2.8
P	6.9	2.2	5.0	1.4	1.9	3.6	3.7	4.0
FIN	5.0	2.7	3.4	-0.5	5.1	3.6	5.9	4.6
S	4.1	1.8	2.3	0.5	3.9	1.3	1.8	2.6
UK	3.1	1.4	3.3	1.3	2.8	2.3	3.5	1.9
EU-15[1]	4.8	2.0	3.3	1.5	2.5	1.8	2.7	2.8
USA	4.0	2.3	2.8	2.0	2.4	2.8	3.8	2.5
JAP	9.7	3.4	4.6	1.4	1.5	3.9	1.0	0.4

[1] EU-15 aggregate includes unified Germany from 1991 onwards

[2] As usual, the forecasts are conditioned upon, inter alia, the technical assumption of "no policy change"

Source: Summary of March 1998 forecasts - Commission services

The leading contributors to the EU's GDP... and the more modest ones

Expressed in Purchasing Power Standard (PPS), the GDP of the European Union totalled 6 765 billion in 1996 — about 6% less than that of the USA and 2.5 times more than Japan's. In PPS terms, Germany accounts for 24% of the Union's total GDP. Between them, Germany, France, Italy and the United Kingdom produced around 72% of European GDP, expressed in PPS. Denmark, Greece, Ireland,Luxembourg, Portugal and Finland contributed 7.8% of the Union's GDP.

Source: Eurostat - Economic Accounts of the European Union — 1996 — National Accounts

At the same time, the USA has recorded uninterrupted growth at a sustained rate since 1992.

Finally, if we take as a reference the European average per capita GDP, Ireland's relative position has improved substantially between 1992 and 1996. A less notable improvement has also been recorded in Denmark, Luxembourg, the Netherlands, Finland, Greece and Portugal. In the last two, 1992 levels were relatively low. Except for France and Italy, where there has been a slight decline, the relative position of the remaining countries is virtually stable (Figure 1).

Progress has thus been observed in particular amongst the "small" contributors to European GDP. (see box opposite).

Figure 1 - GDP per head at current market prices and PPS[1], 1992 - 1997

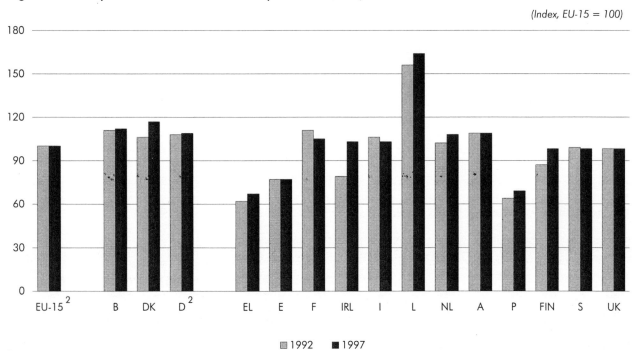

(Index, EU-15 = 100)

□ 1992   ■ 1997

[1] see box p. 10

[2] Data for Germany and EU refer to Germany post 3/10/1990

Source: European Commission - Eurostat, DG II - DG II forecasts - Autumn 1997

Employment stagnated between 1990 and 1994

....

There has never been any doubt that growth is a source of jobs; the figures prove it. Since 1975, job development has closely followed variations in GDP. According to estimates made for the Union as a whole, on average a real-terms growth rate in excess of 2% for EU-15 is needed for there to be net job creation. That was not the case in 1991, 1992, 1993 and 1996, and growth in jobs has suffered as a result. (see chapter on Labour Market).

The sluggishness of the job market is highlighted if we set the total number of jobs in " full-time equivalent" terms against the population of working age (i.e. aged 15 to 64). This indicator attenuates the differences attributable to the greater or lesser use of part-time work in different countries, and is relatively less sensitive to the effects of under-employment. In all EU countries except Belgium, Luxembourg, the Netherlands and Austria, the full-time equivalent employment rate fell, and in Finland and Sweden the fall was particularly steep (Table 2).

This shrinkage in full-time equivalent employment in EU-15 as a whole was to a large extent the result of recession in virtually every Member State between 1990 and 1993/94. Much of what job creation there was could be attributed to the creation of part-time jobs; countries such as Ireland continued to create full-time jobs because of their high growth rate. The overall result was an increase in unemployment levels in most Member States.

Table 2 - Variation in employment[1] rates (in equivalent full time), 1990 - 1996

(As a % of the population aged 15-64)

	EU-15	B	DK	D	EL	E	F	IRL	I	L	NL	A	P	FIN	S	UK
1990	57.6	51.6	68	62.6 [2]	55.3	48.4	59.4	51.1	52.8	57.8	50	65.2	64.5	71	72.6	62.7
1994	55.1	52.2	66.1	58.4	54.7	43.7	56.0	51	50.4	58.3	50.2	65.9	63.4	57.4	62.5	58.8
1996	55.0	52.5	67.1	56.9	55.5	45.1	55.9	52.6	50	57.4	51.5	65	63.8	58.3	63.2	59.3

[1] Employment: employers, employees and self-employed

[2] 1991 for Germany

Source: Employment DG V Report 1997 - European Commission

The background to this social portrait is thus a relatively low employment rate and a rise in unemployment on average over the first half of the decade. Estimates for 1997 and forecasts for 1998 do nevertheless suggest a significant improvement (Table 3). At the same time, job flexibility, i.e. more part-time working, more fixed term contracts of employment, more non-standard working hours, is on the increase (See chapter on Employment).

The share of compensation of employees declined

Compensation of employees is the largest share of total resources: in nearly all Member States gross wages and salaries made up at least 44% of total resources in 1995. It accounted for a relatively small share in Italy - 37% in 1995 -in contrast to Denmark where it was 63% in 1994.

The proportion declined in all Member States between 1980 and 1995 (Table 4).

Table 3 - Variation in total employment

(Annual % change)

	1991 1995	1995	1996	Estimates 1997	Forecasts[2] 1998
B	-0.4	0.5	0.4	0.3	1.2
DK	-0.3	1.6	1.1	2.2	1.2
D	-0.4	-0.3	-1.2	-1.4	-0.1
EL	0.8	1.4	0.7	0.5	1.0
E	-0.5	1.7	1.5	2.6	2.4
F	-0.2	1.0	0.0	-0.1	1.1
IRL	1.9	5.1	3.9	4.1	3.5
I	-1.0	-0.2	0.2	0.1	0.4
L	2.7	2.5	2.6	2.3	2.4
NL	0.7	1.4	1.8	2.3	2.1
A	0.4	0.2	-0.7	-0.1	0.5
P	-0.6	-1.0	0.6	1.9	1.3
FIN	-3.7	1.7	1.0	2.0	2.2
S	-2.2	1.5	-0.5	-1.1	0.6
UK	-0.9	1.4	0.4	1.6	0.6
EU-15[1]	-0.6	0.6	0.1	0.4	0.8

[1] EU aggregate include Unified Germany from 1991 onwards

[2] March 1998 forecasts

Source: Commission services

Table 4 - Share of compensation of employees received, 1980 - 1995

(as % of total resources)

	B	DK	D	E	F	I-	NL	P	FIN	S	UK
1980	52	:	56	52	54	44	55	45	59	:	63
1994	46	63	53	48	50	40	46	44	58	61	55
1995	45	:	:	46	49	37	45	:	52	56	53

Source: "The economic accounts of the European Union, 1996" - Eurostat

Inflation under control

·······························

If households are to plan ahead, for example buying a house or paying for their children's education, then the future must, if not fully known, at least be known to be stable. Consumer price variations form part of that environment. The average rate of inflation in the EU-15, measured here, as the deflator of private consumption in national accounts, fell from 2.6% in 1996 to 2.1% in 1997, whilst the forecast for 1998 is 1.9% (Table 5). Except in Greece (5.5% in 1997), there is very substantial convergence on inflation, ranging from 1.1% in France to 2.5% in Spain in 1997.

The average annual variation in prices was frequently in double figures between 1974 and 1985, ranging from 22.2% in Portugal to 4.3% in pre-1991 Germany. The European average was then 10.7% per year.

Table 5 - Variation in private consumption price, 1974 - 1998

(Deflator of private consumption - annual % change)

	1974 1985	1986 1990	1991 1995	1995	1996	Estimates 1997	Forecasts[2] 1998
B	7.4	2.3	2.7	1.7	2.3	1.6	1.3
DK	9.6	3.7	1.7	2.0	2.1	2.3	2.1
D[1]	4.3	1.5	3.5	1.9	1.9	1.9	1.7
EL	17.5	17.0	13.8	8.6	8.5	5.5	4.5
E	15.4	6.6	5.6	4.7	3.4	2.5	2.2
F	10.5	2.9	2.3	1.6	1.9	1.1	1.0
IRL	13.8	3.2	2.4	2.0	1.1	1.4	3.3
I	15.9	6.1	5.7	5.8	4.3	2.4	2.1
L	7.4	2.4	3.0	2.1	1.6	1.4	1.6
NL	5.7	0.9	2.5	1.5	1.3	2.2	2.3
A	5.8	2.0	3.0	1.5	2.5	1.8	1.5
P	22.2	12.2	7.4	4.2	2.6	2.1	2.2
FIN	10.9	4.5	3.1	0.3	1.6	1.4	2.0
S	10.3	6.7	4.7	2.7	1.2	2.2	1.5
UK	12.0	5.0	4.1	2.6	2.6	2.3	2.3
EU-15	10.7	4.3	4.1	3.0	2.6	2.1	1.9

[1] EU aggregate include Unified Germany from 1991 onwards

[2] March 1998 forecasts

Source: Commission services

Long-term trends unaffected by slowing consumption[1]

•••

Household consumption is frequently used as a proxy for disposable income. Because of the recession and the problems of the labour market, household consumption has slowed down since the beginning of the decade: between 1990 and 1996, average annual growth in real terms was 1.4% against 3.6% between 1985 and 1990 in EU-15. Reflecting the recent improvement, growth in 1996 was 2%.

Compared with the trends of the late 1980s, household spending has slowed in most Member States. In 1993, for example, consumption in volume had slipped significantly in Italy, Spain, Portugal, Finland and Sweden. The decline in spending continued for three consecutive years in Finland, and for two in Sweden and the United Kingdom (Table 6).

Purchasing Power Standard - PPS
Purchasing Power Parities - PPPs

PPS are obtained by means of a conversion rate called a Purchasing Power Parity.

The PPPs are the rates of currency conversion that equalise the purchasing power of different currencies. This means that a given sum of money, when converted into different currencies at the PPP rates, will buy the same basket of goods and services in all countries. In other words, PPPs are the rates of currency conversion which eliminate the differences in price levels between countries.

A given PPS refers to a specific basket of goods and/or services: for example the PPS for household consumption refers to the basket of goods and services consumed by households.

Table 6 - Variations in private consumption, 1985 - 1996

(change in volume - % per year)

	B	DK	D[2]	EL	E	F	IRL	I	L	NL	A	P	FIN	S	UK
1985-1990[1]	2.8	0.5	3.4	2.9	4.7	3.2	5.2	3.8	5.0	2.8	3.0	7.0	3.7	2.4	4.7
1990	2.6	0.0	5.1	2.5	3.5	2.6	2.1	2.4	5.6	4.1	3.2	5.4	0.0	-0.4	0.6
1991	2.8	1.2	/	2.7	2.8	1.3	2.3	2.6	5.8	3.0	2.8	3.9	-3.7	0.9	-2.2
1992	2.3	1.8	3.6	1.8	2.2	1.3	4.2	1.3	-0.4	2.5	2.7	3.2	-5.1	-1.4	-0.1
1993	-0.9	2.2	0.2	0.1	-2.3	0.2	1.6	-3.5	1.1	1.0	0.7	-2.0	-3.0	-3.2	2.4
1994	1.3	6.2	1.4	1.4	0.9	1.4	6.4	0.8	2.1	2.2	2.5	0.9	1.9	1.8	2.5
1995	1.2	2.1	1.9	1.6	1.5	1.6	3.6	1.3	2.3	2.0	1.9	2.5	3.6	0.8	1.9
1996[2]	1.4	2.5	1.8	2.2	1.9	2.1	6.3	1.1	2.4	2.8	1.5	2.5	3.2	1.5	2.9

[1] For 1985 - 1990 annualised average growth rate

[2] Break in the series in 1991

Source: "The economic accounts of the European Union - 1996" - Eurostat

---

[1]   Consumption is measured here in national account terms – (see box p. 194)

Principal expenditure: rent, gas and electricity

Nowadays, rent (including gas and electricity) forms the principal item of expenditure in the consumption of EU households. Next come "food, beverages and tobacco" and "transport and communications". The total of these three items, all of which are usually regarded as essential, comes to more than 53% of private consumption, and more than 72% if health services are also included. The remainder of spending is divided between clothing, leisure and culture, and other miscellaneous expenditure.

This structure of expenditure on goods and services is the consequence of long-term trends which were unaffected by the recession of the early 1990s. The share of "food, beverages and tobacco" has thus continued to decline, falling from 22% in 1985 to 18% in 1995; and this expenditure is now in second place behind rent. Clothing purchases are also declining noticeably.

Purchases for the home remain stable. All other items now account for a greater share of overall spending, notably health services (up 1.5 percentage points in ten years), rents (+1.4) and transport and communications (+0.6) (Table 7).

Broadly, these trends can be observed in most Member States, with differences arising principally from the level of earnings and also from national tradition.

In Greece, Spain, Ireland and Portugal food expenditure is still well ahead of rent. The share of spending on clothing is declining in all Member States, though noticeably less in Italy and Portugal than, for example, in Austria. Expenditure on leisure has grown slightly during the period under review, but much faster than the average in Ireland, the United Kingdom and Denmark at between 11% and 12%, compared with 9% for EU-15 (see chapter on Consumption, Housing Conditions).

Table 7 - Structure of the household consumption, 1985 - 1995

(as a % of total consumption)

	EU-15		
	1985	1995	Trends
Gross rent, fuel and power	18.4	19.8	↗
Food drinks and tobacco	22.3	18.2	↘
Transport and communications	14.8	15.4	↗
Health services	7.4	8.9	↗
Recreation, education and culture	8.2	8.7	↗
Furniture and household equipment	7.7	7.6	=
Clothing and footwear	7.8	6.6	↘
Other goods and services	13.1	14.7	↗

Source: Eurostat - National accounts - SEC

Social Protection data

The data on expenditure and receipts of social protection schemes in the EU-15 contained in this section are drawn up according to the ESSPROS Manual 1996. ESSPROS stands for European System of integrated Social PROtection Statistics, a harmonised system providing a means of analysing and comparing social protection financial flows.

Social protection is defined as follows in the ESSPROS Manual 1996.

Social protection encompasses all interventions from public or private bodies intended to relieve households and individuals of the burden of a defined set of risks or needs, provided that there is neither a simultaneous reciprocal nor an individual arrangement involved.

The list of risks or needs that may give rise to social protection is fixed by convention as follows :

Sickness/health care
Disability
Old age
Survivors
Family/children
Unemployment
Housing
Social exclusion not elsewhere classified

Expenditure

Expenditure on social protection schemes is broken down into social benefits, administration costs, transfers to other schemes and other expenditure.

— *Social benefits* consist of transfers, in cash or in kind for the 8 risks or needs (See. above).

— *Administration costs* are the costs charged to the scheme for its management and administration.

— *Transfers to other schemes* are unrequited payments made to other social protection schemes.

— *Other expenditure* consists of miscellaneous expenditure by social protection schemes such as interest payable by the scheme to banks and other creditors in respect of loans taken up and payment of taxes on income or wealth.

Receipts

Social protection receipts comprise social contributions, general government contributions, transfers from other schemes and other receipts.

— *Social contributions* are the cost incurred by employers on behalf of their employees or by protected persons to secure entitlement to social benefits.

— *General government contributions* relate to the financing of social protection expenditure by central, state, regional or local governments in their role as public authorities rather than as employers. They consist of:
the cost to general government of running public non-contributory schemes ;
financial support provided by general government to other resident social protection schemes.

— *Transfers from other schemes* are unrequited payments received from other social protection schemes.

— *Other receipts* come from a variety of sources, such as from interest and dividends.

Further information: the revised methodology is presented in the ESSPROS manual - 1996

Social protection: benefits and funding

From a macro-economic point of view, social protection accounts for a relatively large part of GDP in every Member State: from 20% in Ireland to 35.6% in Sweden in 1995. The total includes mainly social benefits: retirement pensions, unemployment, sickness and invalidity benefits, family and housing allowances, social exclusion benefits, and others. The revenue used to cover these out-goings is representedby social contributions (employers, employees and others), payments by public authorities from income tax, transfers from other schemes and other receipts (see box opposite).

From the point of view of households and individuals, social protection (whether in cash or kind) tops up existing income and/or makes up for a partial or total lack of resources.

Social protection thus has two dimensions, one economic and the other social. In this section, we consider macro-economic aspects, e.g., the trends and patterns of social expenditure , the structure of funding,... The income aspects are addressed in the chapter on Income (see p. 171).

28.4% of EU-15 GDP in 1995

In 1995, expenditure on social protection accounted for 28.4% of GDP, 0.2 of a percentage point down on 1994[1]. Between 1994 and 1995, real per capita expenditure stabilised and even declined slightly in Denmark, Italy and Finland and also the Netherlands where the decrease was significant. Over the period 1980-1995, the ratio of social protection to GDP rose by around 4 points. This indicator tends to rise when the economy is slowing rapidly, as was the case in 1980-83 and especially 1990-93 (Figure 2).

Figure 2 - Social protection expenditure in EU-12, 1980 - 1994

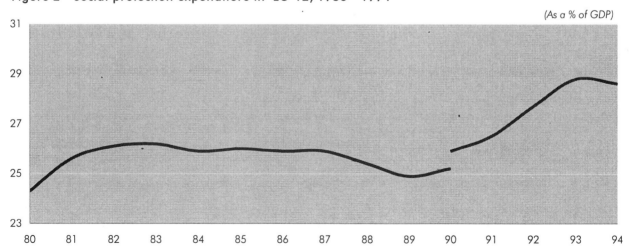

(As a % of GDP)

EU-12: the new German Länder are included from 1990 onwards
Source: Eurostat - ESSPROS/old methodology

---

[1]   Figures established using the new ESSPROS methodology.

Widely varying ratios amongst the Fifteen

The degree of social protection expenditure, which we express here as a share of GDP, varies widely from one country to another within the Europe of Fifteen. For 1995, the proportions lay between 20% and 22% in Ireland, Portugal, Greece and Spain. At the other end of the scale were Denmark (34.3%) and Sweden (35.6%). Germany and the United Kingdom were around the EU average (Figure 3).

The disparities in the social expenditure to GDP ratios are reflected also in the level of expenditure per capita which when expressed in ECU is a factor of 5 between Portugal and Denmark in 1995; in PPS, the factor is 3. Between 1990 and 1995 the increase in volume was steeper in the countries where the baseline was more modest – this being particularly the case with Portugal and Ireland. Even so, Denmark's per capita social protection expenditure rose by 22% from one of the highest baselines. During the same period, there was a slight increase in expenditure in Italy (+ 7%) and in the Netherlands expenditure remained at a level comparable to that of 1990 (Figure 4).

Figure 3 - Social protection expenditure as a percentage of GDP in the EU countries, 1995

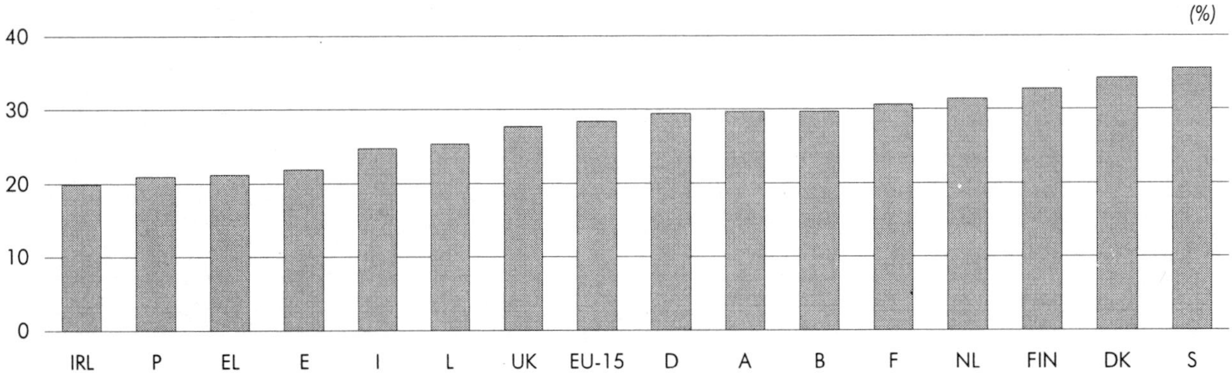

Source : Eurostat - "Social protection expenditure and receipts - 1980 - 1995" (ESSPROS manual - 1996)

Figure 4 - Social protection expenditure per capita

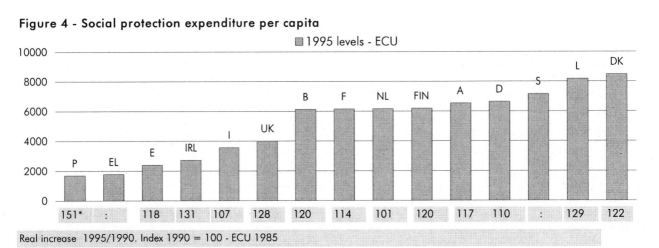

Source: Eurostat - "social protection expenditure and receipts - 1980 - 1995" (ESSPROS manual - 1996)

Several factors contribute to explaining the differences in per capita social protection expenditure amongst the Member States.

First, there seems to be a connection between the level of prosperity (measured here as per capita GDP) and the level of social expenditure per capita. This relationship can be observed in particular in the countries where the welfare state has a long tradition, e.g. the Nordic countries and the Netherlands. The age structure of the population, the level of unemployment, the size and composition of households, also influence social expenditure: for example, the greater the number of retired people, the greater the number of pensions paid. Main conditions of eligibility, duration of payments, rates and overall general conditions also affect the amount of social protection expenditure.

Beyond this, the discrepancies in relative costs of social protection per capita must be interpreted with care (see box opposite). Account must be taken of the social and fiscal deductions likely to diminish transfer incomes such as pensions. That applies particularly in Finland, Sweden, Denmark and the Netherlands.

In the same way, income tax relief (e.g. "quotient familial" in France) is another form of transfer. But these types of tax relief are not counted as social protection expenditure.

Important remarks

• Social benefits are recorded without any deduction of taxes or other compulsory levies payable on them by beneficiaries. Users of the data are warned that for some types of analysis the use of gross benefit data may give rise to misleading conclusions.

• Benefits granted within the framework of social protection can take many forms ; however, within the framework of ESSPROS 1996 "Core system" they are limited to :

— Cash payments to protected persons,
— Reimbursement of expenditure made by protected persons,
— Goods and services provided directly to protected persons.

These are all direct benefits in the sense that they imply a direct rise in the disposable income of beneficiaries.

• Calculations of national values. National values are obtained by consolidating the transactions between, schemes (such as transfers).

Definitions

Employers' social contributions are the costs incurred by employers to secure entitlement to social benefits for their employees, former employees and their dependants. Employers' social contributions are an indirect component of compensation of employees (the direct component being wages and salaries). Generally they are related to employees' earnings but are sometimes assessed by reference to other criteria. Employers' social contributions may be actual or imputed.

Employers' actual social contributions are payments made by employers to social security funds, commercial insurance companies, non profit-making Institutions running contributory schemes. Also, employers maintain segregated reserves in their balance sheets.

Employers' imputed social contributions are the costs incurred by employers by granting social benefits, or by promising social benefits payable in future, to their employees, former employees and their dependants, (i) without involving an autonomous insurer, and; (ii) without maintaining segregated reserves for that purpose in their balance sheets.

Earmarked taxes are the proceeds from taxes and levies which, by law, can be used only to finance social protection.

Further information: the revised methodology is presented in the ESSPROS manual - 1996

To the fore, Old age / survivor benefits
....

Benefits (in cash or kind) – retirement pensions, sickness, unemployment and family benefits – form the bulk of social protection expenditure: around 96% for EU-15 as a whole in 1995. Most of the remaining expenditure consists of overheads.

In most Member states, old age/survivor benefits made up the largest items of social benefits in 1995 : on average, over 44%. In Ireland, the Netherlands, Portugal and Finland, on the other hand, sickness / disability account for the largest share of total social benefits. The EU-15 average for this type of benefit was 36.0%. Unemployment and family / child benefits came third and fourth respectively with 8.4% and 7.6% (Figure 5).

There are major differences between the Member States when it comes to the relative importance of unemployment benefits (Table 8). In 1995, these accounted for over 17% of total benefits in Ireland, and about 14% for Belgium, Denmark, Spain and Finland. In contrast, percentages are relatively small in Italy (2%) and Luxembourg (3%). The total amount of unemployment benefits is not always explained by the level of unemployment in these countries. There are, in fact, substantial differences when it comes to the coverage and amount of unemployment benefits. Also, there are other means of providing income support to the unemployed apart from unemployment benefits ; particularly the housing / social exclusion benefits. In the United Kingdom, Sweden and Denmark this item reached a high level compared with other countries: for example 8% in UK compared to very little in Italy.

Figure 5 - Social benefits by group of functions, EU-15[1] , 1995

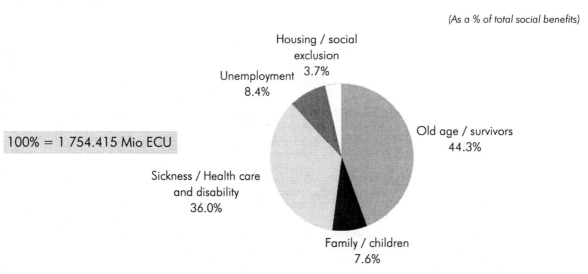

(As a % of total social benefits)

Housing / social exclusion 3.7%

Unemployment 8.4%

100% = 1 754.415 Mio ECU

Old age / survivors 44.3%

Sickness / Health care and disability 36.0%

Family / children 7.6%

[1] Data for Greece are not included

Source : Eurostat - "Social Protection Expenditure and Receipts 1980 - 1995" (ESSPROS manual - 1996)

Also, disability benefits in the last decades have become one way to provide long-term support to old workers unable to find a job. For most Member states, the effect on the pattern of social expenditure development of differential changes in unemployment seems to be relatively small: unemployment benefits represent a comparatively modest element of spending on total social protection.

Changes over 1990-1995 have not modified the structure of social benefits

In nearly all EU-15 countries, the share of social benefits devoted to unemployment increased from 1990 to 1995. This was explained mainly by the rise of unemployment rates due to the recession. In Finland the unemployment share doubled during these 5 years (Table 8). The exceptions were Denmark and Spain, where the labour market situation improved somewhat in 1994 and 1995.

During the same period, changes in the share of pensions (old age / survivors) varied from country to country. It was rather stable in Germany, France, the Netherlands and Portugal. It diminished in Ireland, Austria, United Kingdom and Greece. It increased markedly in Italy. In the other countries, it rose by 1 or 2 percentage points.

Table 8 - Social Protection Benefits by group of functions in the EU-15 countries - 1990 - 1995

(As a % of the total social benefits)

	Unemployment		Old age / Survivors		Family / Children		Sickness / Health care and disability		Housing and social exclusion	
	1990	1995	1990	1995	1990	1995	1990	1995	1990	1995
B	13.9	14.3	40.7	42.5	9.5	8.2	34.4	32.3	1.5	2.7
DK	15.4	14.7	36.8	37.6	11.9	12.4	30.0	28.4	6.0	6.8
D[1]	8.6	9.1	42.8	42.5	8.3	7.5	37.8	38.1	2.5	2.8
EL	4.8	5.9	54.3	49.3	3.7	6.9	36.1	35.5	1.2	2.4
E	15.8	14.3	44.0	45.4	1.7	1.8	37.6	37.6	0.9	0.8
F	8.3	8.2	42.7	43.0	9.4	9.0	35.5	34.9	4.1	4.9
IRL	14.6	17.3	30.6	26.0	11.3	11.7	38.3	40.1	5.1	4.9
I	1.7	2.2	59.6	65.7	4.9	3.5	33.7	28.6	0.1	(2
L	2.6	3.0	45.8	44.7	10.8	13.2	39.1	37.5	1.7	1.6
NL	8.3	10.1	37.4	37.4	5.6	4.7	44.7	44.4	3.9	3.4
A	4.6	5.6	50.0	48.3	10.5	11.3	33.2	33.4	1.8	1.5
P	2.5	5.5	43.1	43.4	7.1	5.8	46.9	44.8	0.4	0.4
FIN	6.1	14.3	34.1	32.8	13.5	13.3	43.7	36.1	2.6	3.6
S	12.3	11.1	35.9	37.1	12.6	11.3	32.3	33.9	7.0	6.5
UK	5.7	5.9	42.6	39.4	9.0	9.0	35.9	37.7	6.8	8.1

[1] D: 1991

[2] Negligible

Source: Eurostat "Social protection expenditure and receipts - 1980 - 1995" (ESSPROS manual - 1996)

In 1995 the share of pensions ranged from 37% to 49%; Ireland (26%) and Finland (33%) having a smaller proportion and, Italy a much larger one. In the latter, pensions represented 66% of total social benefits in 1995. This reflects the large proportion of the population above the official retirement age (62 for men, 57 for women), but also the relatively large numbers below this age who are retired: the employment rate in Italy of people aged 50-64 was 36% in 1996 compared with 47% for the same age group in EU-15 as a whole (see chapter on Labour Market).

Apart from a few exceptions such as Ireland and United Kingdom, the share of sickness /Health care and disability was stable or decreased during the period 90-95. The Netherlands made the largest contribution to this group of functions (44.8%) but this too was less than in 1990, as a result of efforts developed since 1991 to curb expenditure in this field.

Two patterns of funding

The funding of social protection comes partly from social contributions and partly from tax-related general government contributions (see box p. 12). Social contributions are levied mostly on income from employment and particularly on wages. These contributions are paid by the employers and the protected persons, i.e., employees and self employed. In some countries contributions are also levied on benefits such as pensions.

In 1995, for the EU-15 as a whole, the three main sources of funding were contributions by employers (39%), public contributions (32%) and protected person's contributions (24%). In the latter, employees account for nearly 20 percentage points (Figure 6).

Figure 6 - Social protection receipts by type in EU-15, 1995

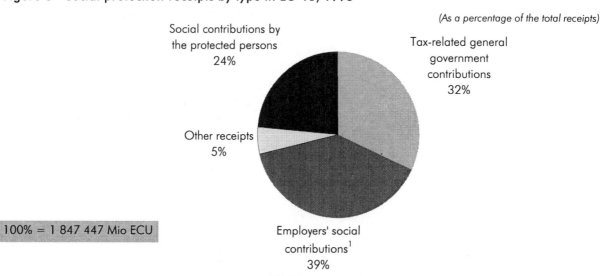

(As a percentage of the total receipts)

Social contributions by the protected persons
24%

Tax-related general government contributions
32%

Other receipts
5%

100% = 1 847 447 Mio ECU

Employers' social contributions[1]
39%

[1] Actual and imputed employer's social contributions (see Box p. 15)
Source: Eurostat - "Social protection expenditure and receipts 1980 - 1995" (ESSPROS manual - 1996)

As regards the structure of social protection funding, there are two major different patterns which reflect the historical developments of social protection in the various Member States. In both 1990 and 1995, social contributions accounted for around two thirds of receipts in Belgium, the Netherlands, France, Germany and Austria (Table 9). At the other end of the scale, the Nordic countries, the United Kingdom and Ireland finance their Welfare state mainly through taxes, i.e., levies on the households overall income. In these latter countries, the government's relative share of total receipts was at least 45% in 1995. It reached 63% and 71% respectively in Ireland and Denmark.

Table 9 - Social protection receipts EU-15, 1990 - 1995

(as a % of total receipts)

| | Employers' social contributions | | Protected persons' contributions | | | | General government contributions | | Other receipts[1] | |
| | | | Employees' social contributions | | Contributions by other protected persons | | | | | |
	1990	1995	1990	1995	1990	1995	1990	1995	1990	1995
B	40.8	42.4	20.5	20.4	4.7	4.5	24.7	20.2	9.3	12.5
DK	:	9.6	:	10.8 (3	:	3.1	:	71.0	:	5.6
D[2]	42.5	40.3	23.6	23.3	4.4	5.4	26.7	28.6	2.8	2.4
EL	:	:	:	:	:	:	:	:	:	:
E	55.8	51.7	9.3	9.2	5.2	5.9	26.7	30.4	3.0	2.8
F	52.0	49.5	22.9	22.1	6.0	5.3	16.7	21.1	2.5	2.0
IRL	24.7	22.3	14.2	12.8 (4	1.2	1.3	58.9	62.8	1.0	0.9
I	52.9	49.0	10.2	11.0	4.8	6.8	29.0	29.8	3.1	3.4
L	28.9	25.4	17.1	17.4	5.5	6.0	40.6	46.1	7.9	5.1
NL	20.1	22.0	30.2	35.5	8.8	10.6	25.0	16.0	15.9	16.0
A	38.1	37.0	21.2	21.9	3.9	4.0	35.9	36.4	0.9	0.8
P	37.1	29.9	18.1	16.3	1.8	2.6	33.8	39.4	9.2	11.7
FIN	44.2	35.3	:	:	:	:	40.5	44.7	7.3	6.4
S	:	37.9	:	4.5	:	0.7	:	48.4	:	8.4
UK	27.5	25.4	15.6	13.2	0.7	0.7	39.4	49.5	16.7	11.1

[1] see box p. 12

[2] D: 1991

[3] Including labour market contributions

[4] Including social contributions paid by pensioners and other persons

Source: Eurostat "Social protection expenditure and receipts - 1980 - 1995" (ESSPROS manual - 1996)

Within this global framework:

— employers' contributions represent the largest share of receipts in Belgium, Germany, Spain, France, Italy and Austria;
— contributions from pensioners and other benefit recipients accounted for 8.4% of total receipts in the Netherlands in 1995. In other Member States either the percentages are quite small or such contributions do not exist. However, information in this field is very partial (Table 10);
— other receipts, e.g., miscellaneous current and capital receipts of social protection schemes were around 12% of total receipts in Belgium, Portugal and the United Kingdom in 1995; it reached 16% in Netherlands.

The share of employers' contributions in total receipts decreased nearly everywhere

In every Member State, with the exception of Belgium and the Netherlands, the share of employer's social contributions decreased between 1990 and 1995. It was particularly marked in Finland – from 44% to 35%, and Portugal – from 37% to 30%. Concurrently, the share of funding from employees increased in some countries such as the Netherlands. More significantly, the proportion of financing from tax-related government contributions rose in all EU countries except in Belgium and the Netherlands. The changes over this period point to some shift in funding: from contributions levied on employers to other sources, more related with total income, thereby spreading the cost of financing more evenly across the population. In this context, contributions from pensioners and other benefit recipients have increased slightly and specially "earmarked" taxes have been introduced, particularly in France.

Table 10 - Social contributions from pensioners and other benefit recipients, 1990 - 1995

(As a % of total receipts)

	B	DK	D¹	EL	E	F	IRL	I²	L	NL	A	P	FIN	S	UK³
1990	1.4	:	3.3	:	0.3	0.9	:		3.2	7.3	1.7	0.1	:	:	
1995	0.9	:	4.1	:	0.4	0.8	:		3.5	8.4	1.8	0.3	:	0.0	

¹ D: 1991

² These contributions are included in the employees' social contributions

³ Negligible

Source: Eurostat - "Social protection expenditure and receipts 1980 - 1995" (ESSPROS manual - 1996)

Living standard indicators

Between 1990 and 1996, the EU Member States had to cope with a marked recession: some of them suffered more than others. Where do the Member States stand today with respect to living standards?

Apart from Luxembourg, the index of GDP per head in 1990 ranged from 58 in Greece to 116 in Germany. Italy, the Netherlands, United Kingdom and Finland were around the EU-15 average. Six years later, the same index varied from 66 (Greece) to 116 (Denmark). Ireland has joined the countries around the EU-15 average (Table 11). The index of consumption per head also provides some evidence of a reduction in disparities (Table 12).

The implicit tax rate on employed labour rose in most EU countries from 1990 to 1995. Some decreases were recorded in Ireland, Luxembourg, the Netherlands and Sweden. In 1995, there were still large disparities between Member States: from 27.0% in United Kingdom and 30.1% in Portugal to 53.7% in Finland and 56.2% Sweden (Table 13).

Table 11 - GDP per head in PPS, 1990 - 1996

(Index 100 = EU-15 based on PPS)

	EU-15	B	DK	D	EL	E	F	IRL	I	L	NL	A	P	FIN	S	UK
1990 (PPS)	100 (14 640)	104	105	116	58	75	110	72	101	144	101	105	59	102	105	101
1996 (PPS)	100 (18 070)	112	116	110	66	76	107	99	102	169	108	111	68	98	100	97

Source: Eurostat - The economic accounts of the European Union - 1996

Table 12 - Private consumption per head in PPS, 1985 - 1996

(Index 100 = EU-15 based on PPS)

	EU-15	B	DK	D	EL	E	F	IRL	I	L	NL	A	P*	FIN	S	UK
1985-1990[1] (PPS)	100 (7 649)	104	91	118	82	77	105	66	102	147	100	92	61	82	94	96
1996 (PPS)	100 (11 240)	106	92	102	72	85	98	82	113	152	94	97	66	74	80	102

[1] Average over the period

Source: Eurostat - The economic accounts of the European Union - 1996

Table 13 - Implicit tax rate on Employed Labour[1] in the EU-15, 1990 - 1995

(in %)

	B	DK	D	EL	E	F	IRL	I	L	NL	A	P	FIN	S	UK
1990	43.8	43.8	38.5	34.1	35.5	42.2	30.7	39.9	30.4	49.7	39.3	32.5	47.6	57.2	24.5
1995	45.7	47.6	44.1	45.9	38.0	44.4	30.1	44.0	29.6	48.8	44.5	36.7	53.7	56.2	27.0

[1] Implicit tax rate on Employed Labour = mainly Employers' and employees' social contributions + wage taxes divided by compensation of employees x 100

Source: Statistics in Focus - Economy and finance 1997/35

Regional disparities globally remained the same

••

Economic disparities in the Union are most evident at regional level. In 1995, GDP per head was below or well below average in all the southern peripheral Mediterranean regions, including southern Italy. A similar situation pertained in the eastern and northern periphery (eastern Germany and northern and eastern Finland) and on the western periphery, in Ireland and parts of the UK (Map 1 p. 24).

The average level in Hamburg, the most properous region in the EU-15, was 4.5 times that in Ipeiros (EL). If we compare the 10 richest with the 10 poorest, the factor is less than 3.5.

The trend between 1985 and 1995 could best be described as stable. The spread between the richest and poorest hardly changed in any of the countries. It widened slightly in Italy and UK; Germany, because of unification, was a special case. In those countries where the differences were relatively small (Portugal, Sweden, Greece, Spain) the differences remained the same (Figure 7).

The top ten regions did not change between 1985 and 1995. Among them were 5 northern capital city regions: Brussels, Ile de France (Paris), Vienna, Luxembourg and Greater London. They took advantage of the growth in service industries in the more urbanised areas. The bottom group was dominated in 1995 by the same Greek and Portuguese regions as in 1985 even though, in some cases, at an improved level (Table 14).

Table 14 - GDP per head for NUTS 2 regions, 1985 - 1995

(Index 100 = EU-15 GDP/head)

Member State	Minimum Values				Maximum Values			
	% of EU average		NUTS 2 regions		% of EU average		NUTS 2 regions	
	1985	1995	1985	1995	1985	1995	1985	1995
B	78	83	Hainaut	Hainaut, Namur	164	172	Bruxelles	Bruxelles.cap
D	(80)	(55)	(Lüneburg)	(Dessau)	187	195	Hamburg	Hamburg
EL	43	43	Ipeiros	Ipeiros	74	74	Sterea Ellada	Attiki, Notio Aigaio
E	47	54	Extremadura	Extremadura	94	100	Baleares	Baleares
F[1]	80	81	Corse	Corse, Languedoc-Roussillon	164	165	Ile de France	Ile de France
I	62	60	Calabria	Calabria	130	133	Lombardia, Valle d'Aosta	Lombardia
NL	77	77	Flevoland	Flevoland	119	131	Noord Nederland	Groningen
A[2]	64	73	Burgenland	Burgenland	156	165	Wien	Wien
P	45	50	Açores	Açores	76	89	Lisboa Vale do Tejo	Lisboa Vale do Tejo
FIN[2]	82	75	Itä-suomi	Itä-suomi	134	123	Åaland	Uusimaa
S	104	92	Oestra Mellansverige	Oestra Mellansverige	131	123	Stockholm	Stockholm
UK	76	71	Northern Ireland	Merseyside	113	139	Greater London	Greater London

[1] France without French overseas departments
[2] Austria and Finland: 1990 and 1995
Source: Eurostat, REGIO regional database

Figure 7 - GDP per head by Member State and extreme values by region, 1985-1995

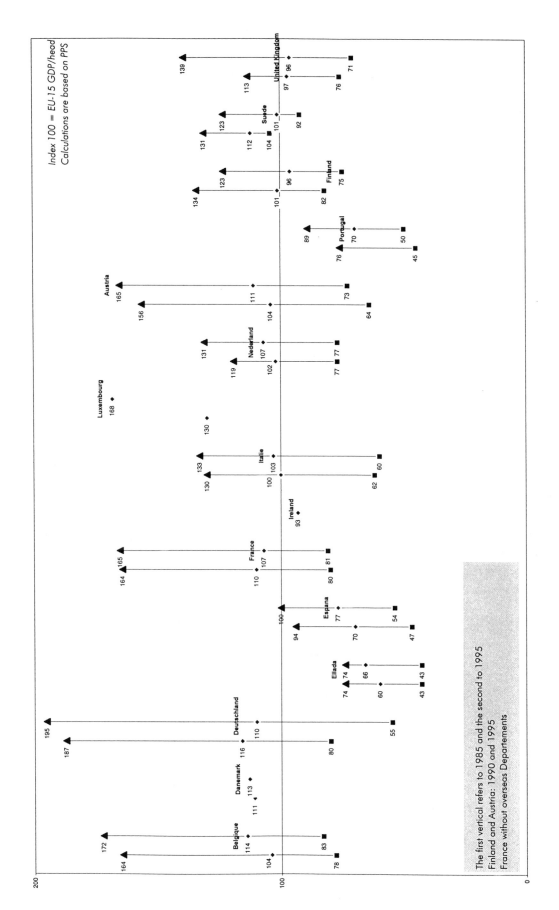

Index 100 = EU-15 GDP/head
Calculations are based on PPS

The first vertical refers to 1985 and the second to 1995
Finland and Austria: 1990 and 1995
France without overseas Departements

Source : Eurostat, REGIO regional database

MAP 1

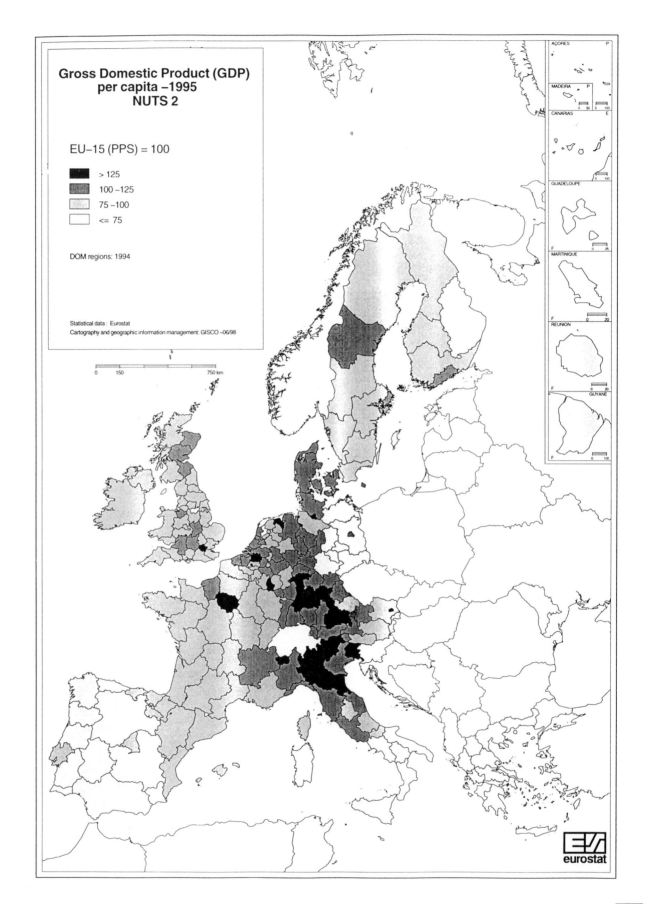

Gross Domestic Product (GDP)
per capita –1995
NUTS 2

EU–15 (PPS) = 100

> 125
100 –125
75 –100
<= 75

DOM regions: 1994

Statistical data : Eurostat
Cartography and geographic information management: GISCO –06/98

0   150   750 km

Eurostat's Regional Statistics

The data cover the main aspects of economic and social life in the regions of the European Union: GDP, demography, employment, unemployment etc. Most of the concepts are those used by Eurostat in compiling or collecting data at national level.

The demographic statistics at regional level provide information on population (annual average, and at 1 January of each year), population density and birth and mortality rates. Data on inter-regional migration are also available for some countries.

The information is presented according to NUTS (Nomenclature of Territorial Statistical Units), which divides the territory of the European Union into 77 regions at NUTS Level 1, 206 at NUTS Level 2 and 1031 at NUTS Level 3. The Grand-Duchy of Luxembourg is classed as belonging to Levels 1, 2 and 3, and Denmark and Ireland as belonging to Levels 1 and 2.

Further information
REGIO – Regional database. Description of contents, Eurostat 1995.

Population

A faster ageing population

Increased longevity in the last 50 years reflects the high welfare standards reached across the EU countries. Nowadays, for the first time in history, it is no longer exceptional for 4 generations of the same family to be alive simultaneously.

However, extended life expectancy was coupled with an important drop in fertility over the last three decades. The result is that the processes of dejuvenation (fewer children) and ageing (more elderly people) of the population are common throughout the EU though at different speeds and intensities. In addition, in various European regions, the population has stopped growing. This phenomenon is expected to extend to the majority of EU regions, sooner or later.

Rapid changes in the age distribution of the European population - fewer children, more elderly people - have become an increasingly important concern at Community level given the direct implications for such areas as health care and pension funding which accompany these phenomena. The ageing of the population and its possible decline in the next 20 years will clearly require many adjustments. At the same time, these trends may create new economic, social and cultural opportunities.

— With its 374 million people, the European Union is currently the third most populous economic entity in the world, however well behind China (1.2 billion) and India (almost 1 billion);

— Today, the total number of non nationals living in the EU-15 as a whole is about 5% of the total population; around 40% of these are EU-15 citizens, living outside their home country;

— The annual population growth rate has slowed considerably on average in the EU: 2.8 persons per 1000 population in 1996 against 8 per 1000 in the 1960s;

— Positive net migration has increased: it compensates the natural decrease which is already occurring in some countries and foreseen for most of the rest of the EU;

— According to Eurostat's baseline population scenario, the Union's population is expected to stagnate and decrease from 2020 onwards;

— The ageing of the population will accelerate. The elderly (aged 60 and over) represented 17% in 1960. In 1997 this proportion had risen to 21% and by 2030 may reach levels of 30%.

Adapting social protection to the demographic ageing of European Societies

1— Making public pension schemes sustainable

Objective: Foster the adaptation of public pension schemes to the ageing of European populations
Key action: Develop comparable projections of pension expenditure using common forecasting methodologies and harmonised economic and demographic assumptions; assess the elements of reform which seem to be most adapted to ensuring the sustainability of public pension schemes while preserving their core aspects of solidarity and presents the conclusions in the 1998 Social Protection in Europe report ,

2 — Providing secure environment for supplementary pension schemes

Objective: Provide a secure environment for supplementary pension schemes
Key action: In the first half of 1997, the Commission will issue a Green Paper on supplementary pensions with a view to identifying, with all parties concerned, including the social partners, the main elements of a framework at European level to provide a secure environment for the efficient operation of supplementary funded schemes.

3 — Meeting new care needs for older people

Objective: Revisit social protection systems to meet the care needs of dependent older people
Key action: Analyse in the 1998 Social Protection in Europe report the experience of Member States which have already implemented care-related provisions with a view to identifying the most efficient patterns of long-term care insurance scheme.

4 — Improving health services

Objective: Improve the efficiency, cost effectiveness and quality of health systems so that they can meet the growing demands arising from the ageing of the population and other factors
Key action: — carry out an assessment of the potential impact of prevention on the reduction of health care costs;
 — clarifiy to what extent and under what conditions, introducing market forces within health care systems can help save costs while fostering a better quality of services and ensuring access for all to health care;
— the Commission will bring together work carried out in the Member States on the efficiency and cost-effectiveness of health care systems, and assess which initiatives can be taken at Comminity level to assist Member States in reducing costs while maximising health gains.

Sources: This abstract is drawn from "Modernising and Improving Social Protection in the European Union" — Communication from the Commission — Brussels 12,03,1997 — COM (97) 102 final.

374 million EU inhabitants

With its 374 million citizens on 1st January 1997, the European Union was the third most populous economic entity in the World, well behind China (1,2 billion) and India (almost 1 billion) but ahead of the USA's 266 million. The population of the twelve Central European countries, potential future member countries of the Union, is around 110 million. Germany has the largest population. Its 82 million people account for about 22% of the Union's population while the United Kingdom, France and Italy each represent just over 15% (Table 1).

The six largest countries by area are France, Spain, Sweden, Germany, Finland and Italy which cover almost 80% of the entire territory. The Netherlands is the most densely populated of the 15 Member States with nearly 400 inhabitants per square kilometre (Figure 1). At the other extreme, the equivalent density figure in Finland is just 15 people.

Table 1 - Total population, 1 January 1997

	EU-15	B	DK	D	EL	E	F	IRL	I	L	NL	A	P	FIN	S	UK
(1000)	373 713	10 170	5 275	82 012	10 487	39 299	58 492	3 652	57 461	418	15 567	8 068	9 934	5 132	8 844	58 902
% share	100	3	1	22	3	11	16	1	15	0	4	2	3	1	2	16

Source : Eurostat - Demographic statistics

Figure 1 - Population density - Number of inhabitants per square km, 1997

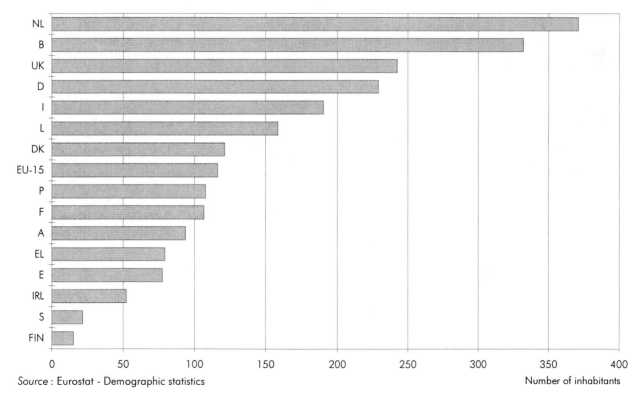

Source : Eurostat - Demographic statistics

Number of inhabitants

The **age dependency ratio** shows the extent to which the young (less than 19) and the old (over 60) are dependent on what is considered to be the active population (aged 20-59). It is assumed that those in the 20-59 age bracket support their younger and older citizens. The ratio is expressed as a percentage.

The United Kingdom is the most urbanised, (defined as having more than 500 people per square kilometre) with 77% of its population living in urban areas. Only 21% of the Swedish population live in towns or cities while the average figure for the Union is about 55%.

The age structure of the population is largely uniform between Member States although there are considerable regional variations. For the Union as a whole, 24% of the population is aged under 20. The elderly population (aged 60 and over) is forming an increasingly large part of the population: 21% on average for EU-15 in 1996.

The age dependency ratio in the Union (see box opposite) has declined from about 100% in the mid-seventies to 80% today. This is due entirely to the decrease in the number of children.

The total number of non-nationals living in the 15 Member States in 1995 amounted to almost 18 million, or about 5% of the total population. About 40% of these were citizens of Member States living in another Member State. The remaining 60% were citizens of countries outside the Union.

Fertility in the Member States: four broad groupings

On average, total fertility rates(1) are below the level required to replace the generations (2.1)

— the **Scandinavian countries** (Denmark, Finland and Sweden) saw their fertility rates begin to recover in the late 1980s and the current figures are among the highest in the Union (1.6-1.8).

— **Germany and Austria** have similar demographic antecedents, with an earlier "baby boom" and no increase in the birth rate for almost 20 years, have very low fertility rates (1.4-1.6).

— **Belgium, France, Luxembourg, the Netherlands and the United Kingdom** have had fertility rates in the 1.5 to 1.8 range since 1975.

— **Southern Member States and Ireland:** the drop in fertility happened later but more rapidly. It is levelling off: 1.2 to 1.4 in the south, 1.9 in Ireland.

[1] The total fertility rate is the average number of children that would be born alive to a woman during her lifetime if current fertility rates were to continue.

Source: Demographic situation in the European Union, 1995 – DGV.

EU population on a downward trend

Population growth is a result of natural increase - the difference between the number of live births and the number of deaths - and net migration. Recent developments in the EU can be summarised as follows:

— population growth has slowed considerably over the last 35 years;
— international migration has gained significantly in importance as a factor of population growth since the mid 1980s;
— completed fertility of the post-war generation has declined considerably although it appears to be levelling out ;
— life expectancy has steadily increased for both men and women.

There has been a significant slowing down of population growth over the last 35 years. In the 1960s, the average annual rate of population growth in EU-15 was just under 8 per 1000 population with the populations of Spain, France and the Netherlands growing by more than 10 per annum. In 1996, the EU-15 reported a population growth rate of 2.8, varying from 0.8 in Sweden to 13.2 in Luxembourg.

There is a marked difference between population trends in the developed and developing world. In 1996, world population increased by almost 81 million people. The Europe of Fifteen accounted for just 1% of this increase while China contributed 15% and India 21%. The USA reported a population growth three times that of the EU. However, in most other developed regions such as Japan and Russia, population growth was less than that of the EU (Figure 2).

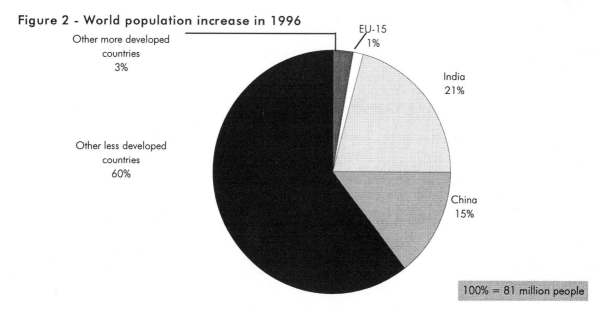

Figure 2 - World population increase in 1996

Source : Eurostat - Demographic statistics

The increasing importance of migration

The impact of migration is evident both in its contribution to population growth and in the consequent effects on the citizenship and age structure of the resident population. During recent years almost half of all those migrating into an EU Member State are nationals of an EU Member State, not necessarily the same one. Returning nationals account for a significant number of immigrants. In Denmark, Spain, Italy, Ireland and the United Kingdom, at least half of all immigrants are returning nationals. Immigration is, however, only one half of the picture and it is generally better recorded than emigration. In order to get a complete view it is necessary to look at net migration. Net migration figures hide the complexity of patterns and size of movements in and out of a country during each reference year, but they provide a useful measure of the impact of those movements on the size of the total population. In 1996, all Member States experienced positive net migration as a significant component in the increased size of their total population (Table 2).

Positive net migration was responsible for 71% of the total increase in the EU population in 1996 (Figure 3). Although this proportion decreased slightly in 1996, it remained the most significant contributor to population growth. Of the total net migration element in the EU's population change, 73% occurred in Germany, Italy and the United Kingdom. Net migration in these three Member States offset the overall decline in the EU which would otherwise have resulted from natural change. In relation to the size of the total 1996 (mid-year) population, positive net migration was highest in Luxembourg (0.9%).

Table 2 - Net migration, 1996

(1000)

EU-15	B	DK	D	EL	E	F	IRL	I	L	NL	A	P	FIN	S	UK
742	16	17	281	22	47	34	13	159	4	21	5	10	4	6	101

Source : Eurostat - Demographic statistics

Figure 3 - Components of population change, annual average, 1960-1996

(per 1000 population)

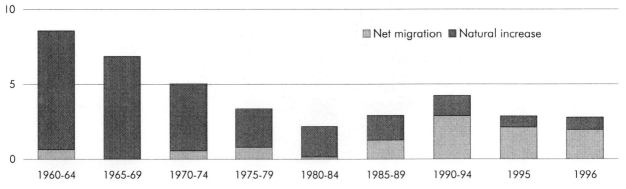

Source : Eurostat - Demographic statistics

The importance of migration's mitigating effect on population decline is particularly clear in Germany and Italy, where in 1996 it offset a natural decrease in the size of the total population. Population growth was also sustained by positive net levels in Greece and Sweden. Countries previously unaffected by the phenomenon such as Spain and Ireland have begun, in recent years, to attract more immigrants, nationals both of other EU Member States and of non-EU States (Figure 4).

The effect of these positive net migration levels over a number of years is also evident in the upward trend in numbers of non-nationals living in the individual Member States of the Union. The total number in 1995 was almost 18 million, a rise of 5 million since 1980. In 1995, about two-fifths of all non-national inhabitants in the Member States were citizens of other EU Member States.

The proportion of non-EU nationals has increased steadily since the 1950s. In 1995, Austria (8%) and Germany (6%) had the greatest share of non-EU nationals. In other countries this proportion ranges from 1% to 4%. In Luxembourg, EU non-nationals represent 29% of the population, by far the highest percentage of the Fifteen. Belgium is a distant second with 5%. In the other Member States, non-national EU citizens comprise less than 2% of their populations.

Figure 4 - Components of population change, in the EU countries - 1996

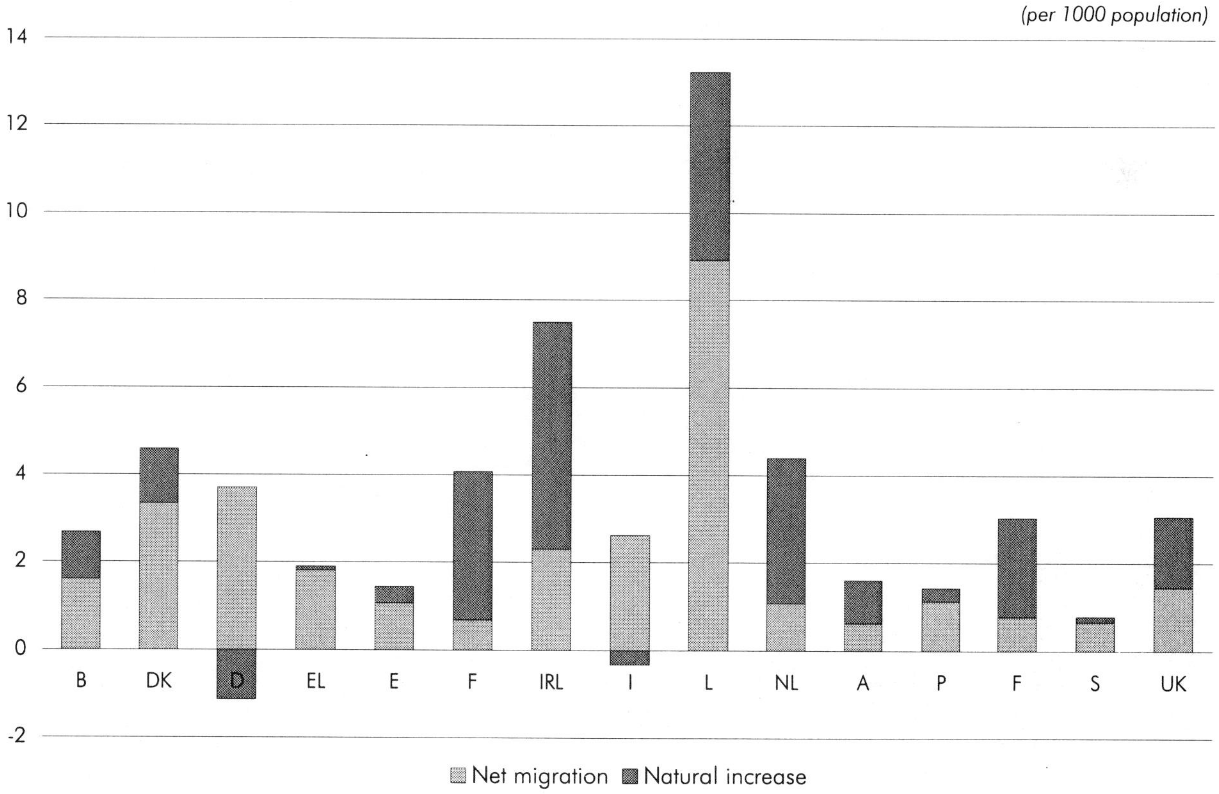

(per 1000 population)

Net migration   Natural increase

Source : Eurostat - Demographic statistics

Numbers of asylum seekers in EU is going down
••

Asylum seeking is one of the elements of international migration which receives most media attention and the one which presents perhaps the most fluctuating picture to interpret.

The data show that 1996 saw an overall decline in the total numbers of applications for asylum in the 15 EU Member States, Norway and Switzerland : from 292 000 in 1995 to 246 000 in 1996, an overall decrease of 16%. This continued the annual decline in total numbers which has occurred since the peak year in 1991 (Figure 5). This decline in total numbers obscures a more complex picture which emerges if the changing set of sending and receiving countries is examined. Eight countries followed the overall downward trend, whilst three, Austria, Belgium and Denmark saw small increases.

Germany has received more than half of all applications during the period since 1988. France and Sweden had been major recipient countries before the asylum numbers peaked, whereas the United Kingdom and the Netherlands took second and third place in 1996.

The changing pattern reflected in the mix of citizenship of asylum seekers shows the impact of recent political events and wars in the sending countries together with the effect of tightened asylum procedures in the Member States. Citizens of Turkey were the largest single group claiming asylum in Europe in 1996. Germany received 82% of these claims. The next most numerous groups across the EU were citizens of the Federal Republic of Yugoslavia and former Yugoslavia. These numbers have been falling annually since the end of 1992, significantly deflating the total numbers. Iraq is now in third place, having provided an annual steadily increasing number of applicants since 1992.

Figure 5 - Asylum applications, 1988 - 1996

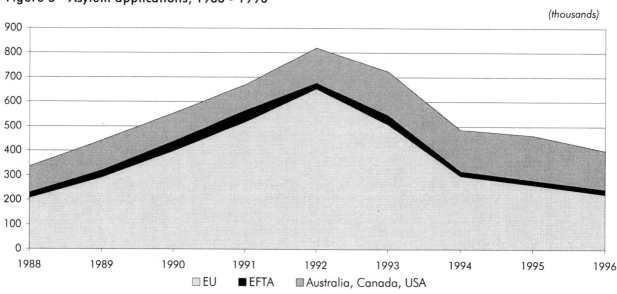

Source : Eurostat - Annual data on Asylum applications

Decline in births halted ... Life expectancy continues to rise

Since the mid 1970s, the total fertility rate in most Member States has not been sufficient on its own to prevent the natural decline in the population. In 1996, the EU-15 rate stood at about 1.44 children per woman, a slight increase on the post-war low of 1.43 recorded in 1995. The decline over the past 50 years is the result of a number of factors: women have become more economically active; more women go on to complete higher education which in turn improves their labour market prospects; the increasing preference of women to either live alone or to co-habit rather than marry and the increasing awareness of and access to family planning services. All these factors lead to postponement of motherhood, voluntary childlessness and declining family sizes with the resultant drop in the fertility rate (see also chapters on Households and Families and Labour Market).

The downward trend in fertility can be observed in all Member States although the timing and extent of the decline vary substantially from one country to another (see box p. 30).

Today, total fertility rates range from 1.15 in Spain and 1.22 in Italy to 1.91 in Ireland (Table 3). The average rate for the Union of 1.44 is much lower than that in the USA (greater than 2) while in most of the developing world the rate is in excess of 3 children per woman (Figure 6).

Table 3 - Total fertility rate, 1996

EU-15	B	DK	D	EL	E	F	IRL	I	L	NL	A	P	FIN	S	UK
1.44*	1.55*	1.75*	1.30*	1.31*	1.15*	1.72*	1.91*	1.22*	1.76	1.52*	1.42	1.44*	1.76	1.61	1.70*

Source : Eurostat - Demographic statistics

Figure 6 - Total fertility rates throughout the world, 1996

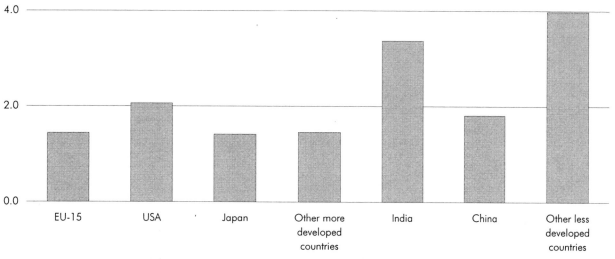

Source : Eurostat - Demographic statistics

Indications are however that the falling trend in the EU is now beginning to level out with even some evidence of a slight upturn. After five years of decline, the number of births in the Union stabilised in 1996 at 4 million. However, it seems very unlikely in the short or medium term that the rate will rise to the replacement level of 2.1 births per woman.

Over the past 50 years, life expectancy of men and women has increased, on average, by about 10 years. In 1996, the male life expectancy was 74.0 years while that for females was 80.5 years (see also chapter on Life Expectancy and Health).

In France in 1996, the life expectancy of baby girls was 8 years longer than baby boys while in the United Kingdom, the difference was around 5 years. Life expectancy is improving throughout the Union albeit at different rates. Since 1960, the life expectancy of men in Denmark has increased by only 2.4 years while in Portugal, it has improved by 9.8 years. Women in both countries saw their life spans increase on average by 3.6 and 11.7 years respectively. These figures reflect the general narrowing in the life expectancy gap between the southern and northern European Member States. Life expectancy levels for men and women in the USA are 72.7 and 79.4 years respectively while the equivalent figures for Japan are 77.0 and 83.3 years. The average Russian however lives 14 years less than the EU equivalent. In China, males and females live around 6 and 9 years less than their EU counterparts.

Changes in the age structure of the population

The elderly population (aged 60 and over) forms an increasingly large part of the population. In 1960, this cohort accounted for 17% of the total population in the Union. By 1997, the proportion had risen to 21%. The main cause of this 'ageing' of the population has been the drop in fertility.

The decline in mortality has gradually become another important factor although this did not take effect until the 1970s. Before this period, mortality rates were falling significantly for the younger age groups. During the last two decades, the decrease in mortality has become more evident among the older age groups.

The age structure of the population is largely uniform across the Community. Around 23% of the population in each Member State is aged less than 20 with the exception of Ireland where the proportion was 33 % in 1997. The elderly population aged 60 and over represented at least 18% of the population in all countries with the exception of Ireland (15%) (Figure 7). Persons aged 80 and over make up around 3-4% of the total population.

Figure 7 - Percentage of the population aged 60 and over, 1997

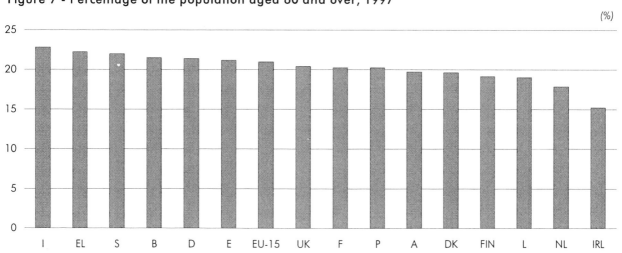

Source : Eurostat - Demographic statistics

Beyond the predictable

Figure 8 shows the future population growth up to 2050 according to internationally consistent but completely different population scenarios (see box opposite). Both the low and baseline projections estimate a sizeable population decline after taking account of both migration trends and the natural increase.

The baseline scenario is calculated on the assumption that in the long term the total fertility rate will vary between 1.5 and 1.8, life expectancy will range from 78-82 years for men and 83-87 years for women and net migration will be 600 000 per annum. According to this scenario, the Union's population is expected to show very slow growth over the next quarter of a century. Current estimates point to stagnation and decrease in the population from 2020 onwards. In contrast, the USA's population growth is expected to be at least double that of the Union over the same period with continuing growth beyond 2020. Furthermore, the Union's share of the total world population will continue to decrease. Today the Europe of Fifteen accounts for 7% of world population. By the middle of the next century, this percentage might fall to just 4%.

According to the baseline scenario, Italy (2008) will be the first to see its population fall while the EU as a whole will experience a decrease about 2023.

The population in Luxembourg, Portugal and Sweden is not expected to decline until the year 2040 (Figure 9).

Figure 8 - Total population, 1950 - 2050, EU-15

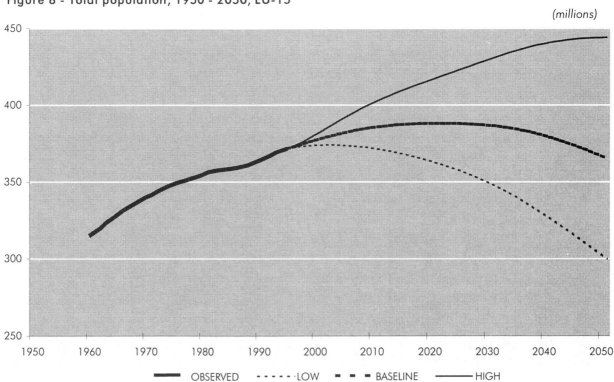

(millions)

OBSERVED · · · · · LOW ▪ ▪ ▪ BASELINE ———— HIGH

Source : Eurostat - Demographic statistics; Eurostat - Long-term population scenarios

There are significant regional variations in terms of population growth or decline. Before the year 2000, 42 regions (out of a total of 206 at NUTS 2 level) will experience a negative growth rate. From 2000 to 2015, this figure is expected to increase to 69 regions (Map 1 p. 41).

Negative population growth is caused either by negative natural growth (deaths in excess of births) or negative net migration. This can be observed in former east German regions and a number of regions in northern Spain, France, Italy and Portugal. In 13 of the declining regions, migration is still positive: examples are the Italian regions along the Ligurian coast and Lombardia, and the French Massif Central. In these cases, the attractiveness of the area has diminished the effect of negative natural growth. In 49 regions, the attraction is so high that net migration exceeds the effect of negative natural growth.

Figure 9 - First calendar year of population decline - baseline scenario

| 1995 | | 2008 Italy | 2013 Germany | 2014 Spain | | 2023 EU-15 | 2026 Finland | 2029 Austria | 2030 United Kingdom, Ireland | 2032 Belgium | 2034 Denmark, France | 2037 Netherlands | 2038 Greece | 2040 Portugal | | 2050 |

Source : Eurostat - Long-term population scenarios

Eurostat's long-term population scenarios

Long-term population scenarios are based on certain key assumptions for fertility, life expectancy and migration. These three factors determine the demographic trend in each country.
Five scenarios have been drawn up:
— Low scenario: low projection for each factor
— Baseline scenario: medium projection for each factor
— High scenario: high projection for each factor
— Young scenario: high fertility, high migration, low life expectancy
— Old scenario: low fertility, low migration, high life expectancy.

Fertility assumptions: Total fertility rate is assumed to vary from 1.3 - 1.6 (low) to 1.8 - 2.1 (high). Only the high projection will achieve the replacement rate (2.1 children per woman) and this in only five Member States (Finland, France, Ireland, Sweden and the United Kingdom).

Mortality assumptions: Life expectancy is still thought to be increasing, but at a slower rate than previously. The low projection expects it to stabilise for men in the range of 73 to 78 years and for women in the range of 82 to 84 years. The high scenario's corresponding values are 82 - 85 years for men and 85 - 88 years for women.

Migration assumptions: annual net migration is assumed to range from 400 000 (low), 600 000 (baseline) to 800 000 (high).

These regions are mainly to be found in a large zone extending from Denmark into Germany, as well as a zone stretching from Austria down along the Italian Adriatic coast. A similar pattern can be observed in south-west France and in various parts of England, particularly in the south-west and Wales. Here the effect of regional attractiveness for migrants is the determining regional population growth factor.

One of the most important factors behind demographic processes are economic parameters. Migration is certainly related to regional differences in economic indicators. Births and deaths may also be related either directly or indirectly. In general, regions with a high GDP tend to also have a high population growth. On the other hand, regions with a high unemployment rate are likely to have low population growth.

Assuming that medical advances continue together with progress in medical care, preventative measures and the development of healthy life-styles, life expectancy at birth for women in the EU-15 may reach 87 years by the year 2050. The equivalent figure for men could be as high as 83 (Figure 10).

Figure 10 - Life expectancy at birth, 1950-2050, EU-15

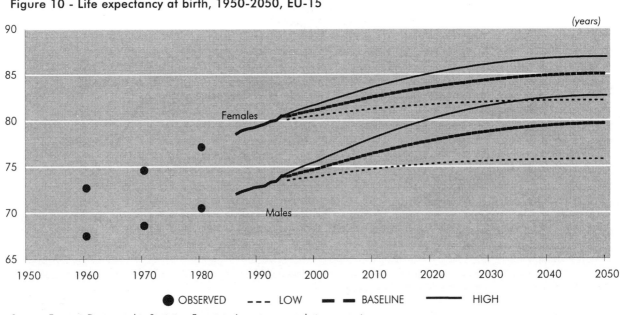

Source : Eurostat-Demographic Statistics; Eurostat - Long-term population scenarios

MAP 1

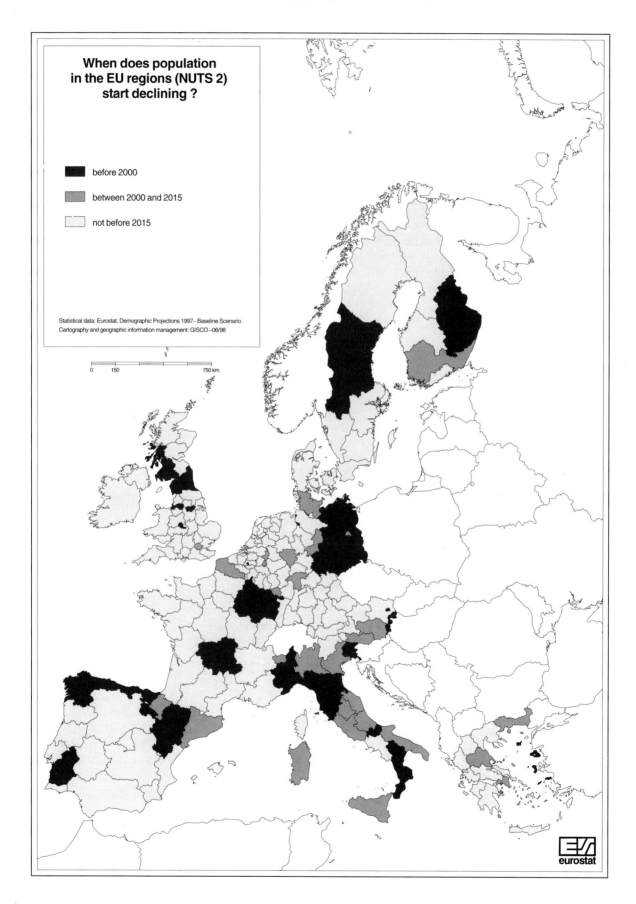

**When does population
in the EU regions (NUTS 2)
start declining ?**

before 2000

between 2000 and 2015

not before 2015

Statistical data: Eurostat, Demographic Projections 1997– Baseline Scenario
Cartography and geographic information management: GISCO –06/98

0   150   750 km

Ageing will accelerate

....

The current annual growth of the elderly population (aged 60 and over) fluctuates around a level of 0.8 million or 1%. This growth rate is expected to continue up to 2005. However, as soon as the 'baby-boomers' start to enter this age group, the annual increase will shift to levels of around 1.1 million. This will continue until the less numerous 'baby-bust' generations born in the early 1970s pass the age of 60.

The share of the elderly in the total EU population is set to increase considerably and by the middle of the 21st century their share of the population may be as high as one-third. Italy and Spain are likely to be the most aged countries with the baseline scenarios indicating that the over 60s will account for 37% of the population in each country by 2050 (Table 4).

Table 4 - Population aged 60 and over as a percentage of total population up to 2050

	1995	2000 scenarios			2020 scenarios			2050 scenarios		
	Observed	Young	Baseline	Old	Young	Baseline	Old	Young	Baseline	Old
EU-15	20.6	21.2	21.5	21.8	25	27	29	27	34	40
B	21.3	21.6	21.8	22.1	25	28	30	26	32	38
DK	19.9	19.4	19.6	19.9	23	26	28	23	29	36
D	20.7	22.2	22.6	22.9	25	28	30	27	34	41
EL	21.5	22.7	22.9	23.2	25	27	29	28	33	41
E	20.6	21.2	21.5	21.8	24	26	28	30	37	44
F	20.0	20.2	20.5	20.7	25	27	29	26	33	38
IRL	15.3	15.3	15.6	15.8	19	22	24	25	32	39
I	22.2	23.4	23.8	24.0	27	29	32	30	37	44
L	19.1	18.9	19.2	19.6	22	25	28	23	29	36
NL	17.7	18.0	18.2	18.5	24	26	29	25	30	37
A	19.8	19.8	20.1	20.4	23	26	28	26	33	40
P	19.8	20.3	20.6	20.9	22	24	26	25	31	38
FIN	18.9	19.5	19.7	19.8	26	28	30	25	31	36
S	22.1	21.5	21.9	22.2	25	27	29	24	29	36
UK	20.5	20.2	20.5	20.7	23	26	27	25	32	37

Source : Eurostat - Demographic statistics; Eurostat - Long-term population scenarios

The rate of increase of the over 60s will be greatest in those countries which currently enjoy the youngest population profiles such as Ireland, Finland, Luxembourg and the Netherlands (Figure 11).

The share of persons aged 80 and over in the elderly population (aged 60 and over) will increase almost continuously after the turn of the century. Particularly after 2025, when the baby-boomers are passing the age of 80, the number of 'very old' persons will rise dramatically. By the year 2050 their share of the elderly population may be more than one-third.

Regions with a high proportion of elderly people are to be found in the central and southern areas of France, the Iberian Peninsula, Italy, Sweden, south-west England and Wales. In most regions, the share of elderly people will be substantially higher in 2025 than it was in 1995 (Map 2 p. 44 and 45).

Figure 11 - Population aged 60 and over: increase 1995-2020

(Baseline scenario - %)

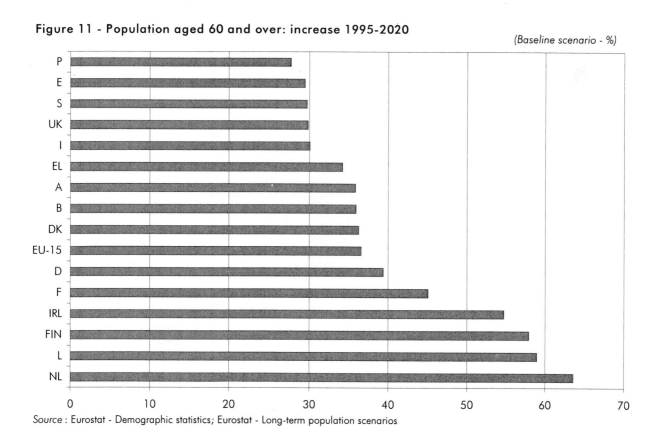

Source : Eurostat - Demographic statistics; Eurostat - Long-term population scenarios

MAP 2 - a

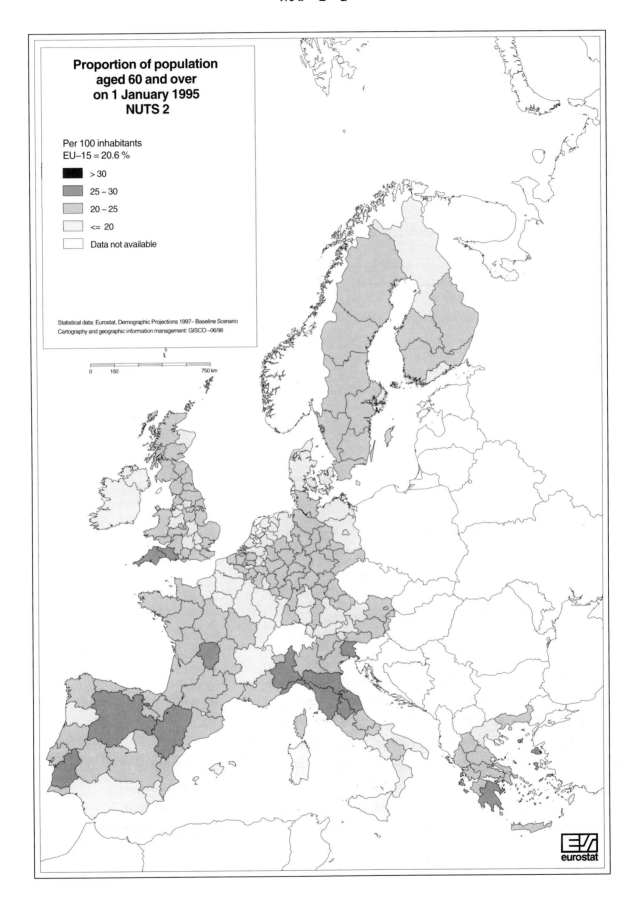

**Proportion of population
aged 60 and over
on 1 January 1995
NUTS 2**

Per 100 inhabitants
EU–15 = 20.6 %

- > 30
- 25 – 30
- 20 – 25
- <= 20
- Data not available

Statistical data: Eurostat, Demographic Projections 1997– Baseline Scenario
Cartography and geographic information management: GISCO –06/98

0   150   750 km

MAP 2 - b

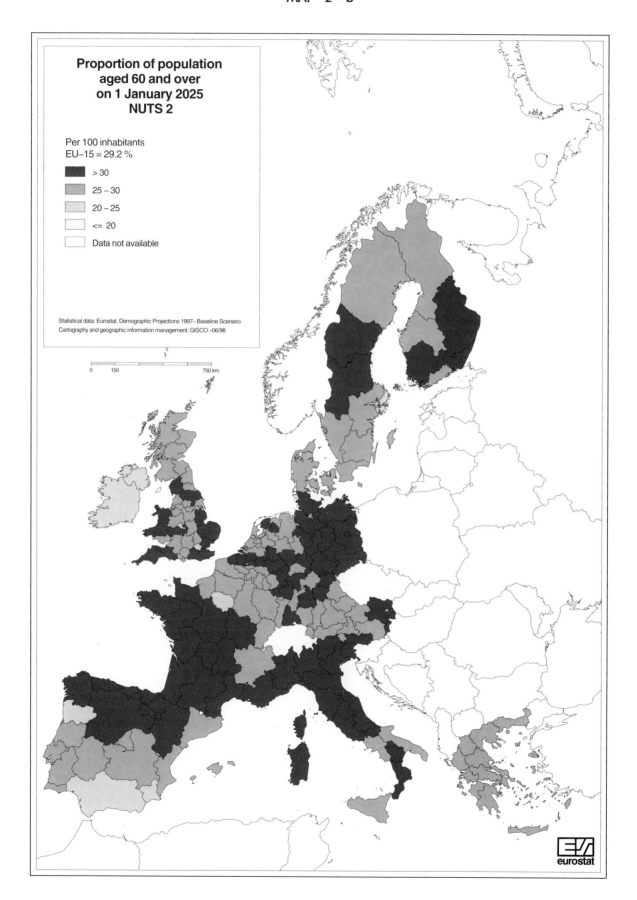

Proportion of population aged 60 and over on 1 January 2025 NUTS 2

Per 100 inhabitants
EU–15 = 29.2 %

- > 30
- 25 – 30
- 20 – 25
- <= 20
- Data not available

Statistical data: Eurostat, Demographic Projections 1997– Baseline Scenario
Cartography and geographic information management: GISCO –06/98

0   150   750 km

Working age population will decline and grow older

Since the mid-70s, the size of the EU-15 population of working age (20-59) has continued to grow by around 1.5 million people per annum. This increase is expected to fall to between 0.2 and 0.6 million in the near future. As the post-war generations begin to leave the (potential) labour force immediately after 2005, a long period of decline will begin (Figure 12). Only if the high scenario hypothesis outlined above - increasing fertility rate and net migration continuing at high levels - were to occur, could we expect stabilisation and even then not until 2035. Italy and Finland will be particularly affected by the decline in the labour force (Figure 13).

Figure 12 - Population aged 20-59, 1950 - 2050, EU-15

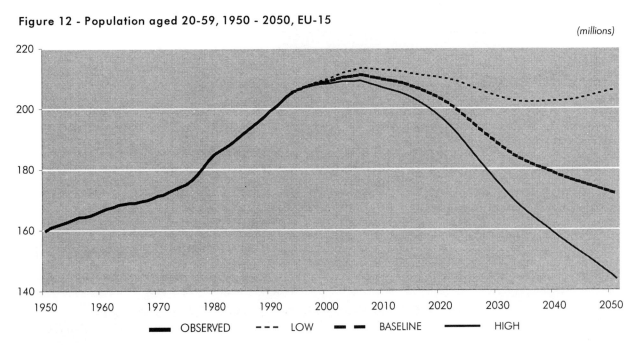

Source : Eurostat - Demographic statistics; Eurostat - Long-term population scenarios

All Member States will experience ageing of the labour force with Italy, Portugal and Spain facing a particularly long period. For the Europe of Fifteen, the population over 40 years of age will account for about 55% of the labour force by 2015 compared with 45% at present (see also chapter on Labour Market).

Figure 13 - Population aged 20-59: change 1995-2020

(Baseline scenario - %)

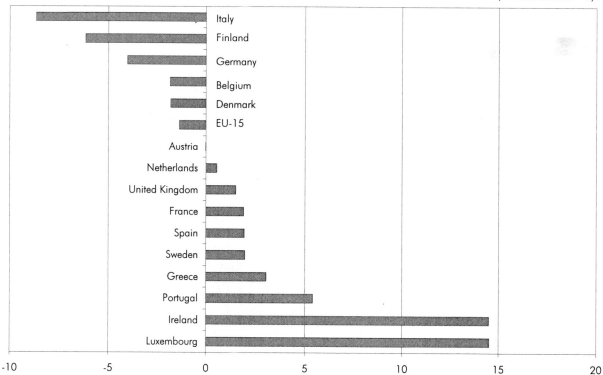

Source : Eurostat - Demographic statistics; Eurostat - Long-term population scenarios

Age dependency will rise considerably
••

While in the short term the age dependency ratio (see box p. 30) is likely to remain fairly constant, it is expected to increase sharply again from the middle of the next decade as the proportion of people in the 60 and over age bracket rises (Figure 14). The increase will be unevenly distributed across Member States over the next 25 years. The Netherlands and Finland will experience increases well above the Union average (Figure 15). According to baseline projections, Italy (119) and Spain (121) will have the highest age dependency ratios by 2050 (Table 5).

This phenomenon may have considerable implications for labour market policies: among the many interlinking factors that will be affected and which may require policy considerations are changes in productivity, activity rates and migration.

Figure 14 - Age dependency ratio, 1950 - 2050, EU-15

(%)

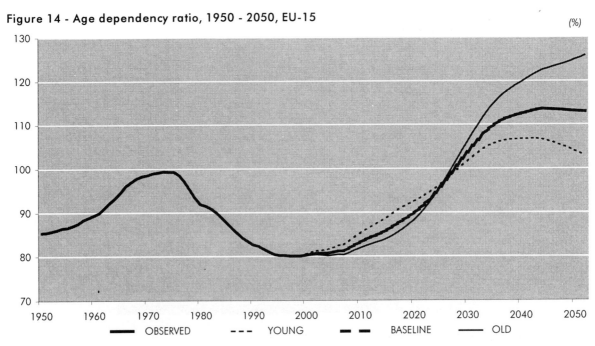

Source: Eurostat - Demographic statistics; Eurostat - Long term population scenarios

Table 5 - Age dependency ratio up to 2050

	1995	2000 scenarios			2020 scenarios			2050 scenarios		
	Observed	Old	Baseline	Young	Old	Baseline	Young	Old	Baseline	Young
EU-15	80.2	80.3	80.5	80.9	90	91	93	125	113	103
B	83.1	83.0	83.5	83.6	94	96	96	121	111	102
DK	76.9	76.1	76.7	77.0	90	91	92	111	101	93
D	73.1	78.8	79.0	79.3	88	87	89	123	110	100
EL	85.0	82.5	83.1	83.1	91	94	94	127	114	106
E	83.9	76.5	76.7	77.2	84	86	89	138	121	110
F	85.7	84.6	84.7	85.4	94	97	101	124	116	108
IRL	96.9	87.0	87.0	86.8	87	88	91	128	114	105
I	77.7	77.6	77.9	78.3	90	92	94	136	119	107
L	75.1	78.5	78.7	79.0	88	88	88	113	102	93
NL	72.6	73.5	74.1	74.1	90	91	91	118	106	99
A	75.6	75.7	76.1	76.3	84	84	87	123	107	98
P	85.1	79.0	79.2	79.3	84	86	87	119	108	99
FIN	79.8	79.9	80.3	80.8	100	101	104	117	109	102
S	87.7	87.1	87.4	87.5	96	98	99	114	105	99
UK	84.6	84.5	84.6	85.0	89	90	93	119	110	102

Source : Eurostat - Demographic statistics; Eurostat - Long term population scenarios

Figure 15 - Aged dependency ratio: increase 1995 - 2020 *(Baseline scenario - %)*

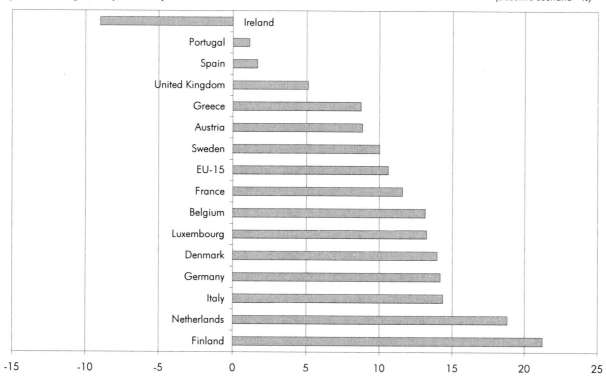

Source : Eurostat - Demographic statistics; Eurostat - Long-term population scenarios

Implications of an ageing population

A number of studies on the effects of ageing on pensions and health expenditure have been carried out both at national and European level. Despite the diverse nature of the social protection systems in the Member States, the main conclusions are relatively similar:

— The challenges will intensify around 2010 when the baby boom generations are likely to retire[1].
— The implications of this for pension funds have been the subject of much debate. Analysis carried out in the 1990s, based on current policies and taking into account the pension reforms introduced by Governments in the 1980s shows that the average ratio of pension expenditure to GDP is likely to rise from 12% to between 15% and 16%. By the year 2030, this ratio will range from less than 10% to as much as 20% in different Member States[2].

In addition, the increasing numbers of older people will increase the demand for health care and social services, resulting perhaps in greater demand for personnel in these sectors.

[1] "The Welfare State in Europe - challenges and reforms" European Economy Reports and Studies N° 4, 1997. European Commission Directorate-General for Economic and Financial Affairs.

[2] D. Franco and T. Munzi "Public Pension Expenditure Prospects in the European Union: a survey of National Projections", European Economy, Report and Studies, N° 3, 1996

Households and families

Changing living arrangements

Over the past 30 years there have been significant changes in the size and composition of households and families throughout the European Union. Households now have fewer members on average than ever before. The explanation lies in declining fertility rates, rising numbers of divorces and increased life expectancy, which has pushed up the number of persons, particularly elderly women, living alone.

Although the traditional one-family household still predominates throughout the European Union, the 'family norm' of a married couple with children is gradually being replaced by other living arrangements. For example, there has been a considerable increase in the number of persons living alone, in the proportion of unmarried couples, particularly amongst the younger generation, and consequently in the number of births outside wedlock. There has also been a substantial rise in the proportion of lone parent families.

Structural changes over the last few decades have seen young people staying longer in education and taking more time to move from training into work. Partly as a consequence of this, the younger generation is now tending to stay longer in the parental home. Two patterns seem to be emerging here, one for the southern Member States and Ireland, the other for the northern countries. In the former, children tend to remain in the parental home until they are ready to start a family of their own. They are more likely to get married. In the northern countries, young people are more inclined to leave home earlier and cohabit.

— For the Union as a whole, there are on average 2.5 persons per household. This figure ranges from 2 in Denmark to more than 3 in Spain and Ireland in 1996.
— More and more people are living on their own. Today, 11% of the population in the EU lives alone compared with 8% in 1981. This figure rises to 44% among persons aged 75 and over.
— Individuals living in couples with children account for a little over half the population. Almost one-fifth of the population in Greece, Spain and Portugal still live in multigenerational households. This compares with a European average of around one in ten.

— Today, around 8% of couples in the Union are cohabiting. Among the young generation, where 31% of those living in a couple are cohabiting, there are wide disparities between countries.

— Fewer people are getting married and those that do are waiting longer. At present, about one marriage in four ends in divorce.

— There has been a sharp rise in the number of births outside marriage, increasing from 10% of all births in 1980 to 23% in 1995. The proportion of children living with just one parent has also risen to almost one in ten. Denmark, Ireland, Sweden and the United Kingdom are well above the EU mean.

— On the whole, female economic activity tends to decrease as the number of children increases although in a few countries, the birth of a first child does not seem to prevent women from remaining in the labour market. Part-time work is one way for women, particularly in the northern Member States, to reconcile their professional and family lives.

— Among working parents, mothers are much more likely than fathers to look after their children and for longer periods. In Greece and Italy, grandmothers play an important role in looking after children.

Households and families
Data sources

A number of different sources have been used to describe the situation of households and families.

The **national population censuses** of 1981/82 and 1990/91 probably provide the most comparable data and allow trends to be examined in all 15 Member States. However, until the next round of censuses in the year 2000, one needs to rely on other sources for more recent data.

The **Labour Force Survey** (LFS) has the advantage of being able to provide relatively recent data (1996) and, in many cases, a time series from 1985. However, as its primary objective is to analyse employment, the sample unit in Denmark and Sweden is the individual (as opposed to the household) and therefore data on the composition of households are not available for these two countries. (For further information, see p. 108).

The **European Community Household Panel** (ECHP) was carried out for the first time in 1994 in twelve Member States. Only the results of the first wave are currently available. It provides valuable and often unique information in the areas of family composition, cohabitation and family responsibilities. (For further information, see p. 172).

Finally, the **annual demographic statistics** of the Member States cover important areas such as marriage and divorce.

148 million private households in EU-15

According to the Labour Force Survey of 1996[1], there were an estimated 367 million persons living in 148 million private households within the fifteen Member States of the European Union. This represents an average of 2.5 persons per household. Every EU country has experienced a decline in its average household size since the beginning of the 1980s. Today, only Spain and Ireland have an average of more than 3 persons per household (Figure 1). In addition to falling birth rates, one explanation is the substantial rise in the number of persons living on their own.

Substantial increase in the number of people living alone

The percentage of one-person households has been increasing in all EU countries since the 1960s. Today, 11% of the population lives alone or, put another way, one-person households make up 28% of all households, compared with 22% in 1981. In Denmark, Germany, Finland and Sweden, they now account for more than one-third of the total (Figure 2).

Figure 1 - Average household size, 1996

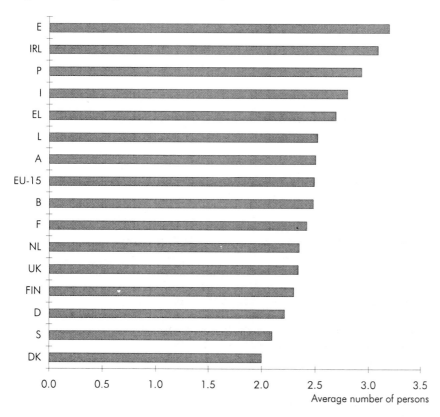

Source : Eurostat - Labour Force Survey. DK - ECHP 1994. S - Census 1990

---

[1]   Data for Denmark and Sweden are taken from 1990/91 population censuses.

There are marked differences between the sexes and across generations regarding the share of the population living alone : 44% of the population aged 75 and over now do so. Women are much more likely to live on their own: 56% of this age group as against 22% of men (Table 1). The longer life expectancy of women (currently 80 years compared with 74 for men) is a significant factor. There are considerable variations across Member States with the proportion of the population aged 75 and over living alone ranging from just over 20% in Spain to just under 70% in Finland.

In comparison with other Member States, young Danes, French, Germans and Dutch are more inclined to live by themselves. For the Europe of Fifteen, there are slightly more young men (12%) than young women (10%) living alone. There is also a strong north-south divide. While the proportion of people aged 20-29 living on their own is rather negligible in Spain, Portugal and Italy, in Sweden 35% of young men and 24% of young women do so.

The increase in one-person households has been accompanied by a considerable fall in the number of large households with more than 4 persons. Around 17% of the population now live in such households compared with 27% in 1981 (Figure 3). Ireland stands out with almost half the population falling into this category.

Figure 2 - Proportion of one-person households, 1996

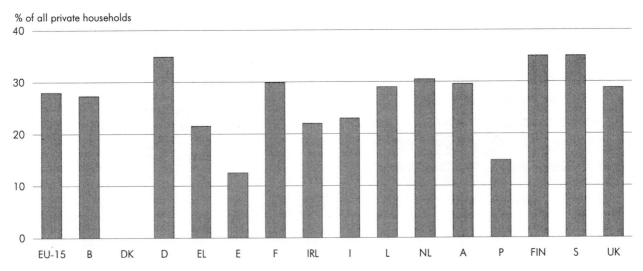

Source : Eurostat - Labour Force Survey. FIN - 1995 Census for data households. S - 1995 Survey of Living Conditions.
        DK - not available (1991 Census gave a figure of 34%)

Table 1 - Percentage of young and old people living on their own, 1996

| | % of population of age group | | | |
| | Age group 20-29 | | Age group 75 and over | |
	Men	Women	Men	Women
EU-15	12 *	10 *	22 *	56 *
B	9	8	26	57
DK	:	:	:	:
D	23	19	26	68
EL	8	7	16	46
E	1	1	10	28
F	16	15	22	59
IRL	5	4	28	46
I	6	4	22	69
L	11	11	23	49
NL	20	16	25	68
A	12	10	19	56
P	3	2	16	33
FIN	26	21	42	80
S	35	24	30	65
UK	13	9	30	58

Source : Eurostat - Labour Force Survey. FIN - 1995 Census data. I - 1995 Multipurpose
Survey on Households. S - 1995 Survey of Living Conditions

Figure 3 - Population by household size

EU-15, 1996

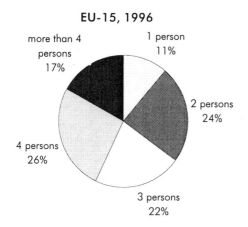

EU-12, 1981

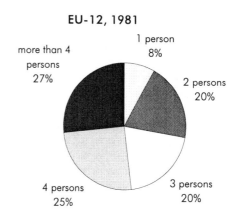

Reading note: In 1996, 17% of the population were living in a household made up of more than 4 persons compared with 27% in 1981.

Source: Eurostat - Population Censuses 1981/82 and Eurostat - Labour Force Survey 1996.

Definition of a family

A (nuclear) family is defined as a married or cohabiting couple with or without children (of any age), or a lone parent with children. In cases where an additional person(s) is living as part of the household, all persons in the household are classified under "other households".

Traditional family structures in decline

Despite the changing nature of family and household structures, the typical household based on the nuclear family (see box opposite) prevails. On average, around 78% of the EU-12 population lives in a nuclear family household (Table 2).

Although couples with children are still the most common family type, this is gradually being eroded by the increasing number of lone parent families and childless couples: today, individuals living in couples with children make up just over half the population in the Europe of Twelve. This holds more or less for all Member States except the Danes (42%) and the Swedes who have a similar structure as their Scandinavian neighbours. Around 60% of the Spanish, Irish, and Portuguese populations are living as part of a couple with children.

Around 30% of the population is living in a household made up of a couple and children under the age of 16. Within this group, the number of individuals living in households with 3 or more children under the age of 16 is quite low, making up 7% of the total population with the notable exception of Ireland where 20% of the population lives in such a household.

Individuals living in couples without children represent 19% of the EU-12 population. In Ireland and the four southern Member States, the proportion of childless couples is considerably lower. It is worth bearing in mind that the figures include couples who have not yet had any children and others whose children have left home.

Table 2 - Proportion of persons living in private households by type of household, 1994

(%)

	EU-12	B	DK	D	EL	E	F	IRL	I	L	NL	P	UK
Total population	100	100	100	100	100	100	100	100	100	100	100	100	100
One-person household	11	11	23	15	7	4	11	7	8	10	14	4	11
Single-parent family	6	7	6	5	4	6	7	9	6	4	5	6	8
Couples without children	19	20	27	24	15	11	21	8	14	20	20	12	22
Couples with children	53	55	42	49	52	60	55	64	55	50	51	58	48
1 child under 16	9	10	9	12	8	10	10	5	7	9	5	11	8
2 children under 16	14	14	14	14	18	15	15	12	12	13	17	14	15
3 or more children under 16	7	9	5	5	4	4	9	20	5	9	10	6	8
at least 1 child over 15	22	23	14	17	23	31	21	27	31	19	19	28	17
Other households	11	6	2	7	22	19	6	13	17	16	10	19	10

Source : Eurostat - European Community Household Panel (ECHP)

Around 6% of the EU-12 population lives in a lone parent family. This type of family accounts for a greater share of the population in Ireland (9%) and the United Kingdom (8%). The overwhelming majority of lone parents are women : they account for around 90% of the total in all Member States and as much as 95% in Austria, with only Italy having a figure below 85% and then only marginally.

Sizeable population still living in multigenerational households in the southern countries

About 11% of the EU population lives in "other households", i.e., households which are neither nuclear family nor one-person households. The vast majority of these are made up of households where all members are related by blood, marriage or adoption. This phenomenon is most apparent in Greece, Spain and Portugal with around one-fifth of the population living in this way.

Reference person

In the first wave of the ECHP, the head of the household is regarded as the reference person (RP) if (i) the head is 'economically active' (working or looking for work), or if (ii) there is no economically active person in the household. Otherwise the spouse/partner of the head, if he/she is economically active, is taken as the RP. If not, then the oldest economically active person in the household is the RP. In addition, to qualify as representative, the person must be normally resident at the household.

The household interview is conducted with the reference person.

Fewer and later marriages and more marital breakdowns

Perhaps the most important step on the path to adulthood is leaving the parental home either to live alone or to form a couple, married or otherwise. Today, there is a tendency for young people to delay this decision. Furthermore, fewer people are deciding to get married and those that do are more likely to divorce than in the past.

Young people are staying longer with their parents ...

Between 1960 and 1980, there was a tendency for young people, particularly in the northern Member States, to leave home relatively early in search of "independence". The following decade saw a reversal of this trend in all countries except the Netherlands. The pattern was accentuated among the 25-29 age-group in the southern Member States with considerably more young Greeks, Spaniards, Portuguese and up to 50% more Italians staying with their parents in 1996 compared with 1987 (Table 3). Today, for the Union as a whole, two-thirds of 20-24 year olds and one-third of 25-29 year olds have not yet left the parental home.

The trend can be explained by a number of factors ranging from the extension of schooling, difficulty in finding employment and suitable housing to more basic changes such as the decline in marriage. In a recent pan-European survey[1], three-quarters of people aged 15-24 thought the main reason young people were staying with their parents, was that they could not afford to move out.

Table 3 - Young people living with their parents, 1987 - 1996

(as a % of each age-group)

	EU-15	B	DK	D	EL	E	F	IRL	I	L	NL	A	P	FIN	S	UK
Age 20-24																
1987	:	63	:	57	63	84	47	64	81	64	55	:	75	:	:	45
1996	66	69		53	73	90	52	60	89	64	51	66	80	24		47
Age 25-29																
1987	:	19	:	20	39	49	14	28	39	26	15	:	39	:	:	15
1996	32	25	:	20	50	62	18	34	59	30	14	31	52	8	:	17

D - new Länder excluded

Source : Eurostat - Labour Force Survey

---

[1]   Eurobarometer 47.2, "The Young Europeans", European Commission, 1997.

... though there is still a strong north-south divide

Changes in family structure still reflect, however, the cultural traditions inherent in many countries. In the northern countries, young people tend to leave home earlier, many in order to live alone or as unmarried couples. This is in sharp contrast to the southern countries and Ireland where the young are more inclined to live longer with their parents and usually wait until they are to marry before leaving. At least 50% of young adults aged 25-29 in Spain, Italy, Greece and Portugal still live with their parents compared with 17% in the United Kingdom, 14% in the Netherlands and as few as 8% in Finland.

Throughout the Union, young women are more inclined to leave home and start a family slightly earlier than their male counterparts (Figure 4).

Figure 4 - Young adults living with their parents, EU-15, 1996

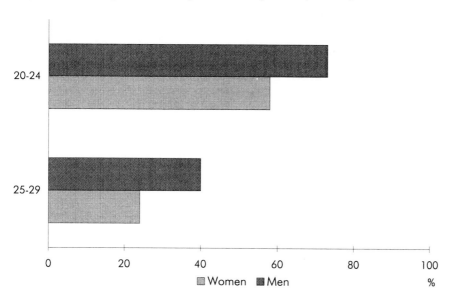

Source : Eurostat - Labour Force Survey

Non-marital unions : a growing phenomenon in most countries

In the last twenty years or so, conjugal life in many countries has increasingly taken the form of cohabitation. Although for the Union as a whole, around 90% of the population living in couples are married, this figure masks significant differences across countries (Table 4). Virtually all couples are married in the southern countries, but in Denmark, this applies to only 75% of persons living in a couple.

There are marked differences between generations in all countries: 31% of young people (under the age of 30) living in a couple are cohabiting compared with 8% of the age-group 30-44 and only 3% of the age-group 45 and over. Among the young generation aged 16-29, there are wide disparities between countries. While more than 70% of young Danish couples are unmarried, only 6-10% of Italian, Spanish and Portuguese couples cohabit.

Table 4 - Percentage of couples living in a consensual union by age-group, 1994

(%)

	Total, 16+	Age-group			
		16-29	30-44	45-64	65+
EU-12	8	31	8	3	3
B	10	27	11	6	3
DK	25	72	28	8	6
D	9	30	8	4	4
EL	2	9	1	1	1
E	3	14	4	1	1
F	14	46	14	4	3
IRL	3	11	2	1	0
I	2	6	2	1	1
L	10	28	10	5	2
NL	13	54	15	4	3
P	3	10	2	1	2
UK	11	38	12	3	1

Definition : Age-groups are based on the age of the reference person (see box p. 57)

Reading note : 31% of couples aged 16-29 were cohabiting in 1994. The remaining 69% were married.

Source : Eurostat - European Community Household Panel (ECHP). I - Multipurpose Survey on Households 1995. NL - 1994 Annual Households Statistics

In spite of this lack of convergence, the opinions of young persons aged 15-24 regarding non-marital unions are rather homogeneous (Figure 5). A small minority, less than 10% in all countries, consider cohabiting to be a "bad thing". On average, around 30% regard as a "good thing" but the vast majority (60%) feel that it is "not for others to judge".

Fewer marriages in all countries ...

Following a slight increase at the end of the 1980s, the crude marriage rate for the Europe of Fifteen has again gone into decline : today, there are just five marriages per year for every 1000 inhabitants, compared with nearly eight in 1970. The downward trend in the number of marriages can be observed throughout the Union (Table 5). The decrease was particularly marked in France (-72%), Ireland (-66%), the Netherlands (-64%) and Finland (-72%). Swedes continue to be the least likely to get married. Two countries, Denmark and Greece have recently experienced a slight upward trend in the crude marriage rate.

Figure 5 - Opinions of those aged 15 to 24 on living together without getting married, 1993

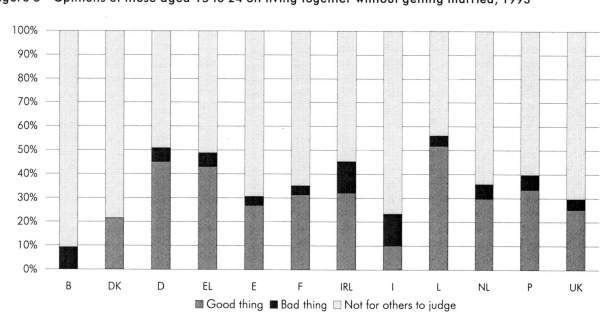

Source : Eurobarometer - Survey 39.0, 1993

Marriage and divorce rates

The **crude marriage/divorce rates** are the ratios of the number of marriages/divorces to the mean population in a given year.

The **total divorce rate**: the mean number of divorces per 100 marriages for a notional cohort which would be subject, for each marriage duration, to current divorce rates.

... and later

In 1980, the average age of a man at the time of his marriage was 26. By 1995, this figure had risen to almost 29 years. Similarly, the average age for women increased over the same period from 23 to 26 years. Throughout the Union, women tend to get married younger than men (Figure 6). The age difference between the sexes is around 2-3 years. Greek women are on average 4 years younger than men. On average, Portuguese and Belgian men tend to get married at a younger age (around 26 years) while Danish and Swedish men are more inclined to wait until their thirties.

About one marriage in four ends in divorce

The number of marriages continues to decline, while existing marriages are tending to become less stable. In most Member States, crude divorce rates reached unprecedented levels in 1995. For the Union as a whole, the rate has increased from 0.8 per 1000 inhabitants in 1970 to 1.8 in 1995 (Table 6).

Table 5 - Trend in crude marriage rates, 1970-1995

(per 1000 population)

	Crude marriage rate		
	1970-74	1990-94	1995
EU-15	7.6	5.5	5.1 *
B	7.6	5.8	5.1
DK	6.6	6.3	6.6
D	7.0	5.7	5.3
EL	7.7	5.7	6.1
E	7.6	5.4	5.0 *
F	7.8	4.7	4.4 *
IRL	7.3	4.7	4.4 *
I	7.5	5.4	4.9 *
L	6.3	6.2	5.1
NL	8.7	6.0	5.3
A	6.8	5.7	5.3
P	9.4	7.0	6.6
FIN	7.9	4.9	4.6
S	5.1	4.2	3.8
UK	8.2	6.0	5.5 *

Source : Eurostat - Demographic Statistics

Figure 6 - Average age at first marriage, 1995

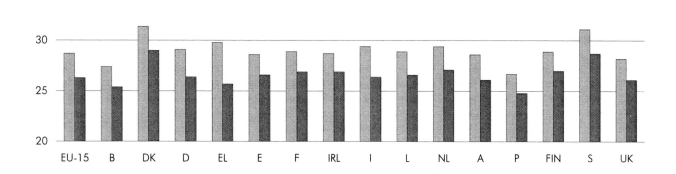

Source : Eurostat Demographic Statistics

Table 6 - Trend in crude divorce rates, 1970-1995

(per 1000 population)

	Crude divorce rate		
	1970-74	1990-94	1995
EU-15	1.0	1.7	1.8 *
B	0.8	2.1	3.5
DK	2.5	2.6	2.5
D	1.5	1.9	2.1
EL	0.4	0.7	1.1
E	-	0.7	0.8 *
F	0.9	1.9	2.0 *
IRL	-	-	-
I	0.4	0.5	0.5
L	0.7	1.9	1.8
NL	1.1	2.0	2.2
A	1.4	2.1	2.3
P	0.1	1.2	1.2
FIN	1.7	2.6	2.7
S	2.1	2.4	2.6
UK	1.8	3.0	2.9 *

Note : Divorce was not legalised in Ireland until 1995.

Source : Eurostat Demographic Statistics

Total fertility rate

The average number of children per woman for a notional birth cohort which would be subject for each age to current fertility rates.

In 1995, the total divorce rate (see box p. 62) in EU-15 was 30 divorces per 100 marriages compared with a rate of 10 per 100 marriages in 1970 (Figure 7): the most recent observations suggest that, if the present rate is maintained, nearly one third of all marriages will be dissolved, a significant increase on the current level.

The trend in the average number of divorces reflects new legislation adopted by some Member States. Nowhere is this more apparent than in Belgium which had the highest divorce rate (0.55) in 1995 owing to the reform introduced in that year which widened the grounds for divorce and simplified the divorce procedure. The United Kingdom and the three Scandinavian countries have also seen their total divorce rate consistently above 0.4 for the years since 1990. At the other end of the scale are the southern countries, particularly Italy which, despite the fact that divorce was legalised in 1970, has the lowest rate in the Union (0.08).

As a result of the increase in the number of divorces, there has been an upward trend in the number of remarriages throughout the Union, particularly among men.

Figure 7 - Trend in the average number of divorces per marriages in EU-15, Germany, Italy and the United Kingdom

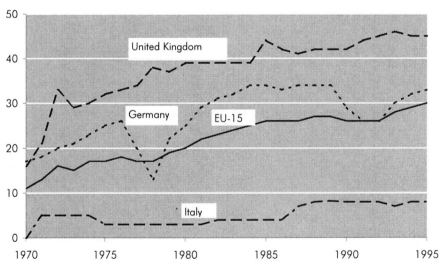

Note : UK - England and Wales only
Source : Eurostat Demographic Statistics

Interpretation: Legislation introduced in Germany in 1977 interrupted the upward trend in divorce. Similarly, reunification in 1990 also ushered in a temporary decline.

Fewer children and later in life

For the Europe of Fifteen, the total fertility rate (see box opposite) has fallen from 2.39 in 1970 to 1.43 in 1995. In 1970, the levels ranged from 3.93 in Ireland to 1.83 in Finland. Today, in spite of a marked fall, Ireland continues to register the highest rate (1.87). Spain and Italy have also recorded particularly sharp declines to leave them with the lowest rates, 1.18 and 1.17 respectively.

In parallel with these trends, women are waiting longer and longer before having their first child : an average of 24 in 1970 has now risen to 26. These combined tendencies mean a sharp drop in fertility among young people.

It is now increasingly rare for a woman to have a baby before the age of 20: from 1975 to the present day, the fertility rates of women aged 15-19 fell by 50%. Greece, France, Italy, and Austria experienced the largest decreases. On average, only 1% of women in this age group across the Union now have children. The United Kingdom stands out with a relatively high fertility rate for this age-group, twice that of the EU average. The fall in the fertility rate is most marked among women aged 20-24. Between 1980 and 1995 in all southern Member States and Ireland, this rate fell to less than half its original level.

By looking at the fertility patterns of different generations, it can be seen that the younger the generation of women, the higher the proportion that is childless. For example, while 15% of German women born in 1950 are childless, this proportion rises to 26% among women born 9 years later. All Member States are experiencing, to varying degrees, an upward trend (Table 7). The proportion of women with only one child is tending to rise in the southern countries. It is relatively stable in the other Member States with the exception of Finland which has experienced a downward trend.

Table 7 - Proportion of childless women by generation, 1945-1960

(%)

	EU-15	B	DK	D	EL	E	F	IRL	I	L	NL	A	P	FIN	S	UK
1945	:	9	8	13	:	6	7	6	10	:	12	:	5	14	12	10
1950	:	10	10	15	:	10	7	9	11	:	15	:	9	16	13	14
1955	:	10	13	22	:	10	8	14	11	:	17	:	8	18	13	17
1959	:	:	13	26	:	12	:	:	15	:	19	:	7	18	13	21
1960	:	:	12	:	:	11	:	:	15	:	18	:	8	18	13	:

D - excluding new Länder, UK - England and Wales only

Source : Eurostat - Demographic Statistics

In a recent Eurobarometer survey, young people aged 15-24 were asked to specify the most important factors that influence the decision to have children. Stability emerged as a prime factor, whether in terms of employment or relationships. Other determinants that were cited by more than 40% of respondents were the possibility of giving the child a good education and having suitable housing.

Almost one in four children born in 1995 had unmarried parents

As the number of people living together outside marriage continues to rise, so too does the number of births outside marriage. The proportion of births out of wedlock increased substantially from 10% in 1980 to 23% in 1995 (Table 8). The picture is far from homogeneous across countries although, for the most part, the percentages are in line with the frequency of unmarried couples (Table 4). For example, in Sweden and Denmark around half the children are now born to unmarried parents while in Greece and Italy, the proportion is less than 10%. However, in spite of the relatively small proportion of unmarried couples in Ireland, the proportion of births outside marriage is rather high (around 23%).

Table 8 - Percentage of live births outside marriage

(as a % of total live births)

	1970	1980	1990	1995
EU-15	6	10	20	23 *
B	3	4	12	15 *
DK	11	33	46	47
D	7	12	15	16
EL	1	2	2	3
E	1	4	10	11 *
F	7	11	30	37 *
IRL	3	5	15	23
I	2	4	7	8 *
L	4	6	13	13
NL	2	4	11	16
A	13	18	24	27
P	7	9	15	19
FIN	6	13	25	33
S	19	40	47	53
UK	8	12	28	34

Source : Eurostat - Demographic Statistics

Almost one in ten children now live with just one parent

The proportion of young children living in lone parent families is increasing in all countries. In 1994, 9% of children under the age of 16 were living with just one parent. This phenomenon is most prevalent in the United Kingdom (16%), Sweden (14%), Denmark (14%) and Ireland (12%). In contrast, percentages for the southern countries, Luxembourg and the Netherlands are significantly lower than the EU average (Figure 8).

The increase in lone parent families and the break-up of traditional family types has seen the emergence of "reconstituted" families, in which one or both parents bring children from a previous marriage into the family. Unfortunately, no comprehensive European data are available at present to quantify this phenomenon.

Figure 8 - Percentage of children (less than 16 years old) living in a lone parent household, 1994

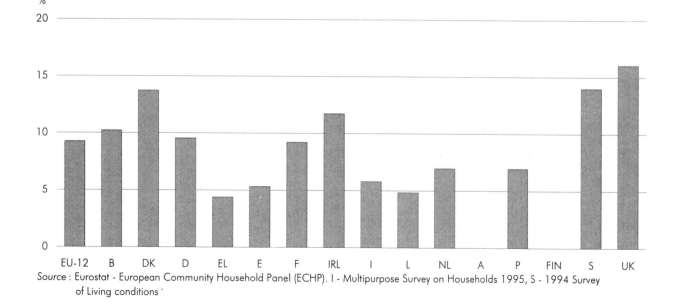

Source : Eurostat - European Community Household Panel (ECHP). I - Multipurpose Survey on Households 1995, S - 1994 Survey of Living conditions ·

Reconciling professional and family lives

Over the past ten years there has been a significant rise in female economic activity (See Employment chapter). This has been accompanied by a drop in fertility rates, an increase in female levels of education and an apparent increase in the view shared by many couples that two salaries are better than one. Today, almost two-thirds of women between the ages of 25 and 59 in the European Union are part of the labour market. Many of them are often faced with the problem of combining both a professional and family life.

The impact of children on female economic activity : a mixed picture

As one might expect, female activity rates generally fall as the number of children increases although the precise effect varies between countries (Table 9). In Germany, Spain, Ireland, Luxembourg, the Netherlands and the United Kingdom, activity rates for women aged between 20 and 45 with one child under the age of 15 are substantially lower (between -15% and -30%) than those without children. This difference increases with the number of children. However, in Belgium, France, Portugal, the female activity rate actually increases, albeit to a small degree, among mothers with one child.

Table 9 - Activity rates for women aged 20-45 by number of children under the age of 15, 1996

(%)

	0 children	1 child	2 children	3 or more children
EU-15	:	:	:	:
B	72	75	76	55
DK	:	:	:	:
D	83	72	60	42
EL	65	58	55	47
E	67	59	53	45
F	78	81	74	50
IRL	77	62	54	41
I	63	56	48	37
L	74	57	43	30
NL	83	66	61	48
A	82	78	67	58
P	73	79	76	60
FIN	82	80	80	66
S	:	:	:	:
UK	86	71	65	48

Source : Eurostat - Labour Force Survey

It is the presence of a second child in Italy and Austria that causes the female activity rate to drop sharply while in Belgium, France, Portugal and Finland it is only mothers with more than two children who are significantly less likely than other women to be in the labour market.

There are a number of factors that may explain these differences across Member States. In addition to the diverse cultural traditions and labour market prospects visible throughout the EU, the provision of childcare facilities, the amount of support available from within the family and the extent to which work is a matter of economic necessity all have a bearing on a mother's decision to work or not.

"Housewives" : considerable differences across the EU

The proportion of "housewives" varies considerably from one Member State to another (Table 10). In Ireland, they account for 60% of the female population aged 25-59. In Spain, Greece, Italy and Luxembourg this percentage is also high, around 40%. In contrast, just over 20% of Portuguese women can be classified as "housewives". Precise figures for the Scandinavian countries are not available but they are understood to be as low as 5-10%. For the Europe of Twelve, around one-third of women aged between 25 and 59 fall into this category.

Table 10 - Mothers giving up work, 1994

(%)

	Housewives as a proportion of the female population aged 25-59	Proportion of housewives aged 25-59 who had to give up work(as a % of all housewives of the same age)	Proportion of housewives aged 25-59 whose main reason for giving up work was children (as a % of all reasons)
EU-12	31 *	39 *	41 *
B	23	26	23
DK	:	:	:
D	27	44	58
EL	42	25	18
E	48	31	22
F	25	44	33
IRL	60	48	41
I	39	24	29
L	44	42	65
NL	35	41	49
P	22	28	12
UK	26	67	49

DK - not available

Source : Eurostat - European Community Household Panel (ECHP)

Among housewives who had stopped working in their last job (see box p. 69), looking after children was by far the most common reason given (41%). Four countries were well above the EU average - the Netherlands and the United Kingdom where the proportion was around 50%, Germany (58%) and Luxembourg where it was as high as 65% (Table 10). For the Union as a whole, marriage was cited as a reason by only 6% of housewives although Greece and Spain had much higher rates (15% and 14% respectively). Other reasons mentioned were breach of contract by an employer (10%), end of contract (9%) and ill-health (8%).

Part-time work: more frequent in the North

Working part-time (see box opposite) is one possible way of combining a professional and family life. Almost one-third of women in employment are working part-time, as against 5% of men (Figure 9). In Belgium, Germany and the Netherlands, female part-time employment is about ten times higher than that of their male counterparts. It is most widespread in the Netherlands (68%), the United Kingdom (45%) and Sweden (40%) and least frequent in Greece (9%) and Italy (13%), (see chapter on Labour Market).

Figure 9 - Percentage of men and women in employment working part-time, 1996

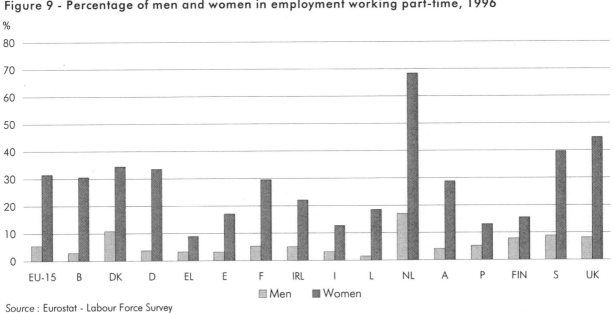

Source : Eurostat - Labour Force Survey

The decision to work part-time is often explained by the need to stay at home. On average for the Community, 55% of women working part-time gave "family obligations" as the main determining factor for this type of work. This proportion was highest in Germany and Luxembourg, exceeding 70% in both countries. This in line with the relatively high proportion of women in these two countries who declared that they had to give up work to look after their children (Table 10).

Among working parents, mothers are much more likely than fathers to look after their children

In families where both parents are in employment for at least 30 hours per week, 75% of mothers and 45% of fathers reported in 1994 that they look after their children (under the age of 16) on a daily basis. This difference in behaviour between the spouses is apparent in all countries, particularly in Portugal where mothers are 4 times more likely than fathers, and in Greece, Spain and Ireland where they are more than twice as likely to look after their children on a daily basis. In contrast, this divergence is relatively small in Denmark and the Netherlands (Figure 10).

Of those working parents who claim that they look after their children on a daily basis, mothers tend to devote much more time to the task than fathers. 69% of women compared with only 20% of men reported that they spent more than 4 hours per day looking after them while, at the other end of the scale, 38% of men against a mere 6% of women did so for less than 2 hours per day (Table 11). This pattern can be observed in all twelve Member States for which data are available.

> **Part-time work**
>
> The classification by part-time or full-time job is based on the self-assessment of respondents in the LFS, except for Austria and the Netherlands where it depends on a threshold on the basis of the number of hours usually worked.
>
> The extent to which a job of a particular number of hours is considered as part-time varies considerably across countries. In Germany and the United Kingdom for example, most people working between 21 and 30 hours a week consider their job as part-time, but, in Ireland and Italy only 1 in 3 persons do likewise.

Figure 10 - Proportion of parents (working at least 30 hours per week) declaring they look after their children (aged under 16) on a daily basis, 1994

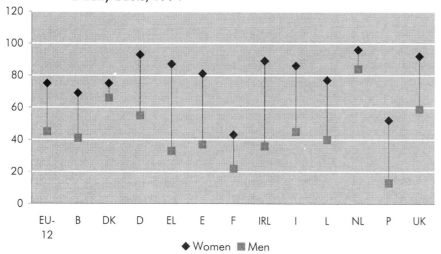

◆ Women ▪ Men

Source : Eurostat - European Community Household Panel (ECHP)

In some countries, grandmothers play an important role in looking after children. For the Union as a whole, 14% of women over the age of 50 say that they look after children on a daily basis without pay. This is likely to consist mostly of grandmothers taking care of their grandchildren. It is in Italy (29%) and Greece (25%) where parents seem to benefit most from this form of free child-care (Figure 11).

Table 11 - Time spent with children per day, EU-12, 1994

(%)

	Women	Men
less than 2 hours	6	38
2-4 hours	25	42
more than 4 hours	69	20

Source : Eurostat - European Community Household Panel (ECHP)

Figure 11 - Proportion of women aged over 50 declaring they look after children on a daily basis without pay, 1994

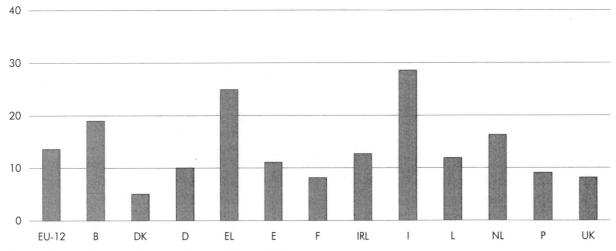

Source : Eurostat - European Community Household Panel (ECHP)

Education and training

Towards a knowledge based society

Now more than ever before, education and training systems must be of the highest quality as the number of jobs for unskilled labour is declining. Education and training must also be relevant and responsive to the rapidly changing demands of our modern knowledge-based society. High youth unemployment and a more competitive labour force have incited young people to stay longer in education and training. The European Commission has actively supported the development of education and training skills. The White Paper entitled 'Teaching and Learning - Towards the Learning Society' (1995) in particular identifies the need for broad based knowledge and for building up the employability of individuals. The chapter emphasises that education and training skills must be developed throughout our lifetimes. Through Programmes such as Socrates and Leonardo da Vinci, the Commission assists the achievement of these goals and seeks to bring about an improvement in European education and vocational training at all levels. By promoting European cooperation and helping to improve the quality of education and training through partnership across national boundaries, such Programmes are seen as making an important contribution to developing the full potential of Europe's human resources.

In the European Union participation in education has been consistently increasing in recent years and the ways of acquiring knowledge are becoming more diverse, as are the forms this knowledge can take. Education possibilities are not limited within the boundaries of individual Member States and mobility in education is openly encouraged. Resources for education of finance and teaching staff remain an important consideration. This chapter examines such issues and identifies some critical points of reference from which our future potential can be assessed and developed.

— About 40 million pupils in compulsory education; around 12 million in tertiary education.
— Females are now participating as much as males in post-compulsory education.
— Nearly 30% of young people aged between 15 and 19 years participate in initial vocational training programmes; such training can be found at the workplace although entirely school-based training programmes are still the most common in the EU.

- Entering tertiary education for the first time is still mainly for those in their late teens and early 20s in many EU Member States; Denmark, Sweden and the United Kingdom are the few countries where taking up tertiary education after age 30 is quite common.
- Pupils in secondary general education are learning on average 1.3 modern foreign languages.
- 6 million teachers in the European Union: this represents about 4% of the total labour force.

From the Presidency Conclusions - Amsterdam 16 and 17 June 1997

'The European Council attaches paramount importance to creating conditions in the Member States that would promote a skilled and adaptable workforce and flexible labour markets responsive to economic change. This requires active intervention by the Member States in the labour market to help people develop their employability. Such action is important if the European Union is to remain globally competitive, and in order to tackle the scourge of unemployment.'

From the Presidency Conclusions - Employment Summit, Luxembourg 20 and 21 November 1997

The Presidency Conclusions of the Luxembourg Employment Summit reinforce some of the decisions made in Amsterdam concerning the vital role played by education and training in the fight against unemployment as demonstrated by the following paragraphs:

'Easing the transition from school to work: ...Employment prospects are poor for young people who leave the school system without having acquired the aptitudes required for entering the job market. Member States will therefore:

- improve the quality of their school systems in order to reduce substantially the number of young people who drop out of the school system early;

- make sure they equip young people with greater ability to adapt to technological and economic changes and with skills relevant to the labour market, where appropriate by implementing or developing apprenticeship training.'

'Member States will ensure that :

- every unemployed young person is offered a new start before reaching six months of unemployment, in the form of training, retraining, work practice, a job or other employability measure;

- unemployed adults are also offered a fresh start before reaching twelve months of unemployment by one of the aforementioned means or, more generally, by accompanying individual vocational guidance.'

Increase in education

The diversity of the education systems across the European Union is reflected by the differing lengths, starting and finishing ages of compulsory schooling. Compulsory schooling of at least eight years is required in the Member States of the European Union. This consists of mainly full-time education although a few countries, namely Belgium, Germany and the Netherlands offer a system of part-time for the last two or three years.

The schooling 'life-cycle' of children varies between countries, with those in Luxembourg starting school at the age of four while school attendance is not compulsory until the age of seven in the Scandinavian countries. The end of obligatory full-time schooling is in general either at age 15 or 16 with Italy being the exception with age 14. Recent reforms in some Member States such as Spain and Portugal prolonging the length of compulsory schooling exemplify the general move towards a better educated population. (Figure 1)

Figure 1 - Duration of compulsory schooling

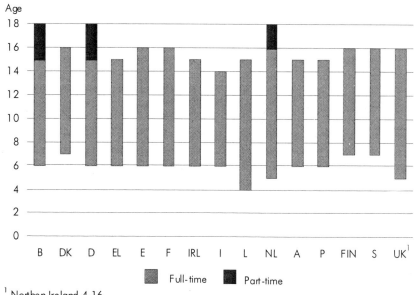

¹ Northen Ireland 4-16
Source : Eurydice

Education starting earlier...

An increase in education participation within the last two decades is evident for all levels of education outside the limits of compulsory schooling with even pre-primary education, the earliest stage of schooling, being affected. This could be the result of a wider acceptance of arguments stressing the importance of such preparatory schooling on a child's development. For instance, increasing numbers of four year olds have been participating in pre-primary education in most Member States of the European Union in the last fifteen years, even if the rates remain relatively low for some such as Greece, Portugal and Sweden at just over 50% in 1995 and in Finland at only 29%. In Ireland pre-primary attendance has not increased at all over this time period remaining at around 50%. For other countries, however, high participation in pre-primary education has been the norm for a long time such as in Belgium since the 1960s and in France and the Netherlands since the beginning of the 1970s. In Luxembourg, participation in pre-primary education for four year olds is even compulsory, although the rate shown here is not 100% as only public schools are included (Table 1).

...and finishing later

At the other end of the education system, tertiary education has seen a considerable rise in demand with the amount of students participating increasing by 75% since 1980/81 in the European Union as a whole (Figure 2). This is not due to a respective increase in the population of young people as the approximate respective age group (18-29) only rose by 3% between 1980/81 and 1994/95. Rather, with unemployment a constant threat, a tertiary education qualification is seen as providing some security in the labour market as the better educated have a competitive advantage and a lower risk of marginalisation. Additionally, studies show that the more a person is qualified, the better their opportunities for lifelong learning. The amount of students in tertiary education has more than doubled in Greece, Spain, Ireland, Portugal and the United Kingdom over the last fifteen years (Table 2).

Table 1 - Trend in the participation of 4 years olds in pre-primary education, 1980/81 - 1994/95

(As a % of children aged 4)

	B	DK	D	EL	E	F	IRL	I	L	NL	A	P	FIN	S	UK
1980/81	100	54	65	38	69	100	54	:	94	96	57	18	18	28	:
1990/91	99	74	71	51	95	100	55	:	94	98	66	46	26	48	:
1994/95	100	79	71	54	100	100	53	96	94	97	71	55	29	58	93

Source : Eurostat - Joint Unesco, OECD, Eurostat data collection (UOE)

Table 2 - Trend in the number of students in tertiary education, 1980/81-1994/95[1]

	EU-15	B	DK	D	EL	E	F	IRL	I	L	NL	A	P	FIN	S	UK
1980/81	6 736 *	217	115	1 525	121	698	1 176	55	1 126	:	364	137	90	113	:	828
1985/86	7 992	248	125	1 842	182	934	1 358	70	1 192	:	405	173	118	128	183	1 033
1990/91	9 656	276	151	2 082	195	1 222	1 699	90	1 452	:	479	206	186	166	193	1 258
1994/95	11 791	353	170	2 156	296	1 527	2 073	122	1 792	2	503	234	301	205	246	1 813

[1] For some countries, the figures for tertiary education in recent years may be affected by the inclusion of programmes that were not included previously

Growth index (1980/81 = 100)

	EU-15	B	DK	D	EL	E	F	IRL	I	L	NL	A	P	FIN	S	UK
1980/81	100	100	100	100	100	100	100	100	100	:	100	100	100	100	100	100
1985/86	119	114	109	121	150	134	115	127	106	:	111	127	131	113	107	125
1990/91	143	127	131	137	161	175	144	164	129	:	132	150	206	146	113	152
1994/95	175	163	148	141	245	219	176	221	159	:	138	171	334	181	145	219

Source : Eurostat - Joint Unesco, OECD, Eurostat data collection (UOE)

Figure 2 - Trend in the number of students in tertiary education
EU-15, 1980/81 - 1994/95

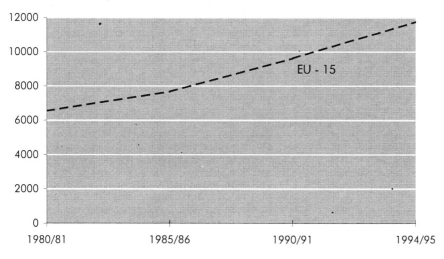

Source: Eurostat - Joint Unesco, OECD, Eurostat data collection (UOE)

More women participating

••••••••••••••••••••••••••••••••••

The considerable rise in the amount of people taking advantage of tertiary education is partly due to the increased participation, in general, of women in post compulsory education. In both upper secondary and tertiary education women have caught up with and, in some cases, overtaken men. In the European Union in 1994/95, there were 102 women per 100 men in upper secondary education compared with 93 fifteen years earlier. In tertiary education the increase was even greater, rising from 79 in 1980/81 to 103 by 1994/95 (Figure 3).

While on the European level the gender gap has disappeared, inequality still persists in some Member States. The lowest female participation is seen in tertiary education in Germany where there were 77 women per 100 men in 1994/95. However, in other Member States and particularly in Portugal, the situation has reversed with women now outnumbering men in tertiary education (Table 3).

Figure 3 - Trend in female participation: women per 100 men, EU-15, 1980/81 - 1994/95[1]

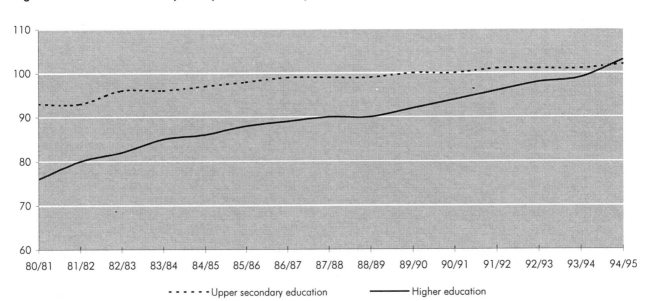

[1] Until 1990/91 data refer to the Federal Republic of Germany prior to 3.10.90.
Source : Eurostat - Joint Unesco, OECD, Eurostat data collection (UOE)

Despite such improvements, men and women still study different subjects and so in this respect some traditional boundaries between the sexes remain. In tertiary education for the European Union as a whole in 1994/95, female students predominated in the arts and medical science (including nursing) while their male counterparts favoured the sciences, mathematics, computer studies and particularly engineering. More than four times as many men as women opted for this latter subject.

Similarly at upper secondary level, women tend to opt for general rather than vocational education. In 1994/95, for every 100 men there were 114 women in general education and 94 women in vocational education. Although this was not the case for all individual Member States as in Spain, Ireland, Finland and the United Kingdom, women actually outnumbered men in vocational education to varying degrees.

Higher attainment levels

As a result of this long term trend of increased demand for education, younger generations are better educated. In 1996, just 31% of those aged between 55-59 in the European Union had completed upper secondary education whereas following a steady rise through the generations, this proportion had risen to 48% for the age group of 25-29. Over the same 30 year period, the proportion of those attaining a tertiary education qualification rose quite dramatically from 13% for those aged between 55-59 to 21% for the younger age group of 30-34, although the proportion can be seen to have levelled out since about the generation of the mid 1950s (Figure 4).

> **The UOE data collection**
>
> The UOE (UNESCO/OCDE/ EUROSTAT) data collection is an instrument through which the three organisations jointly collect internationally comparable data on key aspects of the education systems on an annual basis using administrative sources.

Table 3 - Women per 100 men in upper secondary and tertiary education, 1994/95

	EU-15	B	DK	D	EL	E	F	IRL	I	L	NL	A	P	FIN	S	UK
Upper secondary	102	99	100	85	94	111	95	106	99	90	88	84	109	121	117	117
Tertiary	103	98	108	77	98	111	122	97	110		89	92	131	112	122	104

Source: Eurostat - Joint Unesco, OECD, Eurostat data collection (UOE)

Member States with much lower levels of educational attainment have witnessed a more considerable increase which has lead to a reduction in the differences within the Union. This significant improvement in the level of educational qualifications has occurred in Greece, Spain, Italy and Portugal where the proportion of those aged between 25 and 29 having completed at least upper secondary education is at least twice that of the 50-59 age group.

The rise in the attainment level of the Union's population has been greater for women than for men and young women are now attaining educational levels more or less as high as men. This phenomenon is particularly apparent for tertiary education where the proportion of women completing this level of education has more than doubled between the generations of 30-34 and 55-59 year olds.

Figure 4 - Proportion of the population aged between 25 and 59 having attained upper tertiary education by age group, EU - 15, 1996[1]

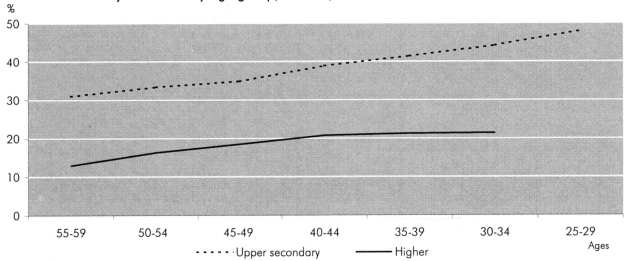

[1] For tertiary education the 25-29 age group is not considered here as many young people of these ages would still be finishing their studies.
Source : Eurostat - Labour Force Survey (LFS) 1996 - Ref p.108

Inequalities in educational opportunities persist

Despite such encouraging developments, inequalities in educational opportunities persist for young people. Studies have shown that the socio-economic or family background can affect the chance of educational success. One illustration of this is the apparent link between participation in post compulsory education and training and the level of education attained by the parents.

In the European Union Member States for which data are available, young people from families in which the head of household has been in tertiary education are less likely to leave the education system at this relatively early stage. For the Union as a whole, the percentage of young people aged 16-19 not participating in education and training was 25% in 1996 for those from families in which the head of household did not progress beyond lower secondary education. This figure was reduced to 9% for those coming from families in which the head of household had been in upper secondary education. Achievement of tertiary education then further reduced this amount to 4%. This situation can be observed to a greater or lesser extent in all countries although the United Kingdom stands out as an exception with the proportion of 16-19 year olds leaving school hardly being affected by the attainment level of the head of household (Table 4).

Table 4 - Proportion of young people aged 16-19 not in education by educational attainment level of head of household, 1996

(%)

Educational level of head of household	Lower secondary or less	Upper secondary	Tertiary
EU-15*	25	9	4
B	10	5	2
DK	:	:	:
D	15	8	4
EL	32	12	6
E	29	9	4
F	12	6	1
IRL	27	11	5
I	34	11	6
L	18	9	3
NL	22	12	7
A	33	20	7
P	31	3	3
FIN	15	11	5
S	:	:	:
UK	8	8	6

Source: Eurostat - Labour Force Survey (LFS) 1996

Vocational education as an alternative to general education

Initial and continuing vocational training have become core issues

Along with the increase in education for the attainment of a knowledge based society, has come a diversification of the types of education offered and of the phases of life during which education is undertaken. Indeed, both the Amsterdam European Council in June 1997 and the Luxembourg Employment Summit in November 1997 declared that the employment relevance of training and lifelong learning should be strengthened (see box p. 74).

Vocational education and training, both initial and that which is continuing throughout an individual's working career, has been identified by Commission policy as a vital means of achieving the goals of full employment, economic growth and competitiveness. For instance, helping young people to attain a certified vocational qualification is one of the priorities laid down in Article 127 of the Maastricht Treaty and the Council of the European Union gave its approval to a global vocational training policy for the Member States in 1994. Implemented as from January 1995, the Leonardo da Vinci action programme is aimed at supporting and supplementing the Member States' initiatives in the field of vocational training.

The Leonardo da Vinci programme

The Leonardo da Vinci is an action programme for pilot studies, exchanges and surveys and analyses designed to propose innovative training practices and improve training systems. The programme implements a vocational training policy in Europe intended to promote quality and innovation in national vocational training systems, to make best use of that innovation and to encourage technological development in vocational training. Moreover, it aims to increase language skills, to promote equal opportunities in training for men and women and to combat exclusion by offering disadvantaged persons a second chance.

This five-year programme, encompassing initial and continuing vocational training and lifelong learning, will run until 1999 and is the follow-up to previous programmes launched from 1987 onwards.

The growing importance of vocational training is underlined by an increasingly intensive effort at Community level. As the need for a policy on vocational training becomes increasingly evident, programmes for supporting initiatives from schools, universities, enterprises and administrations from the Member States are gaining ground.

The Socrates programme

The Socrates action programme continues and extends a number of previous Community programmes, including Erasmus and Lingua. These are combined with new actions to form the first comprehensive European programme for cooperation in all sectors of education. It is a five year programme covering the period of 1995-1999. The programme promotes cooperation in the six areas of tertiary education (Erasmus); school education (Comenius); promotion of language-learning (Lingua); open and distance learning (ODL); adult education; exchange of information and experience on education systems and policy.

The main objectives of Socrates are to develop the European dimension in education; to promote improved knowledge of European languages; to promote the intercultural dimension of education; to enhance the quality of education by means of European cooperation; to promote mobility of teaching staff and students; to encourage the recognition of diplomas, periods of study and other qualifications; to facilitate the development of an open European area for cooperation in education; to encourage open and distance education in the European context; to foster exchanges of information on educational systems and policy.

In order to obtain these objectives Socrates contains provision for a broad range of activities, including transnational projects, networks, partnerships and associations; joint development of curricula, modules, teaching materials and other educational products; exchanges and mobility; transnational training courses for educational staff; visits to facilitate project preparation or sharing of experience; preparation of studies, analyses, guides and data collection activities.

Participation in initial vocational training: great variation in the EU

Member States are dedicating increasing efforts to improve the quality and the attractiveness of vocational education and training programmes offered to young people by developing closer links between the world of work and the education and training world. In the European Union as a whole in 1993/94, around 29% of young people aged between 15 and 19 years participated in initial vocational education and training programmes. The rate of participation, nevertheless, varied considerably across Member States spanning from nearly 12% of the 15-19 year old population in Portugal, to around 55% of the same age group in Austria (Figure 5).

Figure 5 - Participation rates in initial vocational education and training of 15 to 19 year olds, 1993/94

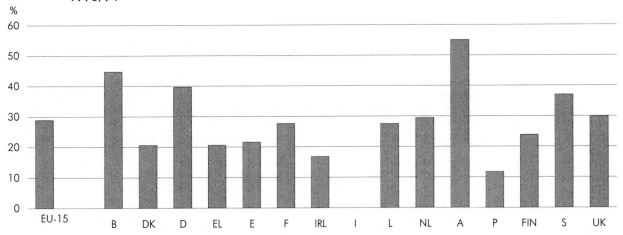

EU-15 estimated.

EL: data covering academic year 1992-1993

FIN & UK: rates for 16-19 year olds not 15-19

L: The fact students attend education/training in neighbouring countries may influence these rates

Source : Eurostat - Vocational Education and Training data collection (VET)

Community action has been particularly aimed at supporting and supplementing measures taken by Member States to enable young women to participate, on an equal basis, in all vocational education and training programmes. From the available statistical data, which shows only a very slight male dominance, it can be said that equal opportunities in vocational training have virtually been reached. In the Union, 55% of participants in initial vocational education and training were men and 45% women in 1993/94. Most Member States were very close to the European average, with the exceptions of Belgium and Ireland where participation was almost the same for men and women, and of Finland where more women than men were enrolled in vocational education and training programmes (Figure 6).

Figure 6 - Participants in vocational education and training by sex, 1993/94

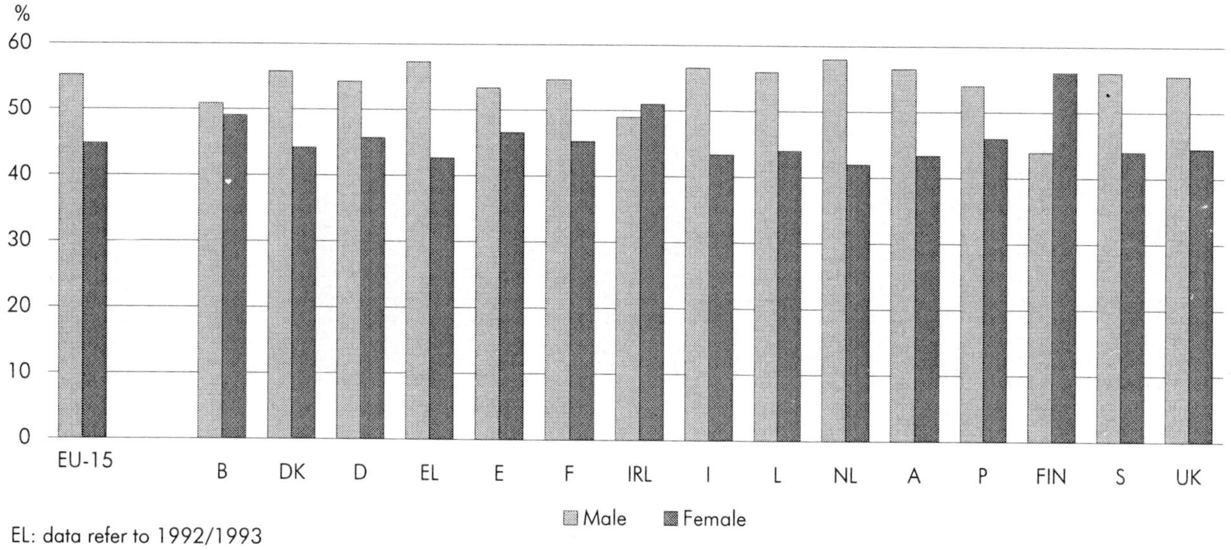

%

EL: data refer to 1992/1993

Source : Eurostat - Vocational Education and Training data collection (VET)

Organisation of initial vocational training: school-based still most common

··

The Member States have adopted different approaches to the organisation of vocational education and training programmes. These approaches lie between the two broad extremes of initial education and vocational training taking place entirely in an education/training institution and that taking place entirely at the workplace. More than half of vocational education and training takes place at least partly at the workplace although entirely school-based training programmes are still the most common in the European Union countries. (Figure 7). In those countries where little or no training time at all is spent at the workplace, efforts are increasingly being made to further involve enterprises in the organisation of vocational education and training programmes. EU policy fully supports this approach which is seen as having several advantages. For instance, it means that students gain knowledge that is more pertinent to the actual workplace, the move from school to work is more gradual and that integration into the workplace is facilitated by contacts already made whilst studying.

Figure 7 - Participants in initial vocational education and training by training place, 1993/94

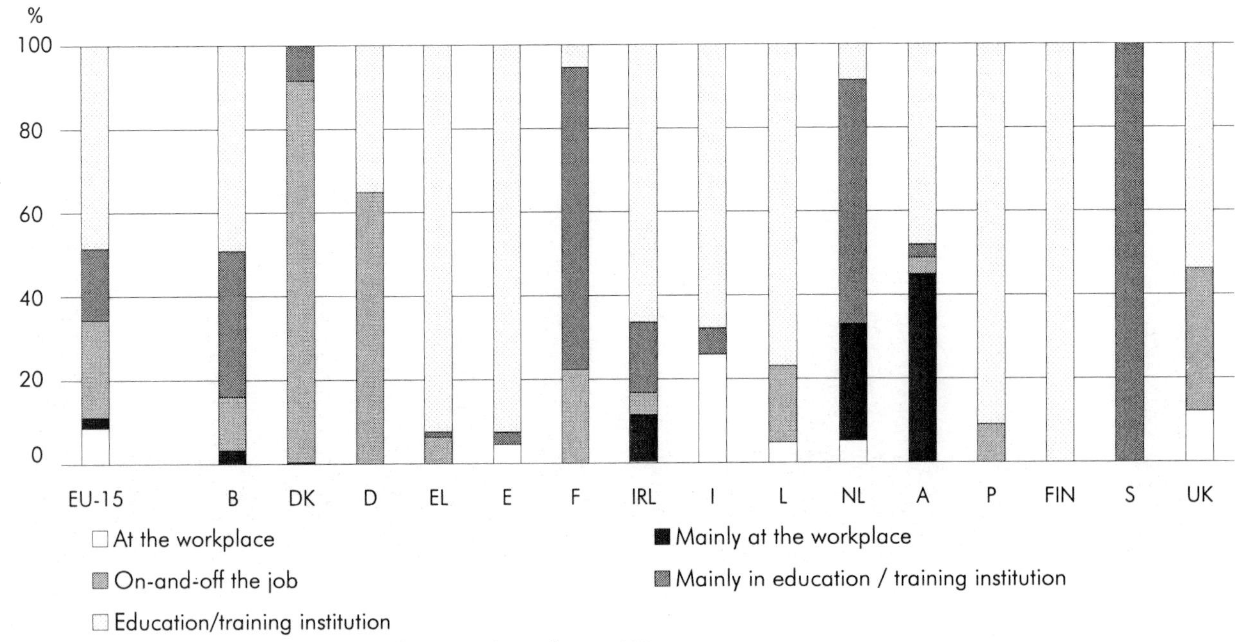

☐ At the workplace ■ Mainly at the workplace

▨ On-and-off the job ▨ Mainly in education / training institution

☐ Education/training institution

Source : Eurostat - Vocational Education and Training data collection (VET)

Lifelong learning

Continuing vocational training: an integral part of working life

Upgrading the existing skills of the workforce and developing new ones is extremely important, both for individuals and for enterprises. For individuals it enhances employability and for enterprises it supports competitiveness. Despite developments in the area of training provision in Member States and the emphasis of Community policy on the concept of lifelong learning, it appears that there is still a long way to go in fully realising this ideal.

In a survey carried out on Continuing Vocational Training (the CVTS) in 1993, 28% of employees of enterprises employing 10 or more people in the then European Union were participating in some form of continuing training provided by the enterprise. In certain countries such as France, Ireland and the UK, this proportion was more than a third, whereas at the other end of the scale the proportion was 13% in Greece and Portugal and 15% in Italy (Figure 8). Sex disparities did not affect the general pattern of these participation rates in continuing vocational training courses across the Union as men and women were seen to be participating almost equally in each Member State.

Figure 8 - Participation rates of employees on continuing vocational training courses [1], 1993

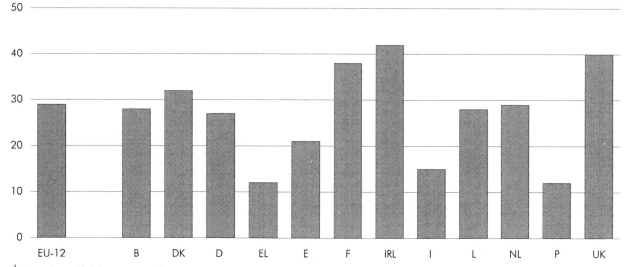

[1] Enterprises with 10 or more employees.

Source: Eurostat - Continuing Vocational Training Survey (CVTS), 1994

The possibility of a link between levels of participation in continuing vocational training and the extent to which initial vocational education is offered in countries is debatable, though not completely ruled out. For instance, some countries such as Portugal seem to exemplify the pattern that low involvement in initial vocational training means low participation in continuing training, suggesting that the worth of vocational education in general might not be valued. Other countries such as Ireland seem to exemplify the pattern that continuing training makes up for low initial training.

More lifelong learning opportunities in large enterprises

Despite differences between countries in the extent of continuing training participation, nearly all countries share the phenomenon of employees in larger enterprises receiving more training than those in smaller enterprises. Thus employees in small and medium sized enterprises have fewer opportunities available to them to develop their skills: for the Union of 12 in 1993, 13% of employees in enterprises with 10-49 employees took part in continuing vocational training courses compared with 44% in enterprises with 1000 or more employees (Figure 9).

Figure 9 - Participation rates in continuing vocational training courses by enterprise size, EU-12, 1993

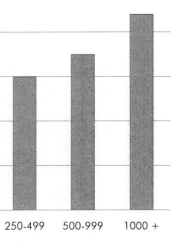

Source: Eurostat - Continuing Vocational Training Survey (CVTS) 1994

The only exception to the pattern was Denmark which was the only country in which the size of the enterprise seemed to have an inverse, but low effect on the participation chances of the employees (Figure 10).

The young and the qualified are more likely to receive training

The European Union Labour Force Survey provides some information on lifelong learning by measuring the participation of individuals in training during the four weeks preceding the interview. According to these results, it emerges that in the European Union only specific groups of people benefit from training with the competitive disadvantage of the older and less educated not being reduced.

As people get older they tend to receive less training. In the European Union in 1996, 7% of people in employment between 30 and 39 years of age were in training. The rate declined to 6% for those between 40 and 49, to 4% for those between 50 and 59 and finally to, below 2% of the over-60s (Table 5). This pattern was repeated in all the Member States, with the exception of Sweden where the 40-49 age group had the highest rate of participation in training programmes of those in employment. Therefore given such findings, it is questionable if lifelong learning has yet been fully achieved considering that it is mostly younger people who are gaining from training opportunities.

Figure 10 - Comparison of the proportion of employees participating in continuing vocational training courses in small and large enterprises, 1993

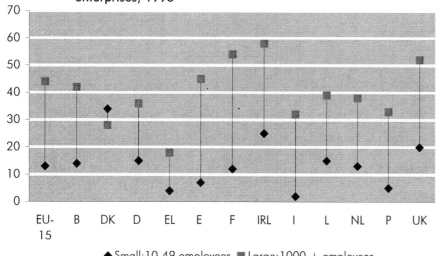

◆ Small: 10-49 employees   ■ Large: 1000 + employees

Source: Eurostat - Continuing Vocational Training Survey (CVTS) 1994

Level of education already achieved was also shown as being another factor which influences the chances of participation in lifelong learning for those in employment. Nearly 11% of people with a tertiary education degree were given training in the European Union as a whole in 1996. This figure was halved for those with upper secondary level education and then was further reduced to one-fifth for people with at best lower secondary education. The phenomenon of people with the highest levels of education being given priority for training was the same for all Member States (Figure 11).

Figure 11 - Participation of those aged 30 and over in training [1] by level of education, EU-15, 1996

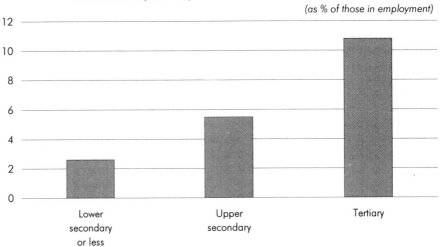

(as % of those in employment)

[1] Training during the four weeks preceding the interview
Source: Eurostat - Labour Force Survey (LFS) 1996

Table 5 - Participation of those aged 30 and over in training[1] by age, 1996

(As a % of those in employment)

	EU-15	B	DK	D	EL	E	F[2,3]	IRL	I	L	NL[2]	A	P[2]	FIN	S	UK
30-39	7	3	19	6	1	4	3	8	4	3	16	9	4	19	19	15
40-49	6	3	18	3	0	2	1	5	4	3	9	7	2	17	20	13
50-59	4	2	13	2	-	1	1	3	2	-	6	5	1	15	16	8
60 and over	2	-	5	1	-	-	-	-	1	-	2	3	-	5	10	3

- unreliable data.

[1] Training during the four weeks preceding the interview.

[2] Information on training is collected only if this is under way on the date of the survey.

[3] Exclusively in-house training is not covered.

Source: Eurostat - Labour Force Survey (LFS) 1996

Lifelong learning opportunities in tertiary education

Although data on this area of education are limited, the age of new entrants to tertiary education indicates the ease of access to university and equivalent studies throughout life in the different Member States of the European Union. In 1994/95, as many as one quarter of all new entrants to tertiary education in the United Kingdom were aged 30 and over. Denmark and Sweden also had a relatively high proportion of those entering tertiary education for the first time from this age group at 17 and 18% respectively. In these three countries, the proportion of those in the 30 and over age group was in balance with the younger new entrants following more traditional routes through education. Conversely, in France, Ireland and Greece hardly anyone entered tertiary education after the age of 21 suggesting that initial linear education predominates over other methods of gaining a degree. (Table 6). Thus, it would appear that certain education systems are more open than others to those wishing to take up tertiary education studies later in life which is one element of education as a lifelong process.

Table 6 - Age structure of new entrants[1] to tertiary education, 1994/95

(%)

	DK	D	EL	F	IRL	NL	A[2]	S	UK
	100	100	100	100	100	100	100	100	100
17 and under	0	0	0	3	19	6	0	0	3
18	0	3	59	40	50	18	18	1	24
19	4	15	24	28	22	20	26	18	13
20	11	21	8	19	4	17	18	19	7
21	15	16	2	8	1	11	9	12	6
22	14	11	2	1	1	7	6	8	5
23	10	9	1	0	0	5	5	6	4
24	7	6	1	0	0	4	4	5	3
25	6	4	1	0	0	1	3	4	3
26	5	3	1	0	0	1	2	3	2
27	4	2	0	0	0	1	1	3	2
28	3	2	0	0	0	1	1	2	2
29	3	2	0	0	0	1	1	2	2
30 and over	17	7	2	0	1	9	5	18	25

[1] Data refer to new entrants to ISCED levels 5 and 6.

[2] ISCED 6 only.

Data not available in B, E, I, L, P and Fin.

Source : Eurostat - Joint Unesco, OECD, Eurostat data collection (UOE)

New ways of learning: how and where

The educational communication process is taking new forms as the information and telecommunications technologies revolution reaches the realms of education and training. It is recognised that such innovations make it easier to acquire knowledge and to develop new, flexible, customised and interactive forms of learning which allows individuals to control the time and pace of their learning and to prepare people for a workplace dominated by computers and a whole range of multimedia applications. As it is believed that in learning we take in 20% of what we see, 40% of what we see and hear, and 70% of what we see, hear and do ourselves, a combination of computers, networking arrangements, and multimedia technology is clearly a formidable educational tool[1].

Recognising the usefulness of these new tools, the Commission adopted an action plan under the title 'Learning in the Information Society' in September 1996, which proposes four main lines of action to promote the use of information technology in the European Union's primary and secondary schools (including vocational). These are encouraging the interconnection of schools, the development of teaching material of European interest by cooperation with TV channels and multimedia publishers, training and support for teachers and trainers to encourage use of new technology in their teaching methods and circulation of information on opportunities offered by audiovisual and multimedia products. Other Commission programmes in this area include MEDIA II, INFO 2000 which are concerned with developing multimedia content.

Lifelong learning too is encouraged by such technological innovations as they also offer learning possibilities outside of the traditional employment and educational environments. With the use of video and audio tapes, TV transmissions, computers, Internet and multimedia educational software, learning at any stage of life can be achieved. Thus exclusion of various sorts such as rural dispersion, people with disabilities or those at home caring for children or elderly relatives can be overcome by these individual modes of learning. Individual lifelong learning opportunities are particularly important for women, who are still much more likely to have childcare and eldercare responsibilities which often make it difficult for them to participate in education and training courses offered in the traditional manner. Additionally, such opportunities are critical for the self-employed and for the increasing group of part-time and casual/fixed contract employees whose employers would have less incentive to invest in skills and development.

---

[1] DGXXII Study Group on Education and Training Report: "Accomplishing Europe through Education and Training, December 1996

The 1993 Continuing Vocational Training Survey (CVTS) showed that as far as training in enterprises is concerned, traditional forms of training such as courses, workplace training and conferences, seminars, workshops etc. were still being offered the most in the European Union. However, the more non-traditional training form of self-learning using computer, video and audio based methods and distance learning was being used by about a quarter of enterprises providing continuing vocational training, as was job rotation (Figure 12).

Internationalisation of education

The European Commission is intent on encouraging cooperation between Member States in the field of education so that countries can benefit from the diverse experiences of others to help improve the general quality of education in the European Union. It is also encouraging the European dimension in education at all levels to strengthen the spirit of European citizenship by improving knowledge of the Union and its Member States and of the purposes of the Union in economic and social terms. Its initiatives in this area include the promotion of foreign language learning, mobility of students and teachers and recognition of qualifications and skills across countries.

Figure 12 - The forms of continuing vocational training offered by enterprises [1] [2], EU-12, 1993

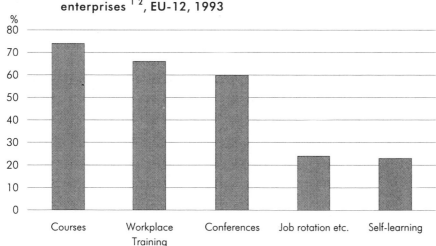

[1] Enterprises with 10 or more employees.

[2] Sum is not 100% as employees can be participating in more than one form of training.

Source: Eurostat - Continuing Vocational Training Survey (CVTS) 1994

Foreign language learning: English widespread

Foreign language learning is of paramount importance in a border-free single market Europe. In its White Paper on education 'Teaching and Learning - Towards the Learning Society' (1995), the Commission stresses the benefits foreign language acquisition holds for occupational and personal opportunities opened by the Union of countries. It cites language proficiency as helping to build up the feeling of being European with all its cultural wealth and diversity, and of understanding between the citizens of Europe. Therefore, one of the main objectives outlined in this Paper is that every citizen of the European Union should be able to communicate in three Community languages thus entailing the learning of at least two by all young people.

Figure 13 - Average number of foreign languages taught per pupil in secondary general education [1], 1994/95

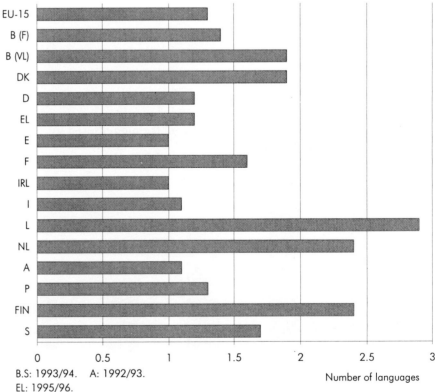

B.S: 1993/94.   A: 1992/93.
EL: 1995/96.

Number of languages

IRL, NL: full time only, NL estimated.

UK: data not available

[1] See note on p. 95

Source: Eurostat - Joint Unesco, OECD, Eurostat data collection (UOE)

In the European Union in 1994/95, pupils enrolled in secondary general education (both compulsory and post-compulsory) were learning, on average 1.3 modern foreign languages[1]. Over half of the Member States were near this European average figure of around one foreign language (ranging from 1.0 in Spain and Ireland to 1.4 in the French speaking Community of Belgium) while other countries revealed figures of pupils learning closer to around two foreign languages (ranging from 1.6 in France to 2.9 in Luxembourg). It can be seen, therefore, that a number of Member States already put more emphasis on foreign language learning which suggests that the objective outlined in the White Paper is not so out of reach in these countries. Although it should be noted that the case of Luxembourg is unique as, together with the Luxembourgish language, it also has French and German as official languages which are both taught in schools as foreign languages (Figure 13).

The teaching of foreign languages in primary school, and even before, has been cited as important for foreign language proficiency. Indeed, experience has also shown that contact with another language at an early age makes command of the mother tongue easier and better. Available data on foreign language learning at primary level show that in European Union countries in 1994/95, if foreign languages were being taught at all it was English that was being taught the most. Belgium and Luxembourg as multilingual countries were exceptions to this phenomenon. Greece, Germany, France, Austria, Portugal and Finland also reported pupils, although very few, learning foreign languages other than English at this level[1] (Table 7). English was also the Union's most popular foreign language in secondary level education.

Table 7 - Most widely taught foreign languages in primary education, 1994/95

(% of pupils in primary education learning selected foreign languages)

	B(F)[1]	B(VL)[1]	DK	D	EL	E	F	IRL	I	L	NL*	A[2]	P	FIN	S[1]	UK
English	1	-	32	6	49	63	14	.	22	-	33	49	30	64	48	:
French	.	35	-	2	5	2	.	-	4	82	-	0	7	1	-	:
German	1	-	-	.	-	-	4	-	1	100	-	-	0	3	-	:

[1] 1993/94.

[2] 1992/93.

* NL : estimated.

Source: Eurostat - Joint Unesco, OECD, Eurostat data collection (UOE)

---

[1] Data refer to foreign languages being studied by each pupil at a specific point in time e.g. In 1994/95 and might therefore underestimate the extent of language learning undertaken throughout their respective levels of schooling.

In order to promote these language skills deemed essential for European integration, action at Community level has been through the Lingua programme which has been integrated into the actions falling under the Socrates and Leonardo da Vinci action programmes on education and training since 1995. The types of activities supported include cooperation between Member States in the joint development of curricula, teaching materials, methods of assessment, modules and training schemes; awarding of grants to enable future language teachers to spend a period of 3-12 months in a country where the official language is the one they will be teaching and the promotion of exchanges of young people enrolled in education or training.

Mobility in education: studying abroad

The EU citizens who pursue their tertiary education studies in a Member State other than their own the most are the Greeks and Irish. There are also many Luxembourgish students to be found in other countries, but Luxembourg is a unique case in that only a limited amount of tertiary education (the first one or two years of some courses) takes place within the country and students are therefore obliged to go abroad in order to continue their studies.

In 1994/95, around 30 000 students with Greek citizenship were enrolled in tertiary education in one of the other Member States of the Union. They represented nearly 10% of the Greek student population. The 11 000 Irish students abroad in the European Union represented 9% of the Irish student population. It should be noted that 86% of them were enrolled in the United Kingdom. Lowest percentages of students enrolled in another Member State were seen for the five larger countries of Germany, Spain, France, Italy and the United Kingdom (Figure 14).

Figure 14 - Percentage of students in tertiary education enrolled in other EU countries [1], 1994/95

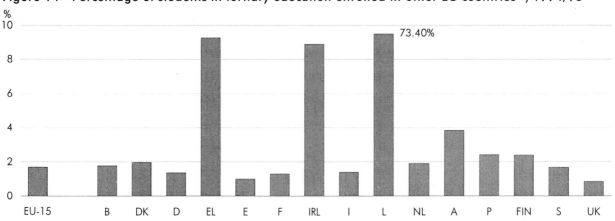

Example: nearly 10% of Greek students were studying in another EU Member State

[1] Data for each Member State are all slightly underestimated as certain countries are unable to provide complete coverage of all non-national students studying in their country.

Luxembourg is a unique case as due to the limited tertiary education provision students are obliged to study abroad. The number of Luxembourg nationals studying abroad therefore far exceeds the number of students enrolled in Luxembourg.

Source: Eurostat - Joint Unesco, OECD, Eurostat data collection (UOE)

According to the Commission's 1995 White Paper, mobility in education will be made easier. The Paper states that the Commission will submit a proposal that any students obtaining a grant in their own country must be able, if they wish, to use it in any tertiary education establishment in another Member State prepared to accept them. Additionally, it recognises the need to work on the removal of obstacles (administrative, legal and those connected with social protection) which act as a brake on exchanges of students, teachers, trainees and researchers alike. Finally, mutual academic and vocational recognition will be developed by the generation of the system of 'credit' transfers and the application of equivalent methods to vocational training. There are numerous Community schemes aimed at encouraging inter-state cooperation and mobility. Results of one such scheme called Erasmus are illustrated in the graph below which shows where tertiary education students obtaining financial aid from the European Commission went to study in 1995/96. In total for this year, 85000 students participated in this student exchange programme which also includes EFTA countries. This figure represented no more than 1% of total tertiary education students in the countries involved. The United Kingdom was the favoured destination with 26% of all Erasmus students choosing to spend a period of their tertiary education studies in a UK institution. This is an indication of the popularity of English as a foreign language and is also presumably the logical result considering the amount of English being learnt in schools in the European Union. France was the next popular destination playing host to 18% of Erasmus students, followed by Germany and Spain at 12% (Figure 15). It is increasingly becoming the case that national governments provide mobility grants to their nationals. This can be taken as evidence that the Commission initiative has been successful in encouraging exchanges to become a normal part of tertiary education. Furthermore, while student mobility retains a position of central importance within the Erasmus programme, improved incentives are now also available to encourage universities to add a European perspective to the courses followed by students who do not participate directly in mobility. New emphasis is consequently placed on teaching staff exchanges and transnational curriculum development.

Figure 15 - Percentage of Erasmus students by host country, 1995/96

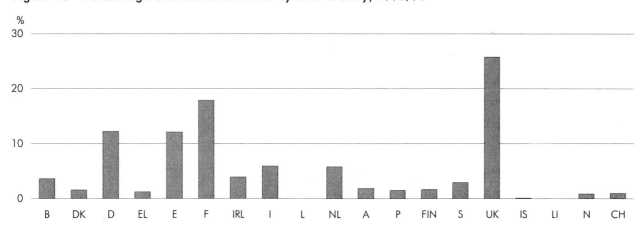

Example: 26% of all Erasmus students went to study in the UK.
Source: Directorate General XXII: Education, Training and Youth.

Resources in education and training

Education is not just about participation; it also has a resource side. The increase in education participation has put pressure on governments and resources and the respective costs remain an important issue in the debate on education.

Six million teachers in the European Union

Taking all levels of education together, the number of people employed as teachers in the European Union in 1994/95 amounted to approximately six million. More than four million of these worked in primary and secondary education.

Figure 16 - Teaching staff as a percentage of the total labour force, 1994/95

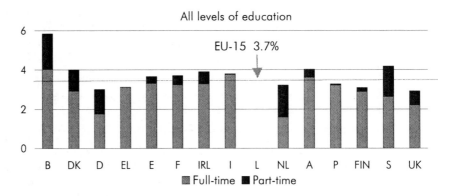

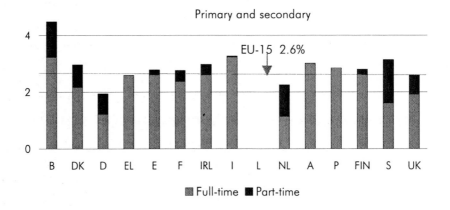

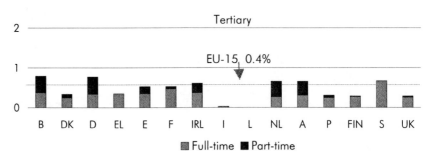

The percentage of the labour force employed in education can be seen as an indication of the amount of economic human resources that are tied up in education. In 1994/95, the percentage of teachers employed either full-time or part-time in all levels of education ranged from less than 3% in the United Kingdom to almost 6% in Belgium. In primary and secondary education combined, the lowest percentage was found in Germany at less than 2% and the highest was in Belgium where it reached more than 4%. At the tertiary level, percentage differences between Member States were minimal (Figure 16).

Some caution, however, is called for in comparing percentages between Member States as definitions of teaching staff may differ slightly. The data may also be affected by a number of other factors such as differences in the size of the school-age population, the magnitude of the ratio of the labour force to the total population, the duration of compulsory education, class size, the number of hours that students attend class each day and the organisation of teachers' working time.

Figure 17 - Direct public expenditure on education as a percentage of GDP, 1994

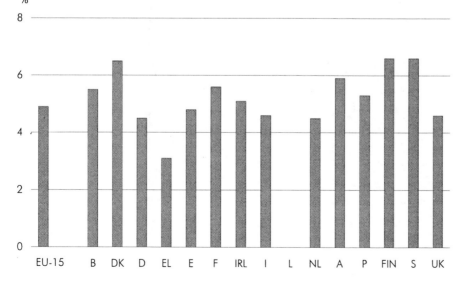

Source : Eurostat - Joint Unesco, OECD, Eurostat data collection (UOE)

Public expenditure on education: 5% of EU GDP in 1994

In 1994 the European Union average for the percentage of GDP devoted to direct public expenditure[1] on education was about 4.9% (Figure 17). In absolute figures, direct public expenditure on education for the Union was about 300 000 million ECU. In general, Member States with the exception of Greece, appeared to allocate similar proportions of resources to education, with the Nordic countries allotting the highest.

The percentage of GDP devoted to direct public expenditure on education by Member States has to be analysed in terms of the supply and demand of education. Thus, it can be influenced by factors such as the size of GDP, the size of the pupil and student population, the unit cost of education, the number of private institutions and the expenditure level of households on education. Nevertheless, the percentage of GDP devoted to education is an interesting indicator for measuring the level of socio-economic development of a country as it reflects governments' degree of priority given to education.

The European Commission is very aware that education and training play a key role in economic growth, competitiveness and in the fight against unemployment and it has invested considerable effort and resources in these areas. During the last ten years, it has financed action programmes at a European level for improvements in the provision of education and training aimed at complementing existing measures being taken in the EU Member States and other EEA countries. Since 1995, all such initiatives have come under the Socrates and Leonardo da Vinci action programmes.

Over the past ten years there has been a considerable increase in the amount of Community funds allocated to the two programmes and their predecessors (Figure 18). This demonstrates the commitment to improving the quality of education and training and to enlarging the number of people and institutions involved in cooperation at European level.

---

[1]   Direct public expenditure refers to the direct expenditure of all levels of government combined (central, regional, local) for all types of educational institutions. It does not include neither financial aid to students (schlarships, grants, students loans) nor transfers and paymentss to other private entities (subsidies to firms and non-profit organisations).

Between 1987 and 1994 the overall budget for Erasmus (tertiary education student mobility) and Lingua (foreign language learning) programmes was about 673 million ECU.[1] The considerable interest generated by these initiatives in the field of education then led the Council and Parliament to increase the Commission's budget in order to enlarge participation and to cover all levels of the national education systems. Thus, in the two first years of its operation, the new Socrates programme was awarded a budget of on average about 160 million ECU per year and its global funding exceeds 900 million ECU for the period of 1995 to 1999.

Between 1987 and 1994 the overall expenditure on the vocational training programmes of Comett (cooperation between universities and enterprises on training in the field of technology), Petra (development of initial vocational training), Force (development of continuing vocational training) and Eurotecnet (training in new technologies) was about 490 million ECU. The amount allocated to vocational training programmes under the new framework of Leonardo da Vinci for the period of 1995 to 1999 is 750 million ECU.

Figure 18 - Community funds allocated to Commission programmes in the areas of education and vocational training, 1987-1996

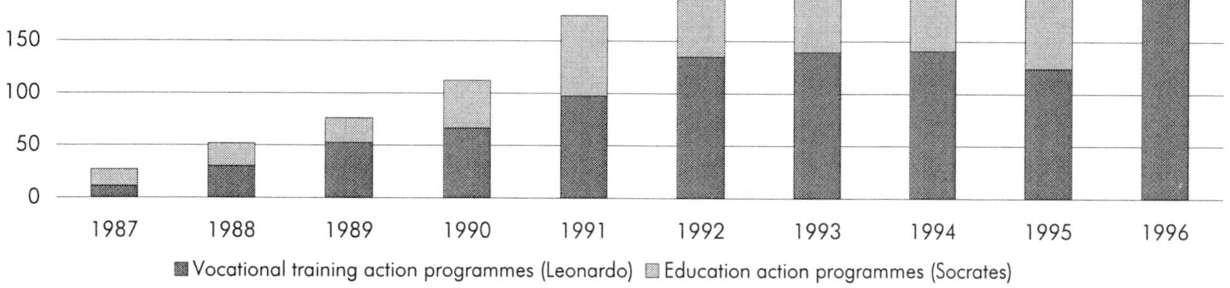

Mio ECU

■ Vocational training action programmes (Leonardo)　▨ Education action programmes (Socrates)

Source : Directorate General XXII: Education, Training and Youth

[1]   Data not available for the other programme concerning education of Youth for Europe (Youth exchange)

Enterprise investment

Information on private expenditure is, unfortunately, very scarce. However, from the Continuing Vocational Training Survey (CVTS) there is some information available on money spent on the provision of training courses by enterprises. The cost of training courses for employees as a percentage of total labour costs provides a relative measure of investment made by enterprises in developing the skills of their workforce.

These figures should be treated with caution. At first glance there would seem to be some differences between Member States in expenditure on CVT but this does not reflect the total picture. This is because the way in which training courses are organised and funded can have a significant effect on the direct cost to enterprises. In some countries training, even for employees, may be financed out of general taxation arrangements which would not be a direct cost to the employer. Additionally, employees who undertake training for their employers in their own time effectively reduce the cost of training to the enterprise.

Figure 19 - Costs of continuing vocational training courses as a percentage of total labour costs of all enterprises, 1993

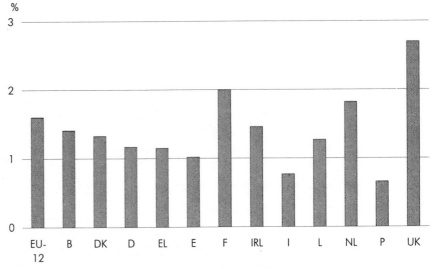

Source : Eurostat - Continuing vocational Training Survey (CVTS), 1994

Labour Market

Creating jobs and combating unemployment:

the challenge ahead

The labour market plays a determinant role in the lives of adults in modern market economies. Not only does stable employment provide income and a share of material well-being, employment can also structure one's social life and give meaning to personal existence. Regular and sufficient income from work gives people a perspective for the future by shaping their household's longer-term plans such as owning a house and by allowing them to invest in their children's education. When people are denied the employment opportunities they are looking for over a long period - either because the transition from school to working life has proved difficult or because long-term unemployment has led to fewer job prospects - a downward spiral of events is frequently set in train. Financial problems are likely to arise and people may find themselves facing poverty. It is therefore not surprising that jobs are one of the prime concerns of the European Union's citizens and that policy-makers are increasingly coming under pressure to fulfil people's employment expectations. The Luxembourg Job Summit in November 1997 was the beginning of a new policy at European level to bring about a change for the better (see box p.104).

Labour market difficulties ... new working arrangements

Although the number of people in employment has been climbing since 1995, a total of more than 3 million jobs were lost between 1991 and 1996. The number of unemployed rose by around 4.6 million over the same period. In addition to those who have lost their jobs, there are those who were previously inactive and

Table 1 - Employment and unemployment in the European Union
Population aged 15 and over EU-15, 1991-1996

(Mio)

	1991	1992	1993	1994	1995	1996	96 - 91	96/91
							(Mio)	% change
Employ-ment	151.6	150.2	147.1	146.7	147.7	148.2	-3.4	-2.2
Unem-ployment	13.6	15.3	17.8	18.5	17.9	18.2	+4.6	+33.7

Sources : Employment: Eurostat benchmark employment series. These series are based on sources which Member States judge to be the best to measure the total number of persons in employment
Unemployment: harmonised unemployment figures (Eurostat: Unemployment — Monthly Bulletin — 2/1998)

103

are now searching for paid employment; for example, young people looking for their first jobs and older people not previously involved in the labour market (Table 1). Three important developments have begun to emerge in recent years. Firstly, the EU labour force is ageing and may well begin to decline at the beginning of the next decade. Secondly, the increase in relatively new forms of employment such as part-time work and fixed-term contracts has resulted in a more flexible labour market. Thirdly, research has shown that the steady improvement in educational levels has had a positive impact not only on people's job prospects but also on economic competitiveness.

The employment guidelines:
A new strategy for employment in the EU

The EU Jobs Summit held in Luxembourg in November 1997 agreed upon a new overall strategy for employment. A central element of this strategy are the **employment guidelines for 1998**. They set out the policies Member States should pursue if the employment rate is to be increased significantly and unemployment is to be reduced . The guidelines centre on **four pillars** for each of which specific guidelines are formulated:

1. Improving employability
— Tackle youth unemployment and prevent long-term unemployment by offering the young and adult unemployed training and etraining measures in addition to work experience before reaching 6 and 12 months of unemployment, respectively
— move from passive to active labour market measures[1]
— ease the transition from school to work by reducing the number of school drop-outs and equipping young persons with skills relevant to the labour market, where appropriate through apprenticeship training

2. Developing entrepreneurship
— make it easier to start up and run a business
— make the taxation system more employment friendly by reducing the fiscal pressure on labour and non-wage labour costs

3. Encouraging adaptability of businesses and their employees
— modernise work organisation by introducing flexible working arrangements such as contracting working time as an annual figure,
    to be completed in a flexible manner (rather than the usual 5 day week), reduction of working hours and overtime, development of part-time working, lifelong training and career breaks
— support adaptability in enterprises by providing incentives for continuing training within enterprises

4. Strengthening the policies for equal opportunities
— tackle gender gaps in employment and unemployment rates
— facilitate the reconciliation of work and family life through policies on career breaks, parental leave, part-time work and increased access to care services and through easing return to work
— promote the integration of people with disabilities into working life

All Member States agreed to produce Employment Action Plans, describing how they intend to implement the Employment Guidelines in their national programmes. The Commission will monitor Member States' efforts and on the basis on the results of this examination will propose a revision to the guidelines for 1999.

---

[1]   Generally-speaking, passive labour market measures refer to the payment of unemployment and other related benefits, and active measures refer to training, placement and job-search assistance, mobility allowances, direct job creation, subsidies to create jobs, reduction on pay-roll taxes, start-up incentives and work offers. In practice, there is no clearcut distinction between the two types of measure mainly because the eligibility conditions for receipt of benefit tend to include participation in active measures.

The ageing of the Labour Force

The active population, or "labour force", is the total number of persons in employment plus the unemployed, in other words all persons who have a job or are seeking a job. From the point of view of the economy as a whole, it is the labour supply on any given date.

In 1996, there were 165.4 million people (aged 15-64) in the labour force of the Europe of Fifteen, i.e. around 30 million more people than in the United States labour market. Community-wide, 43% of the active population were women, one percentage point more than five years before.

The activity rate is a measure of the tendency for people of working age to be economically active (see box opposite). It is affected by a number of factors: firstly, there are the conditions typical of a given society, such as the general value attached to employment, society's role models or the steps taken by government to enable parents to combine a family with a profession. Secondly, the economic situation plays a part: in periods of recession some people withdraw from the labour market because they see no chance of finding employment. Activity rates are also influenced by a country's retirement policy and the duration of young people's education. An employer's preference for full or part-time workers will also impact on the level of participation as will the welfare payments available for the unemployed.

In the EU as a whole the activity rate stands at around 67%, but this average masks substantial differences between the Member States (Table 2). While just under 58% of the population of working age in Italy is available for the labour market, the figure in Denmark is almost 80%. The differences between Member States are determined largely by the large variations in female activity rates. But the picture is by no means uniform for men, either. There are still 13 percentage points of difference between the male activity rates in Belgium (72%) and Denmark (85%).

Labour force definitions

The **population of working age** is all persons aged 15 to 64 years.

The **active population**, or **labour force**, comprises those in employment and the unemployed, aged 15 to 64.

The general **activity rate** shows persons in the active population (labour force) as a share of the population of working age. When activity rates are calculated for the various age groups, the active population is compared with the population of the same age.

Table 2 - Active population and activity rates in the EU - 1996[1]

	EU-15	B	DK	D	EL	E	F	IRL	I	L	NL	A	P	FIN	S	UK
Active population																
Total (1000)	165420	4164	2791	38736	4143	15755	25211	1447	22478	170	7350	3779	4540	2426	4346	28081
Men (% share)	57	58	54	57	61	61	54	61	62	63	58	56	54	52	52	56
Women (% share)	43	42	46	43	39	39	46	39	38	37	42	44	46	48	48	44
Activity rates (%)																
Total	67	62	79	70	61	60	68	62	58	61	70	71	68	72	77	75
Men	77	72	85	79	77	75	75	76	72	76	80	80	76	74	79	83
Women	57	52	74	61	46	46	61	49	43	46	60	62	60	69	75	67

[1] Population aged 15-64

Source : Eurostat - Labour Force Survey

Traditionally, women have had a lower participation rate than men. Although the gap has been steadily narrowing for some time now, there are still only two countries where the rate of economic activity is roughly the same for men and women: Sweden and Finland.

Labour force growth is strongly influenced by rising female participation

Changes in the size of the active population can be attributed to two interacting factors, one demographic and one behavioural. Between 1991 and 1996, the demographic component was positive in all Member States for both men and women; i.e., if there had been no other influencing factors, changes in the population of working age (15-64 years) would have led to a growth in the size of the labour force of more than 4 million people. The behavioural effect is measured by assuming that the activity rates of men and women in different age groups remain constant over the period under consideration. The picture was very different for the behavioural component: in the majority of countries, this component had a negative impact on male activity. The exceptions were Belgium and Greece where the effect was positive and France and the Netherlands which did not experience any change. In contrast, the behavioural component had a positive impact on female activity in nearly all countries. This change was particularly noticeable in Ireland, Spain and Greece - countries where women had hitherto had relatively low levels of economic activity (Figure 1).

Figure 1 - Change in male and female labour force 1996/1991 demographic and behavioural components[1]

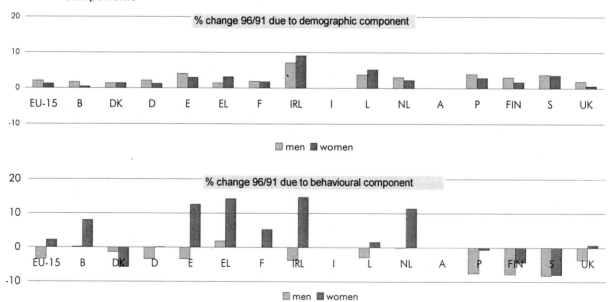

[1] Tha bars show the percentage changes of the labour force between 1996 and 1991 due to demographic and behavioural factors. The sum of the two gives overall change during the period.
Source : Eurostat - Labour Force Survey. I, A: no information due to break in the series

Taking both factors into account, the total change in the labour force is revealed. Between 1991 and 1996, the active population (aged 15-64) in the Community grew by 1.2 million (+0.7%), made up of an additional 2.4 million women and 1.2 million fewer men.

In sharp contrast to the other Member States, female activity rates in Denmark, Finland and Sweden - countries with traditionally high activity rates - declined significantly over the period 1991-1996. In Sweden and Finland, this seems to be a result of the serious economic crisis at the beginning of the 1990s.

Throughout the fifties and sixties, the typical employment "biographies" were as follows. Activity rates were high for men of all working ages except for those approaching retirement. Labour force participation also increased significantly among women but when they reached the age groups at which families were formed and children born, the activity rate stagnated or began to drop. It was not until the children were older that women could contemplate returning to the labour market. These formerly stable patterns of behaviour began to change in the 1970s.

Today, although the activity rate of women in the Union continues to be systematically lower than that of men, there is no longer a significant fall in the rate after the age of 30 (Figure 2). Economic reasons have clearly had a bearing with more couples deciding, out of necessity or choice, to have more than one 'bread winner' in the family. This development has also been accompanied by a decline in fertility rates and an improvement in the educational levels of women. Indeed, female activity is strongly linked to educational attainment: 85% of women with a university degree (or equivalent) were active in 1996 compared with only 52% of women with the lowest levels of education.

Figure 2 - Activity rates by age and sex - EU 15 - 1996

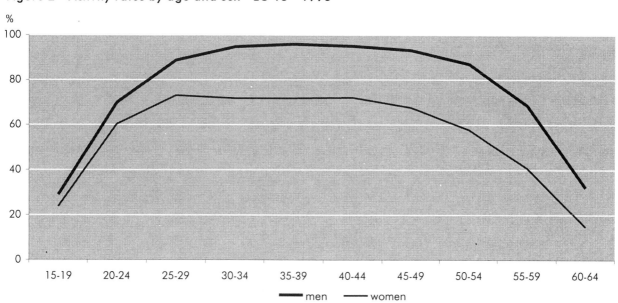

Source : Eurostat - Labour Force Survey

The Eurostat Labour Force Survey

With the exception of table 1, the data in this chapter are drawn from the **European Labour Force Survey**.

The purpose of the Labour Force Survey (LFS)

The LFS is designed to monitor the main changes taking place in the labour market and the trends in employment and unemployment. The main areas covered are :

— the employment characteristics of a person's job(s) : occupational status, sector of employment, working hours, working conditions, fixed-term employment, atypical forms of work etc...

— search for employment (ways of searching, length of search, discouraged workers ...)

— education and training : current participation, levels attained

— each person's situation one year before the survey (longitudinal aspect)

An annual survey of households

The LFS is a sample survey of private households which has been carried out in the Member States in the spring of each year since 1983 (in Austria, Finland and Sweden only since their accession to the EU in 1995). Currently, the sample numbers around 600 000 households or 1.8 million people .

Together with Member States, Eurostat draws up a list of variables, the common codings to be given to responses and the main definitions to be used; since 1983 the survey has used the concepts of the International Labour Organisation (ILO). On this shared basis, each Member State compiles its own questionnaire, determines the size of the sample, conducts the interviews and publishes its national results. Eurostat receives the data, checks them for comparability and publishes the results for all Member States and the EU as a whole.

The main advantages of the LFS are :

i) comparability of results

ii) large sample size allows numerous cross-tabulations since 1983

iii) availability of the data in a centralised micro data base in Eurostat

The data cover private households only, and thus excludes people living in institutions such as boarding schools, hospitals, religious institutions, workers' hostels, etc.

Further reading:

Labour Force Survey - Methods and Definitions - Eurostat 1996
Labour Force Survey 1983 - 1991 - Eurostat 1993
Labour Force Survey - Results 1996 - Eurostat 1997. Annual publication
Unemployment - Eurostat - Monthly bulletin

Although in general female activity rates decrease as the number of children increases, there is no uniform picture across Member States. Differences between countries reflect the level of child-care provision, cultural traditions with regard to work and family life, the availability of part-time work, taxation, welfare support, etc (see chapter on Households and Families).

Young people are joining the labour market much later

Young people are starting their working lives at a later age than in the past. Instead, they are remaining in the education system for longer. In the Union, the extension of schooling is a long-term phenomenon but one which has escalated over the past decade. On the supply side, the level of educational attainment determines not only productivity but also technological and organisational progress. On the demand side, both parents and children have grasped the fact that the possession of educational qualifications increases the likelihood of finding a job (see page 134). Some professions are also now demanding better-qualified people. Moreover, if one's chances of finding a job are slight, postponing the switch from education to work seems a natural reaction which is sometimes also promoted by State measures such as the national targets introduced by France (e.g., 80% of an age cohort should get the baccalaureat) and the United Kingdom (National education and training targets).

In 1987, at least half of all young people aged 18 in the EU had joined the labour market, either through full or part-time jobs (Table 3). By 1996, the same percentage was not reached until the age of 20. In Denmark, half of the young population has had a first contact with the labour market by the age of 16, very often, of course, through holiday or part-time jobs for students. This differs markedly from countries like Belgium, Greece, Spain, France, Italy and Luxembourg where the 50% threshold is reached only after the age of 20.

Table 3 - Youngest age at which at least 50% of young people are in the labour market

	EU-15[1]	B	DK	D	EL	E	F	IRL	I	L	NL	A	P	FIN	S	UK
1987	18	21	16	18	21	19	20	18	20	19	18	:	17	:	:	16
1996	20	22	16	18	21	21	22	20	21	21	17	18	20	19	20	17

[1] 1987 refers to EU-12 ; 1996 to EU-15

Source : Eurostat - Labour Force Survey. The table shows the age at which the activity rate of the young is at least 50%

Given the difficulties faced by young people to find a job and the training placements offered to them by public authorities, the borderline between school and work is becoming increasingly blurred. However, the transition from education to working life still depends on the national education and training systems. In some countries, the typical sequence is initial (general and/or vocational) training followed by a relatively clear-cut entry into the labour market. Belgium, France and Luxembourg are examples: 90%, 81% and 79% respectively of 18-year-olds were in full-time education in 1996. At the age of 24, nearly three quarters of young people in these Member States had completed their full-time education and were in the labour force. The situation is similar, but somewhat less pronounced, in Greece, Spain, Italy, Portugal and Sweden.

In another grouping of countries, young people interact early with the labour market, normally in the form of a combination of work and education/training: the percentage of 18-year-olds who are simultaneously in education/training and active was particularly high in Denmark (57%), Germany (40%) and the Netherlands (43%). Austria, the United Kingdom and Finland also lie well above the EU average. The United Kingdom stands out from all other countries in that 41% of 18-year-olds were already active having completed their full-time education or training (Table 4).

Table 4 - Young people in the phase of transition from education to the labour market - 1996

(%)

Age and activity status	EU-15	B	DK	D	EL	E	F	IRL	I	L	NL	A	P	FIN	S	UK
18 years																
in education/training+non-active	59	90	27	46	67	69	81	66	72	79	40	44	65	54	70	23
in education/training+active	18	3	57	40	3	5	8	6	1	3	43	31	4	29	1	31
not in education/training+active	19	5	15	10	23	21	8	25	20	16	12	23	26	13	26	41
not in education/training+non-active	4	2	1	4	7	5	3	3	7	2	5	2	5	4	3	5
total	100	100	100	100	100	100	100	100	100	100	100	100	100	100	100	100
24 years																
in education/training+non-active	16	14	13	18	10	19	14	8	23	18	10	19	21	22	16	5
in education/training+active	9	5	23	10	2	11	6	4	3	2	24	10	9	21	6	11
not in education/training+active	66	74	59	63	74	64	72	79	59	70	58	67	65	44	68	73
not in education/training+non-active	9	7	5	9	14	6	8	9	15	10	8	4	5	13	10	11
total	100	100	100	100	100	100	100	100	100	100	100	100	100	100	100	100

Source : Eurostat - Labour Force Survey

and older people are retiring earlier

Over the last two decades, labour force participation of older people, particularly those aged 60-64, has declined steadily in nearly all Member States. In the face of increased unemployment, countries such as France have accepted long-standing demands from trade unions to reduce the legal retirement age. Concurrently, some older workers, particularly the low-skilled, have become discouraged and left the labour market. In addition, the number of "early-out schemes" has risen significantly sometimes in order to facilitate mass redundancies or to replace older workers with younger, more qualified people who are often more likely to accept part-time jobs or fixed-term contracts.

As a result, the legal retirement age no longer provides a clear indication for all countries of the age at which people leave the labour market, e.g., Germany and the Netherlands (Tables 5 and 6). In Member States, however, where the replacement income ratio is low in relation to full-time earnings, the legal retirement age is a good indicator of the actual age when membership of the labour force ceases, e.g., Greece and Portugal.

Table 5 - Legal retirement age in the European Union

	B	DK	D	EL	E	F	IRL	I	L	NL	A	P	FIN	S	UK
Legal ret. age															
men	65	67	65	65	65	60	65	62	65	65	65	65	65	65	65
women	60	67	65	60	65	60	65	57	65	65	60	62	65	65	60

Source : Directorate General V 'Employment, Industrial Relations and Social Affairs' :MISSOC 1997

In 1986, just over half (53%) of the EU-12 population aged 55-59 was economically active. There were large variations between the Member States ranging from 37% in Belgium to 72% in Denmark. By 1991, a large proportion of this same generation, now aged 60-64, had left the labour market. Figures ranged from just over 10% in Belgium and France to around 40% in Denmark, Portugal and the United Kingdom.

By comparing the above figures with the activity rates of the next generation of 55-59 year olds in 1991 (and subsequently the 60-64 year olds in 1996), it appears that, for the majority of Member States, older people are now leaving the labour market at a slightly faster rate. Differences were particularly significant for Denmark, Italy and Portugal. In contrast, it appears that older people in Belgium and Greece are tending to leave the labour market at a slower rate (Table 6).

Policies that have encouraged older people to give up work at a younger age are now being questioned. First, the population is ageing and this is giving rise to concerns over the future funding of pensions. In addition, research has shown that the professional experience and know-how of older people in the work force can play an important role in training young people. Possible reforms of the transition from work to retirement are being discussed with an increase in the legal retirement age and the replacement of early retirement by gradual retirement schemes being some of the measures under consideration.

Table 6 - Activity rates of the elderly 1986-1996

(%)

	EU-15	B	DK	D	E	EL	F	IRL	I	L	P	A	NL	FIN	S	UK
55-59 yrs (1986)	53	37	72	59	50	52	51	50	44	37	53	:	42	:	:	67
60-64 yrs (1991)	25	11	38	21	31	30	13	35	23	12	42	:	15	:	:	39
55-59 yrs (1991)	54	34	74	60	48	49	52	50	43	35	58	:	44	:	:	68
60-64 yrs (1996)	23	11	32	20	28	33	12	34	18	11	40	13	15	21	57	37

1987 data for D refer to West Germany : NL - 1985 data
Source : Eurostat - Labour Force Survey

The ageing of the European labour force

Due to the fall in birth rates since the 1970s there are now fewer young people on the labour market. For the Union as a whole, the average age of the labour force has risen from 36 in 1986 to 38 in 1996. This is due largely to the increase in the average age of economically active women. In 1996, Sweden had the oldest active population (aged 15-64) in the Community with an average age of 41, contrasting with Ireland, Austria and the Netherlands, where half of those in the labour force were under 36.

In order to gauge the future of the European labour force, Eurostat recently compiled a set of labour force scenarios for the years 1995 and beyond. The baseline scenario which can be interpreted as the 'best guess' reveals the following trends for the Europe of Fifteen (Table 7):

— The growth of the labour force will slow down during the next decade ; a decline might begin around 2010.

— The number of young people entering the labour force will continue to decrease and after 2000 remain more or less constant.

— The number of people aged 50 to 64 years will continue to increase considerably.

— The proportion of women in the labour force will continue to increase.

Table 7 - The European labour force (aged 15-64) in the 1st quarter of the 21st century, EU-15

	Total	15-24 years old	50-64 years old	share of women	average age
	Mio	Mio	Mio	%	years
1995	167.6[1]	24.0	31.5	42.0	38
2000	174.6	22.4	35.2	43.3	39
2005	180.2	23.0	39.3	44.2	39
2010	183.2	23.5	43.6	44.7	40
2025	175.4	23.1	51.1	44.5	41

[1] Table 1 provides a figure of 166.4 in 1996. The differences can be explained by the different sources used. For example, collective households are included in the projections which are based on Census data but excluded from the LFS.
Source : Eurostat-Labour force projections (baseline scenario) - see chapter on Population.

Qualifications are a key factor in development of the labour force

Regardless of the composition of the active population by age or gender, the key factor is, and will be in the future, the education, training and lifelong learning of the population.

First, low educational levels account for a great deal of the non-participation levels in the labour force. For example, the highest-qualified make up for little more than 7% of the inactive population but 21% of the working population. Conversely, the lowest-qualified represent around two-thirds of the inactive and slightly over one-third of the active population.

Second, people in the labour force have to be equipped with the necessary skills to adapt in a labour market where the expectation of a 'job for life' has become increasingly outdated. In this respect, the higher the educational level of adults in employment, the greater the training opportunities afforded to them (see Figure 11 in chapter on Education and Training). This phenomenon can be observed in every Member State although it is particularly prevalent in the Scandinavian countries, the Netherlands and the United Kingdom.

Level of education and training

The level of school and vocational education referred to here is based on the International Standard Classification of Education (ISCED). To make the figures more readily comparable from one country to another, the seven level categories of ISCED are combined into three stages:

Low: ISCED 1-2: primary + lower secondary education
Medium: ISCED 3: upper secondary education
High: ISCED 5 - 7: higher education

For further details: see chapter on Education and Training

Three factors are at the root of these changes. Firstly, productivity growth has increased at a relatively faster rate in industry and agriculture. Secondly, industries such as the textiles sector have, in a number of cases, relocated in developing countries. Lastly, in the face of a deceleration in growth, certain industries have begun to externalise their own non-industrial functions such as cleaning, wages and accounting and maintenance. These jobs that were formerly counted as part of industry are now regarded as part of the service sector. The changes should therefore be seen partly as a shift from industry to services rather than as a pure increase in services.

Member States to encourage development of self-employment

The extraordinary European Council meeting on Employment held in November 1997 concluded that, in the framework of developing enterpreneurship, Member States will "encourage the development of self-employment by examining, with the aim of reducing, any obstacles which may exist, especially those within tax and social security regimes, to moving to self-employment and the setting up of small businesses, in particular for employed persons."

Table 10 - Distribution of employed persons by economic activity 1986 and 1996

(%)

	EU-15	B	DK	D	EL	E	F	IRL	I	L	NL	A	P	FIN	S	UK
Agriculture																
1986	8*	3	6	5	29	16	8	16	11	4	5	:	22	:	:	2
1996	5	3	4	3	20	9	5	11	7	3	4	7	12	8	3	2
Industry																
1986	34*	32	29	40	26	32	31	30	33	30	28	:	34	:	:	34
1996	30	28	26	35	23	29	27	27	32	23	23	30	31	27	26	27
Services																
1986	58*	65	65	55	45	52	61	54	56	66	67	:	45	:	:	64
1996	65	70	70	62	57	62	69	61	61	74	73	62	57	65	71	71

NL - 1985, D - 1986 refers to West Germany, EU-12 for 1986
Source : Eurostat - Labour Force Survey

The highest rates of self-employment (the self-employed as a percentage of all persons in employment, excluding agriculture) are found in the southern countries of the EU. In the other Member States, the picture is rather similar, especially in the services sector, where in most cases around 11% of persons in employment are self-employed. In all countries, with the exception of the United Kingdom, the self-employment rate is higher in services than in industry (Table 11). Throughout the Union, the rate of self-employment is very much higher for men than for women. On average, men are more than twice as likely as women to be self-employed. This holds true for both sectors.

Over the last decade or so, the self-employment rate has climbed throughout the Union, particularly in the service sector. While the rate in industry rose by around 20% over the period 1986-1996, self-employment in services increased fourfold for the Union as a whole. It should be noted that the phenomenon of the notionally self-employed, i.e. people whose formal status is self-employed but who have no freedom of action or financial independence from their originators, has come increasingly to the fore.

Table 11 - Self-employment rates in industry and services, 1986-1996[1]

(% of all employed who are self-employed)

	EU-15	B	DK	D	EL	E	F	IRL	I	L	NL	A	P	FIN	S	UK
Industry																
1986	9	8	7	5	23	12	8	9	15	4	4	:	11	:	:	10
1996	11	9	6	6	26	16	9	11	17	4	6	5	17	11	10	15
Services[2]																
1986	4	5	3	3	7	4	3	3	6	3	2	:	5	:	:	4
1996	16	18	8	12	32	22	11	15	30	10	11	9	24	11	11	12

[1] EU-12 data for 1986

[2] public administration excluded

Source: Eurostat - Labour Force Survey

Part-time employment : a significant impact on job creation

··

Today, in most of the EU Member States, the patterns of change have become quite similar. The limited increase in employment can largely be attributed to the rise in part-time employment, for both men and women (Figure 3). The general rate of economic growth is still important: in a country such as Ireland where GDP growth has been much higher than the EU average, there has been a larger increase in full-time jobs than part-time ones. In times of labour market difficulty, part-time working is frequently encouraged with a view to providing more people with jobs. Figure 4 shows a positive correlation between the proportion of part-time employed persons and the employment rate for all EU countries. The Netherlands represents an outlier in this picture.

Figure 3 - Contribution of full-time and part-time jobs to the % change in employment, 1991-1996

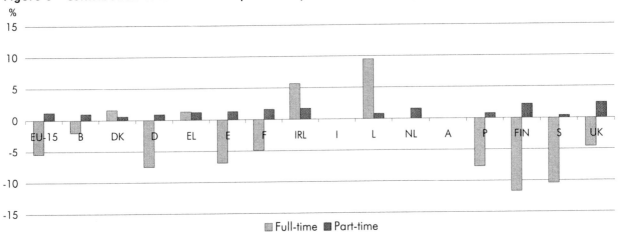

Source : Eurostat - Labour Force Survey, adjusted to be consistent with the benchmark employment series

Figure 4 - Part-time work and the overall level of employment, 1996

employment rate - %

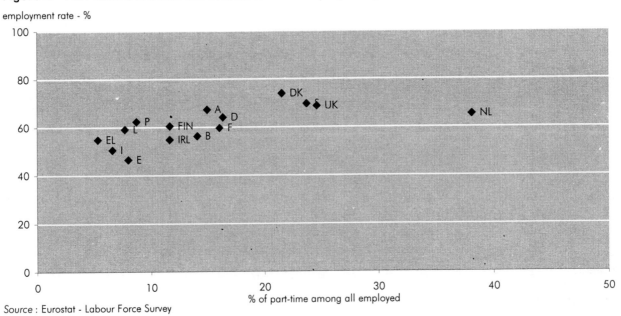

Source : Eurostat - Labour Force Survey

Most part-timers are women

With the exception of Denmark, the percentage of part-time workers has risen noticeably in all countries since 1991. In the United Kingdom and Sweden, one in four employees are now working part-time while in the Netherlands the figure is as high as 38%. There are particularly low rates of part-time employment (below 10 %) in the southern Member States and Luxembourg (Table 12). Men account for only 17% of all part-time workers in the Union. Put another way, 5% of male employees are working part-time compared with 32% of female employees. This phenomenon can be observed in all fifteen Member States. As many as two-thirds of female employees in the Netherlands are working part-time. In Luxembourg and the Netherlands, the extent of part-time working appears to be well in line with the wishes of those concerned. On the other hand, more than 40% of employees working part-time in Portugal, France, Finland and Italy would rather have a full-time job and in Greece, this is the case for 69% (Figure 5). In all EU countries, the percentage of involuntary part-time workers among young people is higher than among people aged 30 and older.

Measurement of part-time working

Part-time working is measured here on the basis of self-assessment by the persons answering the questions (except for Austria and the Netherlands where it depends on a threshold on the basis of the number of hours usually worked).

Figure 5 - Percentage of involuntary[1] part-time employees among all part-time employees

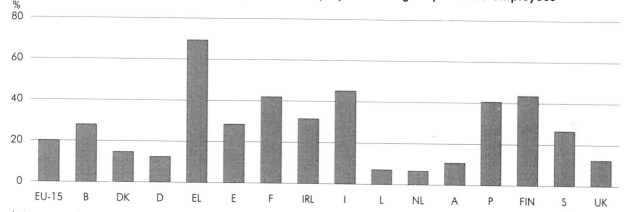

[1] The term involuntary refer to those part-time employees who said they were working part-time because they could not find a full-time job.
Source : Eurostat - Labour Force Survey

Table 12 - Percentage of employees working part-time, 1991 and 1996

	EU-15	B	DK	D	EL	E	F	IRL	I	L	NL	A	P	FIN	S	UK
1991																
Total	14*	13	24	14	3	4	12	9	5	7	32	:	4	:	:	23
Men	4*	2	11	2	2	1	3	4	3	1	16	:	2	:	:	5
Women	29*	31	38	30	5	11	24	17	10	18	59	:	7	:	:	43
1996																
Total	17	16	22	17	4	8	17	13	7	8	38	14	5	11	25	25
Men	5	3	11	3	3	3	5	6	3	1	17	3	2	7	8	8
Women	32	34	35	34	6	17	30	22	12	18	68	29	8	15	41	44

Source : Eurostat - Labour Force Survey

In addition to part-time work, other flexible forms of employment are gaining ground
···

Today, as in the past, most people in employment consider full-time work for an indefinite period to be the 'normal' form of employment. As a longer-term trend, however, this type of employment has lost ground in most countries, with the exception of Denmark, Greece and Portugal. In 1996, 74% of all employees in the Community still had a full-time job of unlimited duration. Luxembourg is well above this EU average with nearly 91%. In contrast, Spain (63%) and the Netherlands (58%) fall below the figure for the Union as a whole. For the former, the explanation lies in the relatively high share of fixed-term contracts, for the latter the extension of part-time employment appears to be the main reason. In all Member States the percentage of male employees with a full-time job of unlimited duration is higher than that of women. The difference exceeds thirty percentage points in Belgium, Sweden and the United Kingdom. It is particularly striking in the Netherlands (50 percentage points) where only about one female employee in four has full-time work for an indefinite period (Table 13).

Finally, if the analysis is restricted to men aged 30 and over, the proportion with a full-time job for an indefinite period is much more homogeneous across the fifteen Member States: in 1996, it ranged from 87% in the Netherlands to 98% in Luxembourg.

The measurement of weekly working time

In the European Labour Force Survey persons are asked about the actual and the usual number of hours worked per week.

The **actual number of hours worked** refers to the actual situation in the reference week of the survey; this means, for example, that someone who was on holidays or ill will report an actual number of zero.

The **usual number of hours worked** indicates the normal situation during a working week. It gives a representative picture of the weekly work involvement of a person over a longer period and is, therefore, used in this chapter.

Table 13 - Percentage of employees who work full-time and have a contract of unlimited duration, 1996

	EU-15	B	DK	D	EL	E	F	IRL	I	L	NL	A	P	FIN	S	UK
Total	74	80	69	73	87	63	75	83	88	91	58	79	84	76	66	70
Males	85	93	80	86	89	67	85	91	92	97	79	89	87	82	83	86
Females	59	62	56	57	85	56	62	74	82	80	28	65	81	70	49	52

Source : Eurostat - Labour Force Survey

Fixed-term employment decreases with age
....

Contracts of a limited duration represent another major element of employment flexibility. For the Union as a whole, one in ten employees aged 20-64 have such a contract. Fixed-term contracts appear to be a characteristic of the Spanish labour market in particular: one-third of all employees work on these terms. With the exception of Finland (16%), no other Member State exceeds the 12% mark. As with part-time working, more women than men are employed for a fixed term in all countries (for the Europe of Fifteen 11% women as against just under 10% men). The gender gap is particularly high in Belgium (8% against 4%) and the Netherlands (15% against 7%).

People in part-time jobs are in general more likely to work for a limited period than those in full-time jobs. The percentage of people with fixed contracts is also much higher among younger people than older employees (Table 14). On the one hand, this results from particular kinds of initial vocational training such as apprenticeship and the dual system. On the other hand, the figures reflect the fact that it is becoming increasingly difficult for young people to start their working life with a job that could be classified as long-term. For many young people, a fixed-term contract has become a trial period where they must first gain experience in order to lay claim to more stable positions.

In general, the proportion of fixed-term contracts does not vary significantly according to level of education. However, the analysis by age group reveals in all countries a relatively high proportion of fixed-term contracts among higher-qualified young people aged 25-29. In fact almost one employee in five aged 25-29 years with a degree has a temporary contract.

Looking at the duration of temporary contracts, there appears to be a relationship between job instability and level of education. Of EU employees with a temporary contract, university (or equivalent) graduates are twice as likely to have contracts of more than one year than those with lower qualifications.

Table 14 - Percentage of employees with a contract of limited duration, 1996

	EU-15	B	DK	D	EL	E	F	IRL	I	L	NL	A	P	FIN	S	UK
20-64 years	10	5	10	8	11	32	12	8	7	2	10	5	10	16	11	6
20-24 years	28	18	31	28	22	73	41	14	16	8	26	9	27	47	36	11
25-29 years	15	9	12	12	15	51	19	7	11	3	13	7	18	30	17	7
30-64 years	7	3	6	5	8	22	7	7	5	1	7	3	5	12	7	6

Source : Eurostat - Labour Force Survey

Full-time jobs with long working hours and part-time jobs with a small number of hours are components of employment flexibility
....

Over the last fifteen years, the usual weekly working time of full-time employees has not changed very much. According to the available statistics, the most significant reductions have been in Denmark and Portugal where the normal working week of full-time employees was around one hour shorter in 1996 than in 1987. In the United Kingdom working time increased by more than 40 minutes.

It should be noted that weekly working time of full-time employees is only one of the factors which determine the total amount of hours worked during the year. Other important elements are the amount of part-time work and the length of holidays.

In 1996 the normal working week of a full-time employee was on average 40 hours for the Europe of Fifteen. In the United Kingdom, the working week of 44 hours was by far the longest amongst all Member States: a full-time employee in the United Kingdom was working on average some 15% longer than his/her counterpart in Belgium (38 hours), which lies at the other extreme. Italy, Denmark and Finland also have a normal working week of under 39 hours on average (Table 15).

Today, the number of working hours and the times at which people work set the structural pattern of people's working lives and also indirectly their private lives. While the comments in this section apply to the number of working hours, the timing of those hours (night work, shift work, etc.) are dealt with in the chapter on Working Environment.

Table 15 - Number of hours usually worked per week, 1996

	EU-15	B	DK	D	EL	E	F	IRL	I	L	NL	A	P	FIN	S	UK
Full-time employees	40	38	39	40	40	41	40	40	39	40	39	40	41	39	40	44
Part-time employees	20	22	19	19	25	18	23	19	25	21	19	22	23	21	24	18

Source : Eurostat - Labour Force Survey

On average, 45% of EU-15 employees usually work for 40 hours or more per week. This proportion varies substantially between Member States. While in Denmark and France less than one in four employees work 40 hours or more, more than 60% of employees in Greece, Spain, Italy, Luxembourg, the Netherlands, Austria, Portugal, Sweden and the United Kingdom fall into this category. The United Kingdom stands out when it comes to the percentage of employees working very long hours: more than one-quarter (27%) of UK employees with a full-time job work 48 hours or more per week, whereas in the vast majority of the other Member States fewer than 10% work as long and in the Netherlands only 2% do so (Table 16).

The average number of hours worked by a part-time employee corresponds to half the number worked in full-time jobs. However, the hours in part-time employment vary considerably from one country to another. In Greece and Italy, the average is around 25 hours a week while in Spain and the United Kingdom it is only 18 hours. The percentage of employees who work very short hours (less than 12 hours a week) is highest in the Netherlands (11%), Denmark (7%) and the United Kingdom (6%) - those countries with the highest overall part-time rate. There have been few significant changes since 1987.

Table 16 - Percentage of full-time employees usually working 40 hours/48 hours or more per week, 1996

(%)

	EU-15	B	DK	D	EL	E	F	IRL	I	L	NL	A	P	FIN	S	UK
>= 40 hours	45	27	19	39	74	82	24	50	63	88	63	66	76	32	84	66
>= 48 hours	9	4	7	6	17	8	7	12	9	4	2	4	11	3	3	27

Source : Eurostat - Labour Force Survey

Throughout the Union, employees work the longest hours in agriculture. In Denmark, Germany, Netherlands, Austria and Sweden weekly working hours are shortest in industry, while in the other ten Member States full-time employees work the shortest hours in the service sector. A closer look at the situation within the service sector permits a further grouping of countries: in ten of the 15 Member States, the longest hours within the service sector were observed in hotels and restaurants and in the other five (Denmark, Ireland, the Netherlands, Finland and the United Kingdom) they were in transport and communication. The shortest working hours were found in public administration (Germany and Finland), in financial intermediation (Austria, Sweden and the United Kingdom) and - in most countries - education and health. Data for this last activity may be slightly biased, however, as it is difficult to calculate accurately the working time of teachers (Table 17).

Table 17 - Usual weekly working hours of full-time employees by economic activity, 1996

	EU-15	B	DK	D	EL	E	F	IRL	I	L	NL	A	P	FIN	S	UK
Agriculture	43	41	44	43	47	44	41	49	41	45	41	41	47	40	40	48
Industry	41	39	38	39	41	41	40	41	41	40	39	40	43	39	40	45
Services	40	38	39	40	40	40	40	40	37	39	40	40	40	39	40	44
Wholesale & retail trade	41	39	39	40	43	42	41	41	41	40	40	40	44	40	40	44
Hotels and restaurants	43	41	39	44	47	44	44	42	43	43	40	41	47	38	41	44
Transport & communication	42	40	40	41	44	42	41	42	40	40	40	41	43	40	40	47
Financial intermediation	40	39	38	40	40	40	41	40	39	40	39	40	38	38	40	42
Real estate, business activities	41	39	40	41	41	40	41	41	40	40	39	40	40	38	40	44
Public adminis., defence	40	38	38	40	40	39	40	39	37	39	39	40	40	38	40	42
Education & Health	39	36	38	40	35	39	37	35	33	37	39	41	36	38	40	43

Source : Eurostat - Labour Force Survey

18 million unemployed in EU-15

Between 1991 and 1996, unemployment rates increased in the vast majority of Member States. Young people, women and the low-qualified were particularly affected. The share of the long-term unemployed increased or remained stable in all countries with the exception of Denmark. Research shows that qualifications improve the chances of finding a job.

Unemployment rose by one-third in the Union between 1991 and 1996

The total number of unemployed in the Europe of Fifteen stood at 13.6 million in 1991, representing 8.2% of the labour force. By 1996, it had climbed to 18.2 million or 10.9% of the active population. The increase in unemployment, which affected all Member States at the beginning of the 1990s, was largely due to recession. Since 1994, the situation has improved in Denmark, Ireland, Finland and the United Kingdom. Over the period 1991-1996, the largest changes occurred in Finland and Sweden where unemployment rates increased by a factor of two and three respectively.

At present, the countries most severely hit by unemployment are Spain (22.1%) and Finland (15.4%). In contrast, rates in Luxembourg, Austria, the Netherlands, Denmark and Portugal are less than 8% (Table 18).

Table 18 - Unemployment[1] 1991-1996

	EU-15	B	DK	D	EL	E	F	IRL	I	L	NL	A	P	FIN	S	UK
Unemployment rate (%)																
1991	8.2	6.6	8.4	5.6	7.0	16.4	9.5	14.8	8.8	1.7	5.8	:	4.0	7.6	3.3	8.8
1992	9.3	7.3	9.2	6.6	7.9	18.5	10.4	15.4	9.0	2.1	5.6	:	4.2	13.0	5.8	10.1
1993	10.7	8.9	10.1	7.9	8.6	22.8	11.7	15.6	10.3	2.7	6.6	4.0	5.7	17.5	9.5	10.4
1994	11.1	10.0	8.2	8.4	8.9	24.1	12.3	14.3	11.4	3.2	7.1	3.8	7.0	17.9	9.8	9.6
1995	10.8	9.9	7.2	8.2	9.2	22.9	11.7	12.3	11.9	2.9	6.9	3.9	7.3	16.6	9.2	8.7
1996	10.9	9.8	6.9	8.8	9.6	22.1	12.4	11.6	12.0	3.3	6.3	4.4	7.3	15.4	10.0	8.2
Unemployed persons 1996 (1000)	18200	410	195	3458	412	3524	3146	174	2732	6	467	166	348	376	439	2347
Index 1996 (1991=100)	134	156	80	158	149	142	135	88	132	200	118	:	182	210	297	93

[1] Data are annual averages and refer to the population aged 15 and over - see box p.132

Source : Harmonised unemployment rates (Eurostat: Unemployment. Monthly Bulletin 2/98)

National unemployment rates often mask important regional disparities within Member States, particularly in Germany (between west and east), Italy (between north and south) and the United Kingdom (also between north and south). In Germany, the unemployment rate in 1996 ranged from less than half the national average of 8.8% in Oberbayern (4.3%) to more than twice it in Sachsen-Anhalt (17.8%). Similarly, in Italy, while the region of Trentino-Alto Adige was largely unaffected by unemployment (3.4%), around 25% of the workforce in the southern regions of Campania and Calabria was unemployed. Other regions in the Union where unemployment rates are considerably higher than the national average include Hainaut in Belgium, Dytiki Makedonia in Greece, Corsica and the overseas departments in France, Groningen in the Netherlands and Alentejo in Portugal (Table 19).

Low unemployment rates can, in some cases, be explained by regional migration, i.e., when people move to another region that offers more job opportunities, this results in a reduction in the labour force in the region of origin and consequently the unemployment rate falls.

While it is meaningful to look at regional disparities within Member States, it is important to bear in mind that the majority of regions in Spain and Finland are among the worst-affected in the Union when it comes to unemployment.

Table 19 - Significant differences in unemployment rates within countries, April 1996

The worst-off regions		The best-off regions	
Regions where the unemployment rate is at least 40% higher than the national average		Regions where the unemployment rate is at least 40% lower than the national average	
BELGIQUE-BELGIE	9.6	**BELGIQUE-BELGIE**	9.6
Hainaut	15.8	West-Vlaanderen	5.5
Reg. Bruxelles-Cap./Brussels Hfdst. Gewest	14.1	Vlaams Brabant	5.1
DEUTSCHLAND	8.8	**DEUTSCHLAND**	8.8
Sachsen-Anhalt	17.8	Bayern	5.3
Mecklenburg-Vorpommern	16.6	Schwaben	5.3
Thueringen	15.8	Tuebingen	5.1
Brandenburg	15.3	Niederbayern	5.1
Sachsen	15.1	Oberbayern	4.3
ELLADA	9.7	**ELLADA**	9.7
Dytiki Makedonia	16.3	Ionia Nisia	5.5
		Notio Aigaio	4.9
		Nisia Aigaiou, Kriti	4.4
ESPANA	22.3	Kriti	3.4
Andalucia	32.4		
Sur	31.3	**ESPANA**	22.3
		Navarra	11.0
FRANCE	12.0		
Départements d'Outre-Mer	31.1	**ITALIA**	12.1
Corse	21.0	Lombardia	6.3
Nord-Pas-de-Calais	16.8	Friuli-Venezia Giulia	6.3
		Marche	5.9
		Veneto	5.4
ITALIA	12.1	Nord Est	5.3
Campania	25.5	Emilia-Romagna	5.3
Calabria	25.0	Valle d'Aosta	5.2
Sicilia	24.0	Trentino-Alto Agide	3.4
Sardegna	21.8		
Sud	20.2		
Basilicata	19.4	**PORTUGAL**	7.4
Puglia	17.9	Centro	4.1
Molise	17.8		
NEDERLAND	6.2	**SUOMI (FINLAND)**	15.7
Groningen	10.1	Ahvenanmaa/Åland	4.7
PORTUGAL	7.4		
Alentejo	12.3	**UNITED KINGDOM**	8.3
		Bedfordshire, Hertfordshire	5.0
UNITED KINGDOM	8.3	Surrey, East-West Sussex	5.0
Merseyside	11.7	Berks., Bucks., Oxfordshire	4.1

Source : Eurostat - Regional Statistics

Most unemployed people seek a full-time job

More than three quarters of all unemployed persons in the European Union look for full-time work. The percentage is particularly high in Spain (95%) whereas it is quite low (46%) in the Netherlands where part-time work is well established as a normal form of employment. Women who are unemployed are in general less interested in full-time work than men are (72% against 85%).

The proportion of the unemployed aged under 25 looking for full-time work is, as would be expected, generally high but there are three exceptions: in the United Kingdom and Denmark, 21% and 29% respectively of young people are looking for part-time work and in the Netherlands the figure is as high as 63%. The education system and the extent of part-time work in each country are clearly influencing factors (Table 20). Given the relatively high level of non-response, the data presented for some countries such as Italy, Portugal and the United Kingdom should be considered as ballpark figures.

Table 20 - Unemployed persons by the kind of job they are seeking, 1996

(as a % of each category)

	EU-15	B	DK	D	EL	E	F	IRL	I	L	NL	A	P	FIN	S	UK
All unemployed																
Full-time	78	79	76	85	90	95	84	80	61	77	46	79	76	80	84	60
Part-time	12	9	15	12	4	5	13	16	12	15	51	19	1	7	10	19
No answer	9	12	9	3	6	0	3	4	27	8	3	2	23	13	6	21
Men																
Full-time	85	86	80	94	90	98	92	92	66	85	68	93	73	79	88	72
Part-time	4	2	11	3	3	2	4	3	3	5	28	5	1	4	4	7
No answer	11	12	9	3	8	0	4	5	31	10	4	2	26	18	8	20
Women																
Full-time	72	72	72	75	90	93	76	62	56	69	26	60	79	81	78	37
Part-time	21	16	19	22	6	7	22	36	21	25	72	39	1	10	18	40
No answer	8	12	9	3	5	0	2	2	22	6	2	1	20	9	4	22
<25 years																
Full-time	79	84	64	90	90	96	89	92	66	80	36	87	77	68	84	62
Part-time	10	5	29	5	4	4	8	7	7	8	63	13	3	14	13	21
No answer	11	11	8	5	6	0	3	1	27	12	2	0	20	19	4	4

Given the relatively high level of non-response, the data presented for some countries should be considered as ballpark figures.
Source : Eurostat - Labour Force Survey

Long-term unemployment remains high

During the Employment Summit in Luxembourg in 1997, the EU Member States agreed on two basic objectives: limiting the duration of unemployment and promoting the re-employment of the long-term unemployed. This is to be achieved by offering the young and adult unemployed training and retraining measures in addition to work experience before reaching 6 and 12 months of unemployment, respectively.

In 1996, 48% of the unemployed had already been jobless for more than one year and, by international statistical agreement, are counted as long-term unemployed. In Denmark (27%), Luxembourg (28%), Austria (26%), and, above all Sweden (19%), the proportion of long-term unemployed was well below the EU average in 1996. Belgium (61%), Greece (57%), Ireland (60%) and Italy (66%) are the countries most affected by long-term unemployment. In relation to 1991, the situation has remained stable in most countries but worsened significantly in Greece, Germany, the Netherlands, Portugal and the United Kingdom. Denmark stands out as the only Member State where there has been a slight improvement (Table 21).

Long-term unemployment among the young varies considerably between Member States reflecting not only the extent or lack of employment opportunities but also the structure of the national education and training system.

Table 21 - Long-term unemployment 1991-1996

(% of all unemployed)

	EU-15	B	DK	D	EL	E	F	IRL	I	L	NL	A	P	FIN	S	UK
All unemployed																
1991	:	61	31	31	47	49	38	60	66	27	41	:	38	:	:	28
1996	48	61	27	48	57	53	38	60	66	28	49	26	53	36	19	40

The long-term unemployed are considered to be those persons unemployed for more than one year.
Source : Eurostat - Labour Force Survey

Higher unemployment among women and young people

For the Union as a whole, the unemployment rate is higher for women (12.5%) than for men (9.6%). This pattern can be seen in 13 of the Member States. In Belgium, Denmark, Spain, Italy, Luxembourg and the Netherlands, the female rate is between 54% and 88% higher than that of men. Women in Greece are more than two-and-a-half times as likely to be unemployed as men. The situation is more favourable for women only in Sweden and the United Kingdom. In the United Kingdom, the rate for men is almost 50% higher than the female rate (Figure 6).

The average unemployment rate amongst the under-25s in the European Union increased from 16% in 1991 to 22% in 1996. This average figure conceals sharp contrasts between the Member States: in 1996, the unemployment rate among young people aged under 25 ranged from 6% in Austria and 10% in Germany to 34% and 42% respectively for Italy and Spain. Over the period 1991-1996, the under-25 unemployment rate increased in all countries except Denmark and Ireland.

Figure 6 - Unemployment rates by gender, 1996

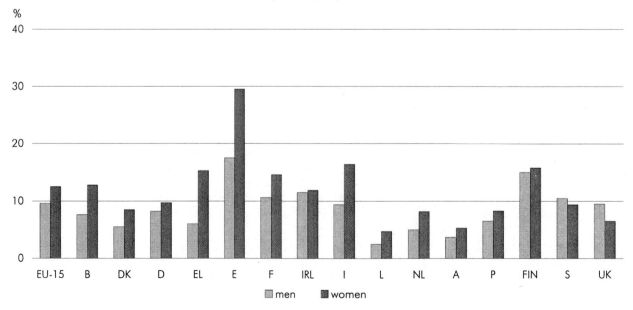

Source : Harmonised unemployment rates (Eurostat: Unemployment — Monthly Bulletin — 2/1998)

Because of the drop in the activity rate of young people aged under 25 and the expansion of training/employment combinations, it is interesting to compare the unemployment rate with an indicator showing the number of unemployed persons aged 15-24 as a proportion of the total population of the same age. For example, while the under-25 unemployment rate in France is around 29%, only one in ten young people in this age group are looking for a job (Table 22). A counter-argument against this kind of yardstick (population) is the fact that many young people, well aware that they risk being unemployed, are consciously prolonging their education and training and "marking time" in the educational system.

Definition of unemployment

For a comparable **measure of unemployment** in the EU, Eurostat applies the recommendations of the International Labour Office (ILO), according to which the unemployed comprise persons aged 15 and over who

— are without work;

— are currently available for work, i.e. can start a job within two weeks, and

— have been actively seeking work during the past four weeks.

The unemployment rate is the percentage of the active population which is unemployed.

The statistics used in the Member States showing persons registered with job centres are not suitable for inter-country comparisons since they are influenced by the provisions of the national labour market administrations.

Table 22 - Youth unemployment, 1996

	EU-15	B	DK	D	EL	E	F	IRL	I	L	NL	A	P	FIN	S	UK
Unemployment rate[1]	22	23	11	10	31	42	29	18	34	9	12	6	17	29	21	16
% of population[2]	10	8	8	5	12	17	10	8	13	4	7	4	7	13	10	10

[1] Number of unemployed aged 15-24 as a % of the corresponding labour force
[2] Number of unemployed aged 15-24 as a % of the population aged 15-24

Source : Harmonised unemployment rates Eurostat: Unemployment. Monthly Bulletin 2/1998

Today, almost one in two unemployed persons under 25 is looking for their first job. In Italy, Greece and Finland the figure is at least three out of four while in Sweden and Denmark it is only one in ten. Youth unemployment is, on the one hand, a result of the general labour market situation. It is also a reflection of how the educational and employment systems manage to complement one another with respect to the integration of the young in the labour market, and, in particular, of how well the education and training system prepares young people for the labour market (Figure 7).

Figure 7 - Percentage of the unemployed under 25 who are seeking a first job, 1996

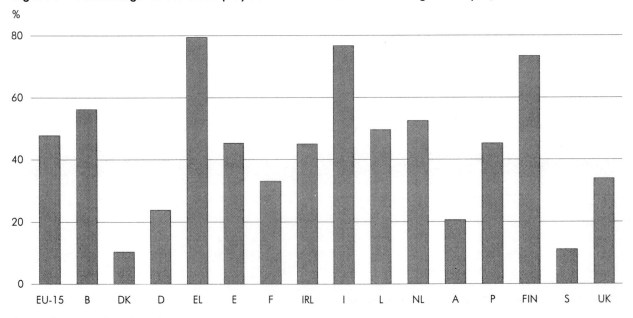

Source: Eurostat - Labour Force Survey

Qualifications improve the chances of finding a job

···

In general, the chances of finding a job rise with the level of education attained. In 1996 for the Europe of Fifteen, the unemployment rate of persons with a higher education qualification was 6%, against 9% for persons who had completed upper secondary level and 13% for those whose educational level is that of compulsory schooling at best.

Higher education qualifications seem to reduce, albeit to differing degrees, the chances of unemployment in all Member States. With the exception of Greece, Spain and Italy, the least-qualified in all countries are more than twice as likely to be unemployed as university graduates. The most significant differences are found in Ireland and Belgium. The picture in Greece is rather unusual in that unemployment seems to affect more those whose highest level is upper secondary education than persons who have not gone beyond compulsory schooling. In Portugal and Sweden, there is no appreciable difference between the unemployment rates of persons who have completed upper secondary level and the lowest-qualified (Table 23).

Table 23 - Unemployment rates by highest completed level of education or training, 1996

(%)

	EU-15	B	DK	D	EL	E	F	IRL	I	L	NL	A	P	FIN	S	UK
level of education or training																
low	13	14	10	15	7	21	15	17	10	4	8	7	7	17	10	9
medium	9	8	6	9	9	18	10	7	8	2	5	5	6	13	10	7
high	6	4	4	5	6	14	7	4	6	.	4	3	3	7	4	4

For further information on the education and training levels, See p. 75

Source : Eurostat - Labour Force Survey

Working Environment

Aspects of today's working life

The term "working environment" encompasses health and safety related to work, including its psycho-social characteristics. It covers therefore all aspects of well-being at work, work-related health problems and accidents at work.

From a historical perspective, the improvement of working life was one of the major objectives of the early labour movement and the emerging welfare states. Research, legislation and negotiations in the context of labour protection have set higher standards in most areas, ranging from physical factors to toxic hazards, from child labour to pension rights and from working hours to leave for training, sickness, family responsibilities and vacations. Accidents at work, which were one of the major scourges of industrial workers at the beginning of industrialisation, have seen a considerable decrease in numbers since the fifties.

Although mechanisation has replaced much of the hard physical work prevalent in the past, it has at the same time resulted in repetitive and monotonous work. There is now a new focus on the psycho-social aspects of work. There is also a general trend towards democratisation of social relations in the work place, and, in the context of work organisation, a move from "taylorism" to more flexible working patterns. Enhanced qualifications and personal responsibility have also become more relevant and are discussed in the chapter on Education and Training and in the section on work-related health problems. These positive developments were partly the result of a new demand for greater productivity and have been accompanied by a tendency towards a more uncertain working status involving more short term contracts (see chapter on Labour Market).

In the light of globalisation and the enhanced competitive environment, the quality of the working environment remains a topical issue. For both the individual and the enterprise, a good and safe working environment is clearly important in order to maintain health and working capacity. The quality of work and its organisation increasingly influences the availability of skilled labour, the motivation of personnel and the development of human resources in general.

Recent data on the working environment in the Union indicate that :

— Working conditions vary considerably depending on the economic sector of activity. In general, persons employed in agriculture, mining and construction are more likely to report exposure to excessive noise, vibrations, extreme temperatures, handling dangerous products and breathing in harmful substances. They also report higher than average levels of work-related skin problems, respiratory difficulties and backache. Finally, the frequency of accidents at work is well above the average in the above-mentioned sectors and the transport and communication sector.

— Persons employed in hotels and restaurants reported the highest levels of exposure to short repetitive tasks and high temperatures. They also have a greater tendency to work at night than persons in most other sectors.

— More than one in four of those interviewed indicated that they suffered from work-related stress in 1996. Around 30% of persons in employment reported work-related backache.

— Around 1 out of 22 employed persons in the Union had an accident at work in 1994 that resulted in at least 3 days absence from work.

— Men are more likely than women to work in high-risk sectors such as construction. Consequently, they have 10 times more fatal accidents (and 3 times more non-fatal accidents) than women.

European Survey on Working Conditions

The European Survey on Working Conditions is conducted by the European Foundation for the Improvement of Living and Working Conditions (Dublin).

Aim: To serve policy makers with indicators on the development of the working environment in Europe.

Reference years: The first survey was carried out in 1991, the second in 1996. The intention is to carry out a survey every four years.

Sample: Multi-stage random sampling of 15 986 individuals for EU-15, made up of around 1 000 per country except Germany (2 087) and Luxembourg (500).

Coverage: All sectors and persons in employment, including family workers. Unemployed and inactive persons were excluded from the survey.

Quality of data: All the questions in the survey are based on the respondent's subjective assessment of the situation. It is however acknowledged that such measures also reflect objective conditions in their work. Nevertheless, data should be used more for relative assessments and comparisons between groups than providing absolute levels for the working environment in Europe. The sub-sample for electricity, gas and water supply does not allow for significant conclusions in all cases.

Last publication: Second European Survey on Working Conditions, European Foundation, 1997.

Community health and safety legislation

During the eighties, health and safety at work became one of the most active aspects of EU social policy in the employment field. Firstly, the Single European Act adopted in 1986 gave new impetus to the occupational health and safety measures taken by the Community. This was the first time that health and safety at work had been directly included in the EEC Treaty of 1957. Most importantly, the directives adopted under Article 118a lay down minimum requirements concerning health and safety at work in the Member States. According to this principle, the Member States must raise their level of protection if it is lower than the minimum requirements set by the directives. Following the Single European Act various other pieces of legislation were adopted, the cornerstone of which was the "Framework Directive" on health and safety at work on which all subsequent directives have been built (see below).

Principal directives

Legislation (Reference to directives in brackets)	Date of transposition
— Single European Act	1 July 1987
— The Framework Directive on Health and Safety at Work (89/391/EEC)	31 December 1992
— Directive on Work equipment (89/655/EEC): Lays down minimum health and safety standards for workplaces.	31 December 1992
— Use of personal protective equipment (89/656/EEC)	31 December 1992
— Manual handling of loads (90/269/EEC)	31 December 1992
— Working time (93/104/EC): Lays down minimum requirements concerning daily and weekly rest periods, annual holidays, maximum weekly working time and certain forms of night-work.	23 November 1996
— Chemical, physical and biological agents at work (several directives adopted)	
— Carcinogens (90/394/EEC)	31 December 1992
— Biological agents (90/679/EEC)	28 November 1993
— Safety and health signs at work	24 June 1994

Work-related health problems

Work-related health problems can be studied by using data on the prevalence of exposure factors in the working environment. A widely-used method is to ask employed persons whether they are exposed to certain factors and, if so, for how long. Such data have been collected by the European Survey on Working Conditions 1996 (see box p. 136).

The physical working environment is covered by the following exposure factors: noise, vibrations and temperature extremes. Just under one in five of those questioned declared that they were subject to excessive noise for about half or more of their working time. Similar proportions reported exposure to vibrations while just over one in eight mentioned temperature extremes. For all four factors, Greece had the highest proportion of respondents reporting exposure (Table 1). A higher proportion of persons employed in agriculture, mining and manufacturing, and construction reported exposure to these physical factors (Table 2).

Noise is a common problem

In 1996, 18 % of persons in employment reported that during about half or more of their working time they were exposed to such levels of noise that they had to raise their voice to talk to people. This amounts to some 25 million citizens of the Union. In 1995, approximately 18 000 cases of hearing disorders caused by work were recognised in the European Union. (Eurostat - European Occupational Diseases Statistics). The risk of hearing damage is associated with the level of the noise and the duration of exposure. The main source of noise is usually various power driven machines, tools or vehicles. The principal groups of workers exposed are plant and machine operators, craft and related trade workers.

Table 1 - Exposure to physical factors, 1996

Self-reported exposure to some physical factors in the working environment[1] (%)

	EU-15	B	DK	D	EL	E	F	IRL	I	L	NL	A	P	FIN	S	UK
Noise	18	15	16	18	27	33	30	18	15	18	14	18	22	22	19	18
Vibrations	17	12	9	17	28	15	25	15	17	17	10	20	24	15	8	12
High temperature	12	9	9	9	29	18	13	8	10	18	12	15	13	9	6	14
Low temperatures	13	9	9	8	31	20	17	12	12	12	11	14	12	9	7	18

[1] The data refer to those persons exposed to the factor(s) for about half ore more of their working time.

Source : European Foundation for Living and Working Conditions: European Survey on Working Conditions 1996

Sources of vibrations are more or less the same as those for noise and the same sectors and occupational groups seem to be affected. On average, 17% of persons in employment claim exposure to vibrations for about half or more their working time. Workers in Greece, France and Portugal all reported much higher levels.

13% of those in employment feel that they work in low temperatures. Similarly, 12% declare that they work in such high temperatures that they perspire even when not working. In addition to the 3 above-mentioned activities, those employed in hotels and restaurants report a higher than average rate for high temperatures (20%) (Table 2).

Exposure to dangerous substances varies considerably between sectors and Member States

For the Europe of Fifteen, 8% of persons in employment declared that they were carrying out work which involves handling/touching harmful products or substances while 17% reported breathing in vapours, fumes or dust during about half or more of their working time. In both cases, Greek stands out with a much higher proportion than any other Member State. With regard to the breathing in of vapours, etc, Spain and Portugal also report much higher levels than the EU average (Figure 1).

Table 2 - Exposure to physical factors by economic activity, EU-15, 1996

Self-reported exposure to some physical factors in the working environment by economic activity [1] (%)

	Vibration	Noise	High temperature	Low temperature
EU-15, All activities[2]	17	18	12	13
Agriculture, Hunting, Forestry, Fishing	32	26	20	32
Mining and Manufacturing	28	30	17	13
Electricity, Gas and Water supply[3]	:	:	:	:
Construction	35	31	18	31
Wholesale and retail trade	11	13	9	14
Hotels and restaurants	9	16	20	5
Transport and Communication	18	19	11	14
Financial intermediation	3	2	5	4
Real estate and business activity	5	8	6	12
Public administration	6	11	8	9
Other services	8	11	8	8

[1] The data refer to those persons exposed to the factor(s) for about half ore more of their working time

[2] NACE Rev. 1

[3] The size of the sub-sample is such that data are not statistically significant for this branch

Source : European Foundation for Living and Working Conditions: European Survey on Working Environment 1996

Figure 1 - Percentage of persons in employment exposed to dangerous vapours, fumes, dust or handling dangerous substances for at least half their working time, 1996

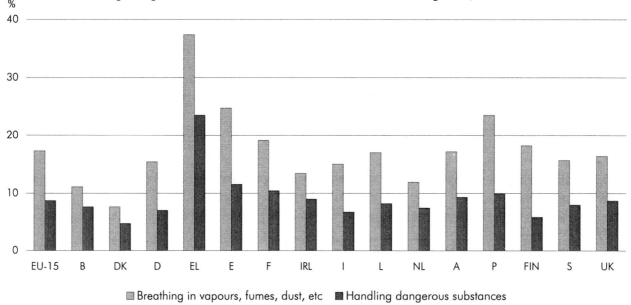

Source : European Foundation for Living and Working Conditions: European Survey on Working Environment 1996

Table 3 - Exposure to chemical and biological factors by economic activity, EU-15, 1996

Self-reported exposures to vapours, fumes, dust or dangerous substances in the course of work and reported skin problems and repiratory aliments related to work (%)

	Percentage of employed persons exposed at least half of the working time to:		Percentage of employed persons reporting a work-related health problem	
	Breathing in vapours, fumes, dust etc.	Handling/Touching hazardous substances	Skin problems	Respiratory difficulties
EU-15, All sectors[1]	17	8	6	4
Agriculture, Hunting, Forestry, Fishing	21	13	7	6
Mining and Manufacturing	27	13	8	6
Electricity, Gas and Water supply[2]	:	:	:	:
Construction	32	12	10	9
Wholesale and retail trade	13	7	4	3
Hotels and restaurants	19	3	5	6
Transport and Communication	19	6	3	3
Financial intermediation	4	1	2	3
Real estate and business activity	8	5	1	2
Public administration	10	7	4	2
Other services	11	8	6	3

[1] NACE Rev. 1

[2] The size of the sub-sample means that the data are not statistically significant for this branch

Source : European Foundation for Living and Working Conditions: European Survey on Working Environment 1996

As it is not possible to gauge the seriousness of this type of exposure, the data do not show the proportion of persons that are exposed to a level which would be harmful to them. They do however bring certain sectors into focus where there is a greater exposure to chemical and biological products and substances.

Persons working in the mining and manufacturing and the construction sectors are most likely to report exposure to breathing in vapours and handling dangerous substances.

Respiratory ailments are due to inhalation of harmful substances in the environment which can cause, e.g., asthma, pneumoconiosis or infections. There appears to be a strong correlation between breathing in harmful substances and respiratory problems. For example, a relatively large proportion of persons in the construction industry, where exposure to breathing in vapours is high, reported work-related respiratory difficulties: 9% compared with an EU average of 4%. Similarly, in those sectors such as agriculture, mining and manufacturing and construction, where a significantly higher proportion of persons declared that they were handling harmful substances, workers also reported the highest rate of work-related skin problems (Table 3).

Table 4 - Exposure to physiological factors and related health problems by economic activity, EU-15, 1996

Self-reported health problems and exposures to the carrying or moving of heavy loads, and painful and/or tiring positions (%)

	Percentage of employed persons exposed at least half of the working time to:				Percentage of employed persons reporting a work-related health problem	
	Carrying or moving heavy loads	Job involving painful and tiring positions	Short repetitive tasks of less than 10 minutes	Repetitive hand or arm movements	Backache	Muscular pains in arms or legs
EU-15, All sectors	20	32	26	46	30	17
Agriculture, Hunting, Forestry, Fishinç	43	59	33	62	49	35
Mining and Manufacturing	20	31	30	52	30	18
Electricity, Gas and Water supply[1]	:	:	:	:	:	:
Construction	41	44	29	59	44	28
Wholesale and retail trade	22	33	29	45	26	15
Hotels and restaurants	20	44	42	61	31	20
Transport and Communication	20	33	22	50	31	18
Financial intermediation	5	18	20	36	20	6
Real estate and business activity	8	22	24	40	20	10
Public administration	9	22	18	31	25	13
Other services	14	27	20	38	27	13

[1] The size of the sub-sample means that the data are not statistically significant for this branch

Source : European Foundation for Living and Working Conditions: European Survey on Working Environment 1996

Backache is a major problem for persons working in agriculture and the construction industry

Exposure relating to the muscular-skeletal system comprises work involving carrying or moving heavy loads, painful and tiring positions and repetitive tasks. Across the Union, almost half of those in employment (46%) indicated that they have to make repetitive hand and arm movements for about half or more of their working time. Workers in agriculture, hotels and restaurants and construction activities have a significantly higher prevalence of exposure (Table 4).

Repetitive hand and arm movements can give rise to muscular-skeletal problems in the upper limbs, neck and shoulder. There appears to be a relatively strong correlation between such movements and muscular pains in the arms (or legs). In the agricultural sector for example, 62% of those employed reported repetitive hand and arm movements (compared with a cross-sector average of 46%) and 35% reported muscular pains in their arms (or legs) (against an average of 17%). The data do not take account of the intensity or the frequency of movements, perhaps one reason why this question elicited a higher response level than the one on short repetitive tasks. Around one in four respondents indicated that they carry out short repetitive tasks of less than 10 minutes for about half or more their working time. The highest prevalence (42%) was found in hotels and restaurants.

Figure 2 - Percentage of persons in employment reporting work-related backache by selected economic activity, EU-15, 1996

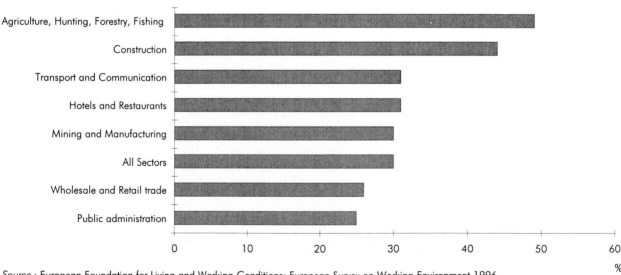

Source : European Foundation for Living and Working Conditions: European Survey on Working Environment 1996

One in three interviewees declared that they had to work in tiring and painful positions. Persons employed in the southern Member States reported a higher prevalence to such exposure than the northern Member States. In addition to the agriculture and construction sectors, a higher proportion of those employed in hotels and restaurants declared that they had also to work in painful and tiring positions. Such positions often comprise several types of work activities such as squatting, kneeling, lifting, reaching above shoulder level or working in awkward positions.

Finally, around one in five respondents said that their job involved carrying and moving heavy loads for more than half of the working time. Significantly higher prevalence (between 23% and 30%) was observed in Greece, Spain, France and Austria. Persons employed in the agriculture and construction branches seem to be more likely than workers in other branches to carry and move heavy loads.

Work involving carrying or moving heavy loads is often linked to back problems. Actions such as lifting and carrying objects will affect in particular the spinal column and the lower back. Work-related backache was reported by 30% of persons in employment and ranks as the highest work-related health problem in the European Union. Persons working in the agricultural and construction branches declared significantly higher levels (49% and 44% respectively) of work-related backache (Figure 2). The humid and cold outdoor conditions often faced by those working in these two branches might constitute an aggravating factor for muscular-skeletal disorders.

Table 5 - Trend in some factors relating to stress, EU-12, 1991-1996

(%)

	1991	1996
Percentage of interviewed persons exposed about half or more of the working time to		
Working at high speed	48	54
Working to tight deadlines	50	56
Percentage of employed persons feeling they have an influence on the pace at which they work	64	72
Percentage of employed persons reporting work-related stress	:	28

Source : European Foundation for Living and Working Conditions: European Surveys on Working
      Environment 1991 and 1996

More than one in four persons in employment report work-related stress

Stress is caused by a multitude of demands in the environment. If there is an inadequate relation between the demands and the capacity of the person to cope with them, it can become stressful for the person concerned.

In 1996 for the Europe of Twelve, just over half of persons in employment said that they spent about half or more of their working time operating at high speed (54%) and working to tight deadlines (56%). This represents a slight increase in relation to 1991 (Table 5). The assumed trend towards the democratisation of social relations in the work place is supported by an increase in the proportion of persons indicating that they have an influence on the pace at which they work. The proportion stood at 72% in 1996, compared with 64% five years earlier.

28% of those interviewed indicated that they suffer from work-related stress. Persons employed in hotels and restaurants reported the highest prevalence of stress related to work (34%). The proportion was also higher than average among those employed in the financial and business activities.

Although persons seem to have more influence over the execution of their tasks, they are also facing relatively more time pressure.

Figure 3 - Percentage of employees usually doing night work, 1996

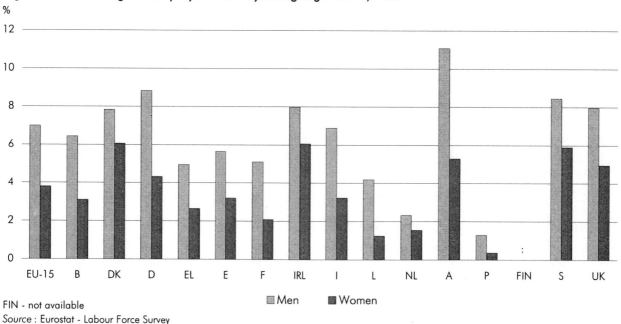

FIN - not available

Source : Eurostat - Labour Force Survey

Trend in shift and night work is slightly upward

In 1996, over 6 million employees in the Union as a whole - some 5.6% of the total - had jobs which involved them 'usually' working at night. This represents a slight increase on the 1992 level of 5.3%. Men (7.0%) are more likely than women (3.8%) to work at night (Figure 3). Another 10 million or so - 9% of the total - 'sometimes' worked at night. The highest prevalence of night work can be observed in Austria where 11% of male employees have jobs which require them to 'usually' work at night. In contrast, Luxembourg, the Netherlands and Portugal stand out with a comparatively low proportion (1%-3%) of employees usually working at night. Night working is most prevalent in fishing, hotels and restaurants, transport and communications and health and social work.

For the Europe of Fifteen in 1996, 12.6% of employees had jobs which involved them usually working shifts, a slight increase on the 1992 level of 11.4% (Figure 4). There are considerable variations between countries ranging from more than 20% in Finland and Sweden to less than 10% in Denmark, Spain, France, Luxembourg, the Netherlands and Portugal.

Shift and night work require people to adapt to varying work schedules, sleeping and meal times. This is known to affect the person mentally and physiologically. Furthermore, shift or night work can also cause psycho-social family conflicts.

> **Definition of working arrangements**
>
> An employee is classified as a shift worker if he/she usually works two or more different work-shifts. Work shifts are defined as distinct periods of work within a 24-hour day. Night work is defined as work done during the usual sleeping hours.
>
> 'Usually' means on about half or more of the working days during the 4 weeks preceding the survey ; 'sometimes', on less than half the days.

Figure 4 - Trend in the percentage of employees usually doing shift work, 1992-1996

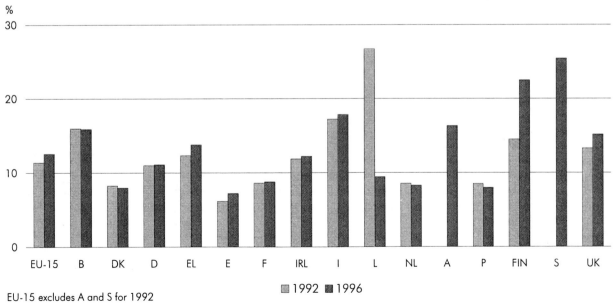

EU-15 excludes A and S for 1992

Source : Eurostat - Labour Force Survey

Around one EU worker in 22 was the victim of an accident in 1994

In 1994, almost 5 million accidents at work - each resulting in more than 3 days' absence - were recorded in the European Union. The European average frequency was thus 4 539 accidents at work per 100 000 persons in employment or, put another way, one worker in 22 was the victim of an accident at work. These figures relate to almost 90% of persons in employment in the Union.

In the same year, 6 423 fatal accidents were recorded in the 15 Member States. This represents 6 fatalities per 100 000 workers or 4 per 100 000 if road traffic accidents and deaths from strictly natural causes which occurred during working hours (e.g., heart attacks) are excluded (Table 6). Although the figures are rather small, they are nonetheless significant particularly if one considers the numerous pieces of legislation in the area of health and safety at work.

High risk branches: construction, agriculture, transport and part of the manufacturing industry

These proportions differ of course depending on the economic activity of the enterprise, and the age and sex of workers. The construction industry has the highest frequency: 9 014 accidents resulting in more than three days' absence and almost 15 fatal accidents per 100 000 workers, corresponding to 2 and 2.5 times the respective averages. It is also higher than average in agriculture and transport and some manufacturing sectors: food and beverages, wood, glass, ceramics and construction materials and basic metals and fabricated metal products. Indeed almost 50% of all the accidents recorded in 1994 took place in the manufacturing and construction industries. In contrast, as one might expect, the frequency is considerably lower in wholesale, retail trade and services.

Frequency of accidents decreases with age but their seriousness increases

In 1994 there were 5 802 accidents per 100 000 for the under-26 age group, 4 374 for the 26-45 group and 3 935 for the over-45 group. Young people are more likely to be in jobs where there is a relatively high risk of accidents. Their actions or lack of experience may also place them at greater risk (Table 7).

In contrast, the frequency of fatal accidents increases considerably with age: 3.8 per 100 000 for the under-26 group, 4.7 for the 26-45 group and 8.6 for the over-45 group. The inclusion by Spain and France of deaths at work from natural causes, the frequency of which increases with age, partly explains this situation. There were 373 such fatalities in these 2 countries in 1994.

Table 6 - Accidents at work by type of economic activity, EU-15, 1994

Economic activities	Persons in employment (1000) [1]	Accidents with more than 3 days' absence		Fatal accidents [2]	
		Estimated number	Number per 100 000 persons in employment	Number	Number per 100 000 persons in employment
A: Agriculture, hunting and forestry	5 613	348 309	6 496	770	14.0
D: Manufacturing	30 147	1 515 556	5 071	1 330	4.6
of which :					
Manufacture of food products; beverages and tobacco	2 947	215 798	7 360	257	9.2
Manufacture of wood and wood products	1 203	105 051	8 852	56	4.8
Manufacture of other non-metallic mineral products (glass, ceramics, construction materials)	1 117	72 155	6 518	99	9.1
Manufacture of basic metals and fabricated metal products	4 263	365 537	8 650	259	6.2
F: Construction	10 249	858 129	9 014	1 457	14.7
G: Wholesale and retail trade	19 549	487 656	2 552	519	2.8
H: Hotels and restaurants	4 650	179 489	4 121	82	1.9
I: Transport, storage and communication	7 003	421 133	6 139	917	13.7
J: Financial intermediation + K: Real estate, renting and business activities	14 270	225 828	1 638	298	2.2
Total 8 branches	91 480	4 036 100	4 539	5 373	6.1
of which fatal accidents excluding road traffic accidents and natural causes				3 413	3.9
Others and unspecified	40 376	881 966		1 050	
Total all branches of activity	131 856	4 918 066		6 423	
of which fatal accidents excluding road traffic accidents and natural causes				4 084	

[1] Actual coverage of these statistics.

[2] Including road traffic accidents (except for UK and IRL) and for E and F only, deaths from strictly natural causes occurred in the course of work

Source : Eurostat - European Statistics on Accidents at Work

Economic activity is also a factor in this age-related pattern of fatal accidents at work: 47% of workers in agriculture are over 45 and 28-31% in the other branches with a high risk of fatal accidents (construction, transport and, to a lesser extent, manufacturing). They represent only 22-26% in the other common sectors of activity (29% on average in the eight branches).

Other factors may also explain the higher risk of fatal accidents among older workers: they may have a higher mortality rate than younger people suffering the same degree of injury ; they may be at workstations with a higher risk of serious accidents at work (including road traffic accidents) ; or they may be less vigilant or agile, etc.

Table 7 - Frequency of accidents at work, 1994

(Number per 100 000 persons in employment)

| | Accidents at work with more than 3 days' absence | | | Fatal accidents at work Road traffic accidents and deaths from natural causes included [1] | | | excluded |
	Total	under 26 years	over 45 years	Total	under 26 years	over 45 years	Total
EU- 15	4 539	5 802	3 935	6.1	3.8	8.6	3.9
B	4 415	7 138	3 198	7.1	7.1	10.8	6.0
DK	2 653	2 740	2 195	4.0	.	.	2.8
D	5 583	8 039	4 529	5.2	2.9	8.3	3.7
EL	3 702	3 440	4 127	4.6	.	.	4.3
E	6 166	7 284	5 135	13.4	6.7	20.3	7.0
F	5 515	8 223	5 068	8.3	5.0	14.5	4.3
IRL	852	:	:	3.9	.	.	3.9
I	4 641	5 991	4 534	8.5	7.5	12.0	5.3
L	7 269	10 013	4 897	.	.	.	.
NL	4 287	5 914	2 910	:	:	:	:
A	5 259	8 143	4 029	7.6	4.4	13.3	3.4
P	7 361	8 026	6 532	12.0	9.5	19.2	9.7
FIN	3 914	4 302	3 376	3.7	.	.	3.6
S	1 123	1 087	1 158	5.7	3.2	8.3	2.1
UK	1 915	:	:	1.7	:	:	1.7

[1] When the deaths due to a road traffic accident or from strictly natural causes, in the course of work, are considered as accidents at work in the Member State - see box p. 152

Source : Eurostat - European Statistics on Accidents at Work.

Men are more likely to have an accident

Men are three times more likely to have an accident - resulting in more than 3 days' absence - and ten times more likely to have a fatal accident: 5 960 accidents and 8.2 deaths per 100 000 male workers compared with 1 936 and 0.8 respectively for women. This result is a function of men's jobs and sectors of activity which tend to be more high-risk than those of women. There are also relatively more women who work part-time, thus reducing their exposure to risk. Other factors such as attitudes to personal safety may play a role but cannot be quantified.

Frequency of accidents: recent downward trend in Germany, Spain and France

European Statistics on accidents at work, drawn up on the basis of harmonised concepts, are at present available for the years 1993 and 1994. In order to look at recent variations in accidents at work, one has to resort to national data that are based on similar concepts to those of Eurostat. Four countries are able to provide such data: Denmark, Germany, Spain and France. The definitions and coverage of the data differ somewhat for each of these Member States and the frequencies are not standardised. The absolute levels are therefore not directly comparable from one country to another.

Figure 5 - Number of accidents at work - resulting in more than 3 days' absence - per 100 000 persons in employment

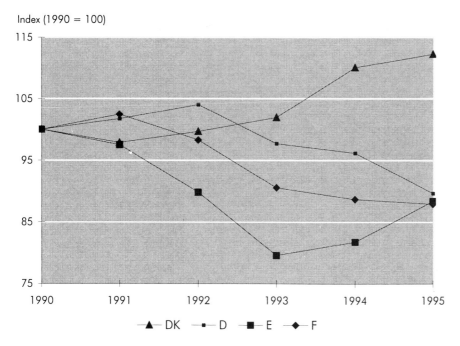

Index (1990 = 100)

Source : Non-harmonised national data

On the other hand, the results are indicative of the general trend in accidents at work in the Union from 1990 to 1995. For 3 of these 4 countries, the number of accidents at work per 100 000 persons in employment fell by approximately 12% between 1990 and 1995 (1991-95 for Germany). The evolution is different in Denmark with an increase in the number of accidents at work of 12% over this period (Figure 5).

Data exist also over a longer period for France and Germany: over the last forty years there has been a sharp downward trend (-60%) in the frequency of accidents at work in these 2 countries.

Satisfaction with working conditions: highest in Denmark and lowest in Greece

Indicators on satisfaction are examined in terms of main economic activity, type of job, working environment, job security and working time. Each of these indicators uses a numeric 6-grade scale which is presented to the interviewee, ranging from 'not satisfied at all' (=1) to 'fully satisfied' (=6). Table 8 presents the average scores for each Member State. The ratings constitute only subjective reactions and should not be regarded as proxy indicators of actual working conditions. They do however provide a rough indication of how employed persons view their situation on the labour market.

The responses are concentrated towards the upper end of the 6-grade scale, which is normal for ratings of this character. There is a clear variation between countries for all four indicators, with Denmark and Luxembourg well above the EU average and Greece, Italy, Portugal, and to a lesser extent Spain experiencing significantly lower ratings. The results for Denmark and Luxembourg may be related to the relatively high level of earnings in these 2 countries (see chapter on Earnings).

Table 8 - Satisfaction with working conditions, 1994

Average score on a 6-grade scale (1=not satisfied at all and 6=fully satisfied) among employed persons aged 20-64   (%)

	EU-12	B	DK	D	EL	E	F	IRL	I	L	NL	P	UK
Main activity	4.2	4.4	5.0	4.4	3.4	4.0	4.4	4.4	3.6	4.8	4.7	3.7	4.3
Type of work	4.3	4.5	4.9	4.5	3.6	4.2	4.3	4.7	3.8	4.7	4.4	4.1	4.5
Working environment	4.3	4.5	4.9	4.5	3.6	4.2	4.3	4.7	3.8	4.7	4.4	4.4	4.5
Job security	4.2	4.5	4.7	4.4	3.8	4.0	4.1	4.4	4.1	4.8	4.5	3.9	4.0
Working time	4.5	4.7	5.1	4.6	3.8	4.2	4.7	4.7	4.0	4.7	4.9	3.9	4.5

Source : Eurostat - European Community Household Panel (ECHP)

Least satisfaction in agriculture
·······································

Persons employed in agriculture recorded lower than average levels of satisfaction for all 3 selected indicators. Other branches where persons seem to be slightly less satisfied include hotels and restaurants concerning the "type of work", the construction, mining and manufacturing branches when it comes to "job security" and the construction, transport and communication sectors as regards "working environment" (Table 9).

The satisfaction ratings seem to fit well with the general findings of this chapter. For example, the agricultural and construction sectors, where ratings are lowest, have the highest rates of accidents at work and the highest prevalence of exposure to factors such as excessive noise and carrying heavy loads.

Table 9 - Satisfaction with working environment by economic activity, EU-12, 1994

Average score on a 6-grade scale (1=not satisfied at all and 6=fully satisfied) among employed persons aged 20-64

	Type of work	Working environment	Job security
EU-12, All sectors	4.3	4.3	4.2
Agriculture, Hunting Forestry, Fishing	3.9	3.9	4.0
Mining and Manufacturing	4.4	4.2	3.9
Electricity, Gas and Water supply	:	:	:
Construction	4.3	4.0	3.7
Wholesale and retail trade	4.4	4.4	4.1
Hotels and restaurants	4.1	4.3	4.0
Transport and Communication	4.3	4.1	4.2
Financial intermediation	4.5	4.6	4.5
Real estate and business activity	4.5	4.5	4.0
Public administration	4.7	4.4	4.5
Other services	4.6	4.4	4.3

Source : Eurostat - European Community Household Panel (ECHP)

European Statistics on Accidents at Work

Aim:

Data are collected in accordance with Council Directive N° 89/391/EEC of 12 June 1989 concerning the implementation of measures aiming to promote the improvement of safety and health of workers at work. The Directive stipulates that the employer has to "keep a list of occupational accidents resulting in a worker being unfit for work for more than three working days". The Council Regulation of 4 July 1995 on the transposition and the application of Community social legislation confirmed that the Commission had to complete the work in progress for the harmonisation of statistics on accidents at work. The data collection has been developed in co-operation with Directorate-General V (Employment, Industrial Relations and Social Affairs).

Data :

The statistics are compiled annually from national administrative sources but according to harmonised concepts and definitions. They cover both accidents at work resulting in more than three days' absence and accidents resulting in the death of the victim. These statistics include accidents caused by third parties, road traffic accidents during working hours and acute poisonings, but not commuting accidents or occupational diseases. The aim is to cover all persons in employment: wage and salary earners, employers, the self-employed and family workers in all branches of activity. The 1994 data cover almost 90% of persons in employment. The first results refer to 1993 and 1994.

Frequencies for the common branches of activity:

In order to make comparisons, the (actual) number of accidents at work per 100 000 persons in employment is calculated ("the frequency"). In 1994, this was calculated only for the 8 main branches of activity completely covered by all 15 Member States. These 8 branches (NACE Rev.1 Sections) correspond to a total of 91.5 million persons in employment in the EU in 1994: agriculture, hunting and forestry - manufacturing - construction - wholesale and retail trade and repairs - hotels and restaurants - transport and communication - financial intermediation - real estate, renting and business activities. The frequency for Europe as a whole is calculated excluding the self-employed, employers and family workers in the United Kingdom (accidents with more than three days' absence) and excluding the Netherlands (deaths). Moreover, the structure of a country's activities influences its total frequency. To correct this effect, a "standardised" number of accidents at work per 100 000 persons in employment is calculated per Member State by giving each branch the same weight at national level as in the European Union total. The source for the reference population is Eurostat's European Labour Force Survey.

Country-specific characteristics :

Caution is called for when comparing the national results as the methodology is being introduced gradually in the various countries. For 1994 there are a number of national specificities. Data for the Netherlands and Austria include accidents with 1 to 3 days' absence. Data for Ireland and the United Kingdom exclude road traffic accidents and Northern Ireland. Spain and France include accidents that are strictly related to natural causes but that occur during working hours (e.g. heart attacks). Lastly, for certain countries civil servants, employers, self-employed persons, family workers, as well as those persons employed in rail, sea or air transport are either not covered or are only partially so.

Earnings

A key factor in prosperity

Most people's prosperity is related, directly or indirectly, to earnings levels. The direct connection is obvious in the case of people who are employed and whose earnings largely determine their living standards. Those who are not employed may be living in a household in which other members are earning, or else they may depend upon other forms of income which are indirectly linked to earnings levels. Pensions, for example, are usually determined by the amount which the person earned while working. Unemployment benefits and social security payments are also related to earnings, with differing national practices as to the relative influences of the individual's previous earnings or the general level of earnings.

How much people earn is affected by a complex web of interacting factors. Depending upon the type of job, collective bargaining by an organised group of workers may have an important influence. In other situations, a minimum wage may be fixed by national legislation. There may be a variable scope for negotiation between the individual employee and the employer when the employment contract begins, or at a later time. In this connection a considerable role is played by the employee's abilities, adaptability and commitment, which are all difficult to measure in statistical terms. Those factors which can be measured include some which relate to the job (the working hours, location and activity) and others which relate to the employee (including age, education and experience). This chapter examines the relative importance of a number of these topics in the context of earnings levels in the European Union.

The importance of earnings as a social indicator is noted in the Treaty of Amsterdam, specifically in relation to equality between the sexes. The following principle is set out in Article 141 :

Each Member State shall ensure that the principle of equal pay for male and female workers for equal work or work of equal value is applied.

How far this principle is currently translated into practice is one of the issues which are discussed in this chapter.

— Gross earnings in most Member States showed a rise in real terms in the period 1980-96, the biggest increases being in Finland (manual workers in manufacturing industry), and United Kingdom (non-manual workers in retail trade and credit institutions). Particularly large increases took place in credit institutions. In the new Länder of Germany, wages have risen considerably since reunification, as part of the process of convergence.

— Earnings are higher in the northern Member States than in the south. They are also generally more evenly distributed in these countries, although the United Kingdom is one of the countries with the most unevenly distributed earnings.

— Employees who completed higher education usually have considerably higher salaries; finishing secondary school has a relatively smaller impact on salary differentials.

— Managerial and professional staff earn about 30% more than technicians and associate professionals. Clerks and sales workers earn about the same as manual workers.

— Part-time workers are usually female, often young and generally in low-status occupations, all of which tend to depress their earnings levels. They may average as little as 60% of the hourly earnings of full-timers.

— Women earn less than men in all occupations, the differences being smallest in the new Länder of Germany, Belgium, Luxembourg and the Scandinavian countries. Even when allowance is made for structural differences, women's earnings remain below 90% those of men in every Member State.

— Depending on the Member State, net earnings represent anywhere between 53% and 81% of gross earnings. These variations are due to the fact that social security and taxation rates differ considerably between countries. Family situation does not greatly affect social security contributions, but is important in the calculation of tax.

— Minimum wages are currently in force in seven Member States, the highest (in Luxembourg) being over twice in PPS the level of the lowest (in Portugal). Trends at constant prices are not the same between countries. Minimum wages represent between 42% and 59% of the average salary in manufacturing industry.

Sources

— Harmonised Statistics of Earnings
— Statistics on the structure and distribution of earnings, 1995
— Net earnings of employees in manufacturing industry in the European Union
— Minimum wages 1997, A comparative study

Gross earnings have risen in most Member States between 1980s and 1996

In manufacturing industry...

Although the economic situation between 1980 and 1996 was not always favourable, (See chapter 1) the hourly earnings of manual workers in manufacturing industry in thirteen Member States of the EU over this period underwent a moderate increase in real terms. The exceptions were Belgium, where a worker's purchasing power remained the same, and Italy, where real earnings fell by an average of 0.6% per year. In the countries where earnings rose, the increase in most cases averaged between 0.5% and 1% per year in real terms, reaching 2.6% annually for Finland and 1.6% for Germany (old Länder) and the United Kingdom (Figure 1). In the exceptional case of the new Länder of Germany (for which the first available data dates from 1992), the effects of convergence with the western part of the country caused an average rate of annual change in real terms of 7.4%.

The trends in gross hourly earnings for manual workers in manufacturing industry in the United States differed greatly from those in the EU during this period, with real wages diminishing by 0.7% annually from 1980 to 1996.

> **"Gross earnings"** refers to the amount paid, by the employer, direct to employee, before the employees' tax and social security contributions are deducted. Gross earnings therefore include the compulsory contributions of employees, the most important of which are tax and social security.
>
> Figures on earnings are not compiled for Germany as a whole owing to the difference in the level of earnings between the former Federal territory and the new Länder and East Berlin

Figure 1 - Average rate of annual change (real terms) of gross hourly earnings of manual workers in manufacturing industry, 1980-1996

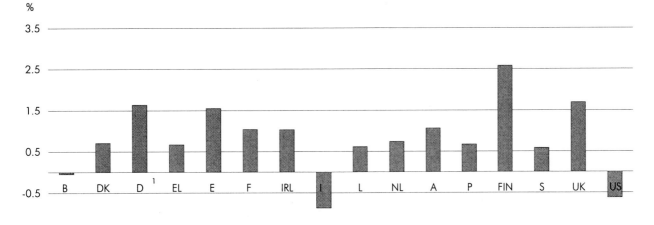

[1] F.R. of Germany prior to 3.10.90

Sources : Eurostat, Harmonised Statistics of Earnings
For the United States, Bureau of Labour Statistics

Harmonised Statistics of Earnings

These statistics present the average gross hourly earnings for manual workers in industry and the average gross monthly earnings for non-manual workers in industry and some services. As the statistics cover a long time series, it is possible to analyse earnings trends over prolonged periods. The series of harmonised statistics on earnings are compiled from national data obtained on the basis of definitions and methods which are not completely comparable harmonised. Consequently these data are more suited to depicting trends rather than making very detailed comparative analyses between countries.

In the EU, the increase in real-terms of monthly earnings for non-manual workers in manufacturing industry in relation to those of manual workers (hourly earnings), have been more marked in Belgium, Germany (new Länder), Spain, Ireland and the United Kingdom (Table 1). In a second group of countries the trends were more favourable for manual workers: old Länder of Germany, France, the Netherlands and Finland. In the remaining countries, developments in earnings for both manual and non-manual-workers differed by only marginal amounts. The rather low annual increase may however hide a significant improvement over the medium and long terms. For example the annual real increase of between 1 and 2% which is evident in several countries for both manual and non-manual workers, point to an overall increase in purchasing power of 17 and 37% over the period 1980-1996.

These findings must be interpreted with caution, since they may conceal structural labour changes amongst the manual and non-manual workers in the total labour force. The fact that there are less non-manual workers than manual workers in manufacturing industry, has different statistical effects.

Table 1 - Average rate of annual change in real earnings in manufacturing industry, 1980-1996

(% per year)

	B	DK	D[1]	D[2]	EL	E	F	IRL	I	L	NL	A	P	FIN	S	UK	US
Manual workers (on hourly basis)	-0.04	1.06	1.64	8.4	0.6	0.6	1.04	0.2	-0.63	0.62	0.66	1.06	0.67	2.58	0.59	1.69	-0.63
Non-manual workers (on monthly basis)	0.44	0.98	1.41	10.05	0.63	1.36	0.81	1.69	:	0.69	0.21	1.33	0.88	2.12	0.34	2.47	:

[1] F.R. of Germany prior to 3.10.1990

[2] New Länder and East-Berlin

Source : Eurostat - Harmonised Statistics of Earnings
For the United States, Bureau of Labour Statistics

... and in retail trade and credit institutions

Apart from manufacturing industry, trends in monthly earnings of non-manual workers can only be followed in selected economic areas such as for example in retail trade and credit institutions. In these two cases, the trend between the 1980s and 1995-6 was generally upward, with Spain an exception as far as retail trade was concerned and Greece in the case of credit institutions. Credit institutions showed a noticeably greater increase than retail trade in real terms, and in both areas the country with the highest average annual growth rate was the United Kingdom with 3% in credit institutions and 2.8% in retail trade. In the new German Länder, an average rate of annual changes in real terms of 11.1% in credit institutions and 8.8% in retail trade was observed between 1992 and 1996.

It should be emphasised that these observations are based on average earnings in all occupations, without taking account of structural effects. It is possible that employers such as credit institutions have taken on more qualified personnel during this period which has caused salary levels to rise.

In the United States, the trend in retail trade earnings during 1983-95 was downward at -1.1% per year in real terms. No data are available for credit institutions.

Figure 2 - Average rate of annual change of gross monthly earnings in real terms of non manual workers, 1980-1996

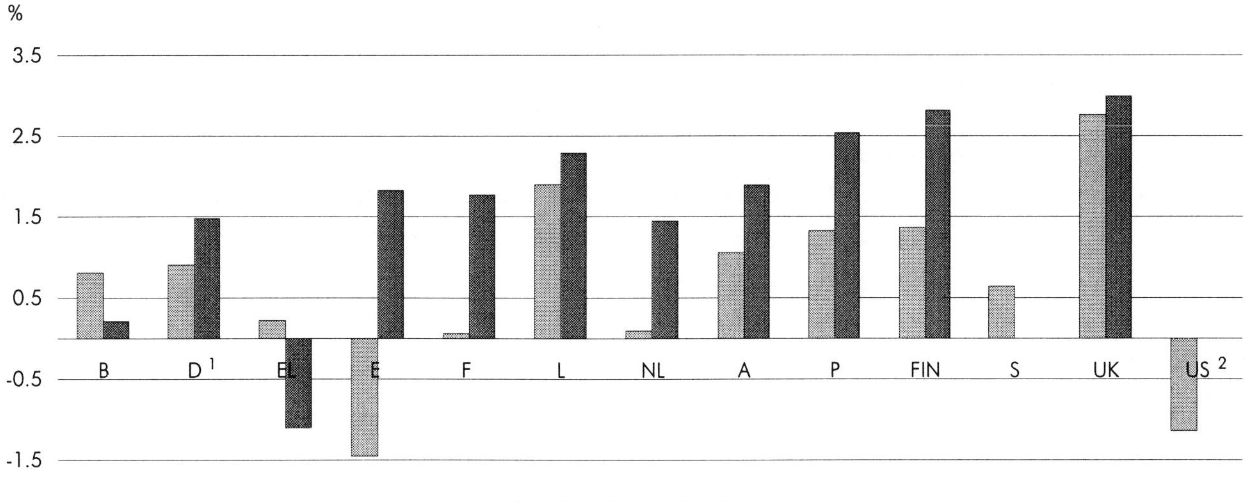

[1] F.R. of Germany prior to 3.10.1990

[2] 1983 - 1995

Sources : Eurostat, Harmonised statistics of earnings
For the United States, Bureau of Labour Statistics

What factors influence earnings?

Earnings levels differ considerably between the Member States, and are generally higher in the north of the EU than in the south. The Structure of Earnings Statistics for the year 1995, which cover employees in industry and in some branches of services, show that the highest median earnings are found in Denmark, the western Länder of Germany, Luxembourg, the Netherlands and Belgium, while the lowest are in Greece, Spain and Italy (Figure 3). Similar results are obtained if other yardsticks are used such as the top decile (above which 10% of the employees are) or the bottom decile (below which 10% of employees are), though slight variations may be observed due to the fact that earnings are more widely dispersed in some Member States than in others.

Earnings are most equitably distributed in the Nordic countries; the top decile figure is only just over twice the bottom decile figure (about 2.1) in Sweden and Finland. In France and Greece the top decile figure is about 3.2 times as great as the bottom decile, and the greatest differences are in Spain and the United Kingdom (about 3.4) which therefore have the most unevenly-distributed earnings.

Figure 3 - Distribution of gross monthly earnings, 1995

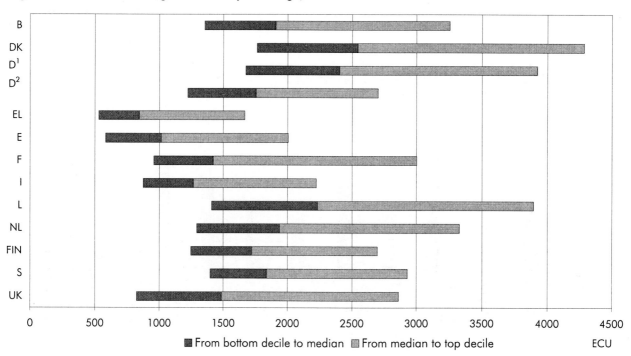

From bottom decile to median   From median to top decile   ECU

[1] F.R. of Germany prior to 3.10.1990
[2] New Länder and East-Berlin
median = the level above and below which 50% of the employees fall
Source : Eurostat, Structure of Earnings Statistics

An employee's position on the earnings scale is influenced by many factors, which are of differing degrees of influence and may also be interrelated. Among those factors relating to the employee, are gender, age, educational and professional experience. Other factors concern rather the company, such as the region where it is located, its size and the industry in which it is engaged, while yet others may be linked to the job itself, including the occupation, supervisory responsibilities and working hours.

The effect of education

In 1995, employees who had received higher education earned between about 30% and 40% more each month than those who had completed upper secondary school, and this figure rises to over 50% in France, Italy, the Netherlands, Finland and the new Länder of Germany. The earnings difference between those who completed the highest level of secondary school and those whose education ended at an earlier stage was rather less, at about 20% in most EU countries, and under 10% in Greece, France, Finland and the Netherlands (Figure 4).

Structure of Earnings Statistics

The Structure of Earnings Statistics collected in all the Member States for the year 1995 (1994 for France) were the first to be compiled in all fifteen current Member States on the basis of comparable methodologies.

They include information relating to employees (including sex, age, occupation, education, length of service, etc.) and to the firms employing them (such as size, location and economic activity).

Currently data are available only for twelve countries, and those for Greece are restricted to industry.

The figures given here are gross and include additional payments such as overtime, shift supplements and regular bonuses. They refer only to full-time workers, except where otherwise indicated. Earnings of trainees are excluded.

Figure 4 - Average gross monthly earnings by level of education, 1995

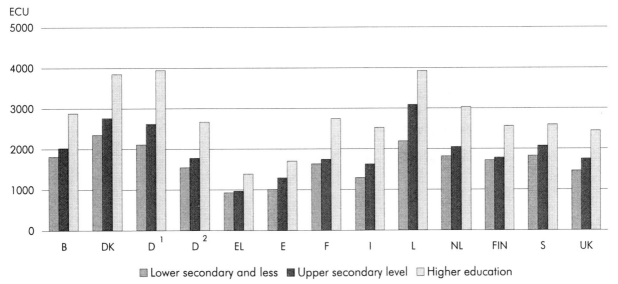

[1] F.R. of Germany prior to 3.10.1990

[2] New Länder and East-Berlin

Source : Eurostat, Structure of Earnings Statistics

Professionals are much better paid
....

The level of qualification which an employee has obtained shapes the type of job which he or she is later able to obtain. People with higher educational qualifications such as university degrees are usually found in managerial and professional occupations, where earnings are typically about 30% more than in the next highest-paid group, technicians and associate professionals. This differential is as high as 50% in Spain and 80% in France and Italy. The other two main occupational groups comprise clerks and sales workers, that is, relatively low-paid non-manual staff, and manual workers (the traditional 'blue collar jobs'). Average earnings in these two groups are roughly the same, with manual workers earning rather less in Germany, Italy, Belgium and Luxembourg and rather more in the other Member States (Figure 5). Cross-country comparisons should be treated with caution due to the different national classification practices regarding occupations.

Figure 5 - Average gross monthly earnings by occupation, 1995

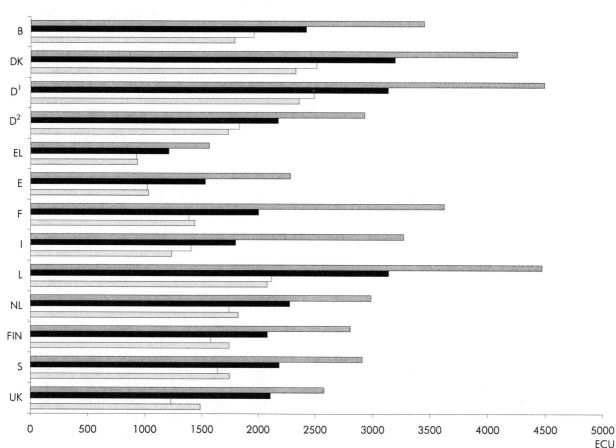

☒ Managerial and professional ■ Technicians and associate professionals ☐ Clerks and sales workers ☒ Manual workers

[1] F.R. of Germany
[2] New Länder and East-Berlin
Source : Eurostat, Structure of Earnings Statistics

Salaries rise with increasing experience

The longer the worker remains with the same employer, the more his or her earnings increase. It seems however that this pattern is becoming eroded as jobs become shorter in duration, and this factor already has less influence on earnings in northern countries such as Sweden, Finland and the United Kingdom than in France, Italy or Spain.

As an employee gains more work experience, his or her earnings tend to increase. The trend is steepest in the person's twenties and thirties and then usually flattens out. In most countries there is even a tendency for employees near the end of their working lives to earn less than their slightly younger colleagues. In France, Belgium, the Netherlands and Italy the oldest employees are the best-paid of all (Figure 6).

Structure of Earnings Statistics

Scope of the survey

This survey excludes persons who are self-employed or who work in local units employing less than ten people, and also employees in agriculture and fishing, public administration and defence, education, health and social work, other community, social and personal service activities, private households or extra-territorial organisations.

Further information:

These statistics may be consulted on-line in Eurostat's New Cronos database, together with a full description of the methodologies used at EU and national levels. Both the data and methodologies may also be obtained from the Eurostat data shops.

Figure 6 - Average gross monthly earnings by age group in selected countries, 1995

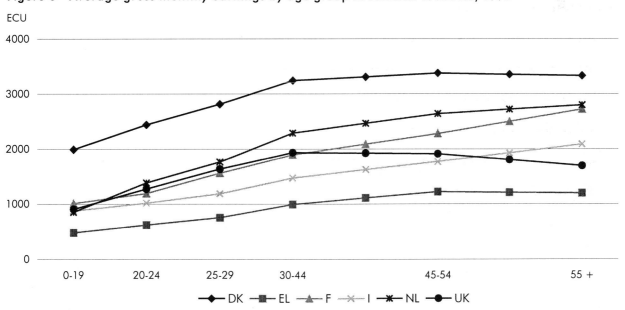

Source : Eurostat, Structure of Earnings Statistics

Part-time jobs are usually low paid
....

An increasing number of people work part-time, either from choice or involuntarily. They may be unable to find full-time work or else they have other obligations to fulfil, such as studies or family commitments. Compared with those working full-time, part-timers earn far less on an hourly basis (Figure 7). The difference is greatest in Spain, France, Luxembourg, the Netherlands and above all, in the United Kingdom, where employees working part-time earn less than 60% as much as those working full-time. However it is not so much the fact of working part-time which affects earnings. Rather, part-time jobs are poorly paid because they represent a concentration of the factors associated with low pay. They are often taken by young people (sometimes as an interim measure during or just after their studies), they usually require minimal qualifications, and they are mostly in low-status occupations such as cleaning offices or hotel rooms, or serving in cafés and restaurants. Above all, four out of five part-time workers are female, and in most Member States the gap between men's pay and women's is one of the most striking features of earnings distribution.

Figure 7 - Average gross hourly earnings by full-time / part-time, 1995

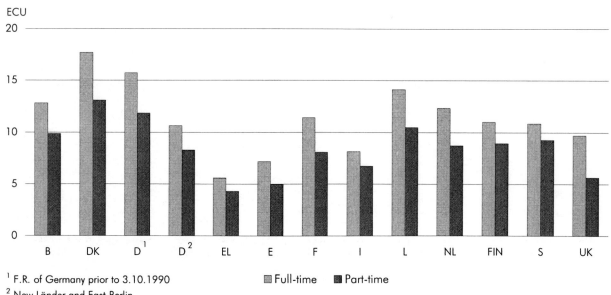

[1] F.R. of Germany prior to 3.10.1990
[2] New Länder and East-Berlin
Source : Eurostat, Structure of Earnings Statistics

Scandinavian countries come nearest to gender equality

In all the Member States, women's average full-time earnings are less than men's, the differences being least in the new Länder of Germany, Sweden, Luxembourg, Belgium, Denmark and Finland and greatest in Greece, the Netherlands, the United Kingdom and Spain (Table 2). This may partly be accounted for in terms of the different characteristics of the male and female workforce, for example the fact that women have on average lower educational qualifications, are more likely to be found in certain types of job which are poorly remunerated or have lower-paid occupations even where they have the same qualifications as men. If the structural effects are discounted by applying the distribution of male employees by occupation and activity to the earnings of women in the same category, then women's earnings come closer to men's. In some countries, and depending on the choice of characteristics, carrying out this exercice can account for a substantial proportion of gender differences, but in other cases it has a relatively small (or even negative) effect. Even when the adjustment is made there is still no Member State in which women's average hourly earnings exceed 90% of men's.

In the special case of Germany, there is a marked difference between the situation in the new Länder, where women traditionally filled an important rôle in the labour force, and the rest of the country. Women's hourly earnings in the new Länder come closer to men's than anywhere else in the European Union. Women are also to be found in highly-paid occupations and activities, so that the elimination of structural effects has the reverse result from that in most other countries.

Table 2 - Hourly earnings of women as a percentage of men's, 1995

Full-time workers, excluding bonuses and overtime

	B	DK	D¹	D²	EL	E	F	I	L	NL	FIN	S	UK
Occupations:													
Managers	73	74	69	79	77	70	68	74	67	62	81	79	67
Professionals	82	87	80	84	71	78	79	83	84	74	84	91	84
Technicians & associate professionals	86	80	73	80	74	83	86	82	88	72	79	88	73
Clerks	84	85	80	84	78	77	92	79	84	76	94	97	94
Service workers, shop & market sales workers	80	84	69	74	64	78	88	82	81	71	86	95	83
Craft & related trade workers	84	90	76	76	59	71	80	77	79	75	82	90	63
Plant & machine operators & assemblers	79	89	79	80	72	74	80	75	68	69	82	95	76
Elementary occupations	84	84	81	82	81	83	87	84	81	76	83	90	82
All	83	83	77	90	68	74	76	76	84	71	82	87	73
After discounting structural effects of activity & occupation	88	85	78	83	71	80	82	86	82	71	83	89	76

¹ F.R. of Germany prior to 3.10.1990

² New Länder and East-Berlin

Source : Eurostat, Structure of Earnings Statistics

From gross to net earnings : some cases

The following discussion is based upon a number of typical family situations, such as an unmarried employee with an average salary, a couple with two children with two average salaries and a couple with two children, one salary. In each case, the calculation of net earnings is based upon average gross earnings in manufacturing industry.

Levies are relatively small in Portugal compared with Germany

In 1996 the average gross monthly earnings of a single employee in manufacturing industry ranged from 2856 PPS in Germany (old Lander) to 786 PPS in Portugal, that is a ratio of almost 4 to 1. In terms of net earnings, i.e. after deduction of taxes and social security contributions, this ratio is 2.4 to 1: 1514 PPS for Germany and 640 PPS for Portugal. These countries also represent the extremes as far as the net earnings as a percentage of gross earnings are concerned.

The net earnings of a single employee with an average salary in manufacturing industry in 1996 represent around 81% of gross earnings in Portugal and 53% in the old Länder of Germany (Figure 8).

Figure 8 - Monthly gross and net earnings in two cases, 1996

PPS

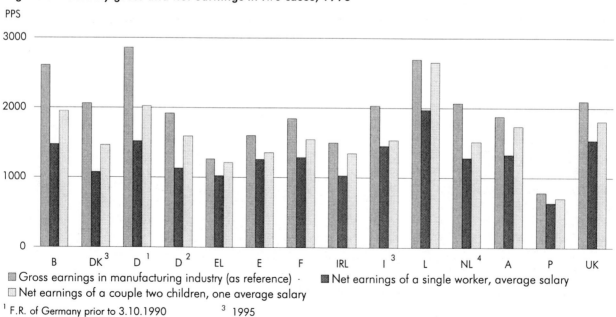

■ Gross earnings in manufacturing industry (as reference) · ■ Net earnings of a single worker, average salary
▨ Net earnings of a couple two children, one average salary

[1] F.R. of Germany prior to 3.10.1990   [3] 1995
[2] Germany New Länder and East-Berlin   [4] 1994

Source : Eurostat - Net earnings of employees in manufacturing industry in the European Union

If this employee is married with two children and the spouse does not work, the net earnings amount to 71% of the gross earnings in the old Länder of Germany and 90% in Portugal. If the spouse's earnings are added in Portugal the net earnings are in this case 75% of the gross earnings (that is, less than is the case for an unmarried employee), while in Germany it is 59%. Portugal and Italy are the only two countries where net earnings as a percentage of gross earnings are higher for an unmarried employee than for a family with two children and two incomes. Earnings may be boosted by family allowances, which for a couple on one salary with two children could add as much as 15% to their earnings in Greece or 12% in Austria, but at the other end of the scale only 4% in Ireland and nothing at all in Spain. (Table 3)

Taxes and social security: considerable variety between the EU countries

The percentage paid in social security contributions and tax varies very considerably between the EU countries. Whereas the employee's family circumstances hardly affect his social security contributions, they have a noticeable effect upon the percentage paid in tax (Figure 9). The highest social security contributions are those paid in the Netherlands (where an unmarried employee pays 23.6% of his gross earnings in social security contributions), in Germany (20.3%), in France (18.9%) and Austria (17.8%). The lowest figure is that for Denmark (only 2.5%).

As far as taxes are concerned, these vary in the case of an unmarried employee in manufacturing industry from a maximum of 44% in Denmark to a minimum of 3.4% in Greece.

> **Net earnings**
>
> *Availability of data*
>
> Although complete data are not yet available for Sweden and Finland, the indications are that the situation is similar in these countries to that in Denmark.
> In these Nordic countries, the social security contributions for an employee of manufacturing industry are typically between 4.5% and 6.5% of gross earnings.

Figure 9 - Composition of gross monthly earnings for an unmarried employee in manufacturing industry, 1996

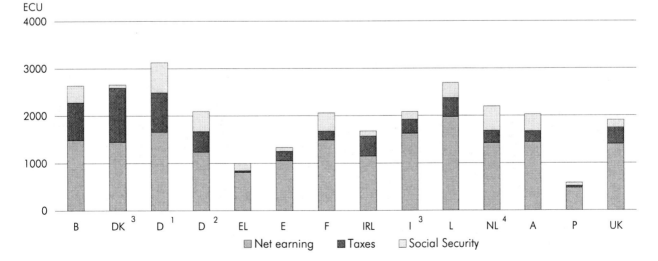

¹ F.R. of Germany prior to 3.10.1990   ² Germany New Länder and East-Berlin
³ 1995   ⁴ 1994

Source: Eurostat, Net Earnings of employees in manufacturing industry in the European Union

Differences between countries concerning the percentage of social security contributions and taxes payable by the employee reflect the patterns of financing social protection expenditure (See chapter 1). As shown above, a Danish worker in manufacturing industry pays income tax amounting to 44% of his or her wages because in this country, social security is financed mainly through taxation. This is considerably more than in other countries where taxation is usually considered high, such as Belgium (30.1%), Germany (26,7%) or Ireland (25.1%).

As a general rule the countries with the highest gross earnings are also those with the highest taxes and social security contributions. As a result, net earnings differ less between the countries than gross earnings. On the other hand there is some compensation between taxes and social security contributions in the sense that where one of these tends to be high the other tends to be low.

The effect of family circumstances on the amount of tax due

The effect of family circumstances on the amount of tax due varies greatly between the Member States. A couple with two children living on one salary paid no tax in France or Luxembourg in 1996, while an unmarried worker with a similar salary paid 9% or 15% respectively. However in Greece, Austria and the United Kingdom, there is almost no difference in the percentage of tax paid by an employee in these different family circumstances. This is compensated for by higher family allowances. In all the other countries, a couple with two children living on one salary pays between 30% and 50% less in tax than an unmarried employee. When a family with two children has a second wage, the percentage of taxes paid increases to a level close to that paid by unmarried employees in most countries.

Table 3 - Net earnings in manufacturing industry by family status, 1996

Gross earnings = 100

	B	DK[3]	D[1]	D[2]	EL	E	F	IRL	I[3]	L	NL[4]	A	P	UK
Single worker, average salary	56	54	53	59	81	79	70	69	72	73	62	71	82	73
Couple with two children, two average salaries	59	58	59	66	87	80	75	73	68	89	66	79	75	78
Couple with two children, one salary	75	71	71	83	96	85	84	80	76	99	73	84	89	79

[1] F.R. of Germany prior to 3.10.1990

[2] New Länder and East-Berlin

[3] 1995

[4] 1994

Source : Eurostat - Net earnings of employees in manufacturing industry in the European Union

Minimum wages in seven European Countries

In general, in the European Union, private sector salaries are negotiated by the social partners by way of collective bargaining. In addition the possibility exists in some countries to apply a national minimum wage through legal means. At present, 7 Member States of the European Union apply such a national minimum wage: Belgium, Spain, Greece, France, Luxembourg, the Netherlands and Portugal. In both Ireland and the United Kingdom, governments are committed, as a priority, to the introduction of a minimum wage in the future. The countries discussed here are those where there is currently a national minimum wage.

Minimum wages: how is the level fixed?

In Spain, France, Luxembourg, the Netherlands and Portugal, a national minimum wage is fixed at an hourly, weekly or monthly rate by legislation, in most cases after consultation with the social partners, and this minimum is enforced by law. Belgium employs a similar system whereby an 'average minimum monthly wage' is fixed by a central agreement which is regarded as applicable to all industries. In Greece a general minimum wage is agreed by negotiation at national level and a distinction is made between manual and non-manual workers.

The statutory minimum wage usually applies to all employees in the economy and all occupations, but may be modified to take into account age, length of service, skills, the physical and mental capabilities of the employee or the economic conditions affecting the firm. The laws governing such systems also contain mechanisms to review the minima, often as a result of tripartite bargaining between government, unions and employers, in the light of changes in prices, wages and other economic conditions. Sometimes the minimum wage is the subject of automatic re-assessment - for example it may be increased in line with the consumer price index or economic growth or else it may be subject to discretionary increases - increased by legislation (see box p. 168 summarising the different systems of national minimum wages in the European Union).

Table 4 - Changes in the minimum wages in real terms
        Indices 1980 = 100

	B	EL	E	F	L	NL	P
1985	103.7	128.2	96.3	113.8	101.1	87.8	85.8
1990	103.8	115.6	94.7	118.3	108.7	85.8	91.5
1997	104.5	107.2	92.8	128.8	131.7	78.7	99.5

Source : Eurostat, Minimum Wages 1997 - A comparative study

Summary of statutory national minimum wages in the European Union
(Situation as on 31 December 1997)

	B	EL	E	F	L	NL	P
Date of introduction in current form	1975	1991	1980	1970	1973	1969	1974
Coverage	Private sector employees aged 21 or over	All employees aged 19 or over for non-manual workers 18 or over for manual workers	All employees aged 18 or over	All employees aged 18 or over	All employees aged 18 or over	All employees aged 23 or over	All employees aged 18 or over
Method of fixing	Negotiation by social partners	Annual negotiation by social partners	Set by government	Set by government	Set by government	Set by government	Set by government
Method of updating	i. automatic indexation ii. periodic review	Annually according to government forecasts of inflation	Annually according to government forecasts of inflation	i. automatic indexation ii. annual review	i. automatic indexation ii. periodic review	Twice annually	Annually according to government forecasts of inflation
Type of rate	Monthly	Monthly for non-manual workers; daily for manual workers;	Monthly and daily	Hourly	Monthly	Weekly	Monthly
Present level in national currency	BEF 43 343 per month	GRD 138 316 per month GRD 6 195 per day	ESP 66 630 per month ESP 2 221 per day	FRF 39.43 per hour	LUF 46 275 per month	NLG 517.80 per week	PTE 56 700 per month
In force since	1.10.97	1.07.97	1.01.97	1.07.97	1.02.97	1.07.97	1.01.97

Source : Eurostat, Minimum wages 1997, A comparative study

Statutory minimum wage represents between 42% and 59% of the average salary in 1997

The development between 1980 and 1997 of the average minimum monthly wages at constant prices in the 7 countries concerned shows three groups of countries with different trends. In Belgium, Greece, France and Luxembourg, the minimum wage increased in purchasing power, in particular in Greece between 1980 and 1985 and in France and Luxembourg where it rose by over a quarter on the whole period. In Belgium and Portugal, the minimum wages in real terms remained relatively stable in the same period. On the other hand, during these 17 years it fell by almost a quarter in the Netherlands and by almost 9% in Spain (Table 4).

Another way of assessing how the value of minimum wages has changed over time is to compare them with the growth in average wages (Figure 10).

As a proportion of the average gross earnings of a single male worker in manufacturing industry, the national minimum wage in Greece, France and Luxembourg increased slightly over the period 1980-1996. In Belgium the situation was stable during this period. The increase in Greece was significant with the minimum wage rising from 39% to 44% against the benchmark. The position of those on the minimum wage in France and Luxembourg improved by 2% and 4% respectively. In the other three countries, the proportional value of the minimum wage decreased, with the most pronounced deterioration being in the Netherlands, where it went from 65% to 49% of the reference figure. Spain and Portugal also witnessed a widening in the gap of 5% and 15% respectively.

Figure 10 - Minimum monthly wages as a proportion of average gross earnings

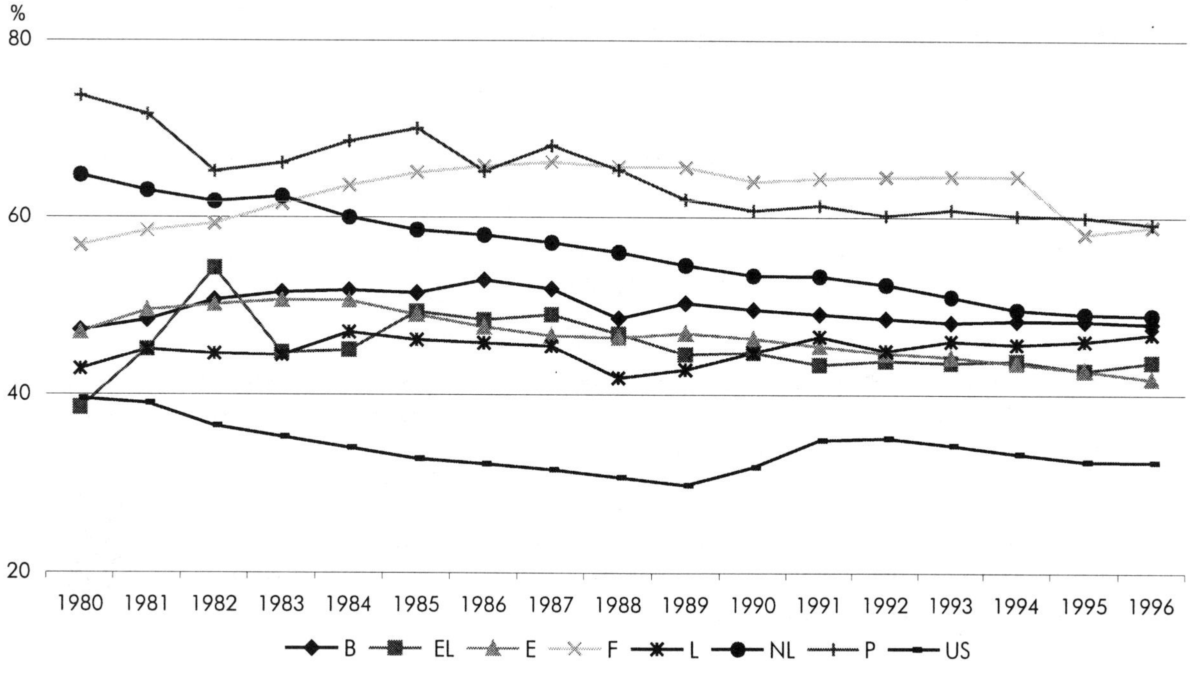

Source : Eurostat, Minimum wages 1997 — A comparative study

In 1996, the minimum wage level was highest in France and Portugal where it stood at 59% of the average earnings of a single male manual worker in manufacturing industry and lowest in Spain at 42%. In the United States the corresponding figure was 33%.

The level of statutory minimum wages varies from 501 to 1094 PPS in 1997

Concerning the level of the statutory minimum wage, two groups of countries may be distinguished: one comprising Luxembourg, Belgium, France and the Netherlands with levels close to 1000 PPS per month in 1997 and a second group in which the level is about the half of this amount (Figure 11).

It should be emphasized that the figures given here are gross, that is before deduction of income tax and social security. It is not possible at present to give the equivalents of these figures in net terms, but the taxes applied to minimum wages may vary from one country to another.

The number of people who earn the minimum wage is available for only four of the seven Member States concerned. In 1996 about 13% of workers in Luxembourg received minimum wages, 11% in France and about 5% in Portugal. In the Netherlands, the share of employees earning the minimum wage or less was 3,7% in October 1994. As a general tendency, twice as many women as men earned the minimum wage.

Figure 11 - Monthly minimum wages in PPS, 1997

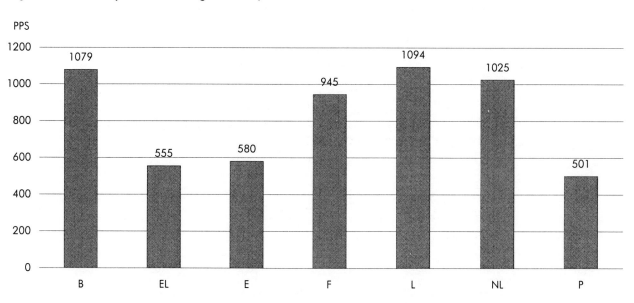

Source : Eurostat, Minimum Wages 1997 - A comparative study

Income

Disparities and poverty

Total household income is made up of income from economic activities and various social transfers such as pensions minus social security contributions and taxes. At the same time, it is the basic source of household consumption and investment.

Income impacts significantly on people's daily lives and future plans: it determines the extent to which people can make ends meet, what people can and cannot afford, and, in certain cases, whether or not they fall into poverty or even exclusion.

In general, the more prosperous a country, the smaller the income disparities. From the available data, every monetary/non-monetary indicator indicates that disparities are highest in Portugal, Greece and Spain. For certain indicators, Ireland and the United Kingdom join this group of countries. In contrast, the smallest disparities can be found in Denmark and Germany.

— In 1994, net monetary income per adult equivalent ranged from 13 000 to 15 000 PPS per year in the majority of EU countries; exceptions were Luxembourg at the upper end (22 000), and Greece and Portugal at the lower end (8 000 - 9 000).
— For the EU, 70% of income results from some form of economic activity. In Greece, self-employment accounts for 25% of total income, compared with around 5% for Belgium, Germany and the Netherlands.
— On average, the 10% least well-off Europeans received 2.5% of total income; the 10% most well-off received 10 times more, i.e. 25%.
— This ratio between the 20% most and least well-off households is less than 3 in Denmark and exceeds 5 in Greece and in Portugal.
— Individuals living in working households where no-one has a full-time job are more likely to be in the lowest income levels.
— In 1994, 59% of Portuguese households declared that they were unable to afford a week's holiday; in Germany the corresponding figure was 11%.
— 7 million Europeans aged 25 and over were affected by long-term unemployment (12 months and more) in 1997. Research has shown that this can often lead to exclusion in the long run.

Social Cohesion

"The promotion of social cohesion requires the reduction of the disparities which arise from unequal access to employment opportunities and to the rewards in the form of income. Such inequality tends to have serious social consequences through the marginalisation of sections of society, such as the long-term unemployed, the young unemployed and the poor. The incidence of poverty is also a result of policy choices affecting inter-personal income transfers. These are all measurable aspects of social cohesion which are considered in the analysis of this report".

This abstract is drawn from, European Commission, First Report on Economic and Social Cohesion, 1996.

The European Community Household Panel – ECHP

The ECHP is a survey that involves annual interviewing of a representative panel of households and individuals in each country, covering a wide range of topics: demographic and employment characteristics, income, health, education, housing, etc. The longitudinal structure of the ECHP makes it possible to follow up and interview the same households and people over several consecutive years. Accordingly, these data allow us to study the dynamics of transition from school to working life, from the labour market to retirement, from employment to unemployment and so on. These are crucial issues in developing an understanding of the dynamics of poverty and exclusion.

The survey is based on a harmonised questionnaire, the Community version of which was drawn up by Eurostat, and subsequently adapted by "national data collection units" to suit the particular characteristics of each country. The first wave of the ECHP was conducted in 1994, in the then 12 EU Member States. The sample totalled some 60.500 households (about 170.000 individuals) selected randomly. Austria (in 1995) and Finland (1996) have joined the project since then. The results are presented for the 13 Member States which participated in ECHP Wave 2, with the exception of Finland which began the survey in the following year, and Sweden where the survey has not been conducted.

The statistical procedures used in the construction of household income variables in Wave 2 have, in certain respects, been improved over those in Wave 1. Nevertheless, some further refinements may be made when combined longitudinal data for waves 1 and 2 are released by Eurostat in the near future. To that extent, the results presented in this chapter should not be considered as "final".

For a detailed description of the ECHP methodology, see *"The European Community Household Panel (ECHP): Volume 1 – Survey methodology and Implementation"*, Theme 3, Series E, Eurostat, 1996.

Majority of countries have similar level of income

In 1994, the standard of living in the majority of EU countries was largely similar ranging from 13 000 to 15 000 PPS per annum per adult equivalent. The exceptions were Luxembourg with a considerably higher figure (22 000), and Greece and Portugal where the average was much lower, 8 000 - 9 000 (Figure 1).

The standard of living in a country is based on the concept of equivalised net monetary income which is derived by dividing the total net monetary income of the household by the number of adult equivalents. Total net monetary income covers all income from work (wages, self-employment income), plus all social transfers such as pensions and income from capital and property, minus social contributions and taxes deducted at source (see box p. 175).

Figure 1 - Mean equivalised net monetary income, 1994

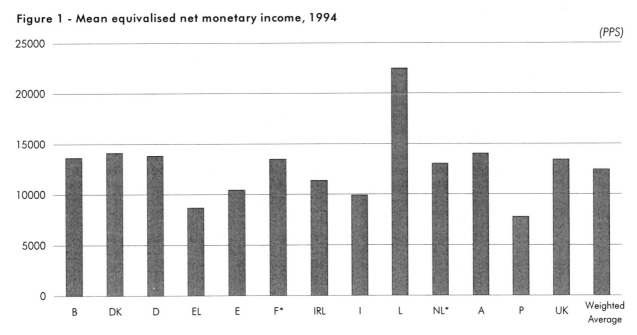

(PPS)

Source: European Community Household Panel - 2nd Wave

In most countries over 70% of income arises from work (employment and self-employment), around 25% from pensions and other social transfers, and the remaining (under 5%) from capital and other private sources.

In Spain and Portugal, wages account for a relatively high proportion of total income. Self-employment represents 25% of total income in Greece and 15% in Ireland compared with around 5% in Belgium and Germany. Pensions form the largest share of all social transfers. They represent 9% of total income in Danish households and up to 21% of that in Italian and Austrian households. With the bulk of their resources coming from gainful employment and less than 20% from social transfers, Spain and Portugal are the two countries least dependent on the welfare state for income (Table 1).

As with the conclusions drawn for wages and social welfare, the more prosperous the country in terms of GDP per capita, the higher the average net monetary income.

Table 1 - Components of income, 1994

(Sources of mean equivalised net monetary income - %)

	B	DK	D	EL	E	F*	IRL	I	L	NL*	A	P	UK	Weighted Average
Mean/ equivalised income-PPS	13 553	14 119	13 851	8 803	10 375	13 500	11 043	10 017	22 124	13 060	13 810	7 773	13 139	12 306
Total	100.0	100.0	100.0	100.0	100.0	100.0	100.0	100.0	100.0	100.0	100.0	100.0	100.0	100.0
Income from work	60.2	72.8	71.9	70.2	79.2	:	72.4	73.1	70.8	:	66.2	78.3	70.1	:
employment	54.6	65.9	66.4	45.4	67.3	:	57.1	59.8	63.6	:	59.6	67.8	62.3	:
self-employ.	5.5	6.9	5.4	24.8	11.9	:	15.3	13.3	7.2	:	6.5	10.5	7.8	:
Non-work private income	6.3	4.0	4.6	9.5	3.7	:	1.8	3.4	4.5	:	3.4	2.7	4.2	:
of which capital & property	4.6	3.2	3.6	6.9	3.0	:	1.5	2.4	2.9	:	1.8	2.1	3.3	:
Social transfers	33.5	23.2	23.3	19.6	17.5	:	26.1	23.8	24.4	:	30.5	19.0	25.7	:
Pensions	17.5	9.0	16.5	17.9	11.4	:	12.9	20.8	16.1	:	21.9	13.9	10.0	:
Sickness/ Invalidity	3.7	2.9	1.4	0.8	2.8	:	2.0	1.7	2.0	:	1.4	1.7	3.6	:
Unemploy.	5.3	5.4	2.3	0.2	2.9	:	6.1	0.7	0.5	:	1.4	1.4	0.7	:
Housing/ social assistance/ other personal	0.5	4.0	1.0	0.3	0.2	:	0.8	0.2	1.1	:	0.5	0.1	7.3	:
Family related/Educ.	6.5	2.9	2.1	0.4	0.1	:	4.2	0.5	4.6	:	5.4	1.8	4.2	:

Source: Eurostat - European Community Household Panel - 2nd Wave

Definitions and methods

- **Households**

In the ECHP a household is defined in terms of two criteria: sharing the same dwelling and common living arrangements. These can include meals taken together or a shared room, and/or a joint budget, and/or the use of common equipment.

- **Total net monetary income of the household**

In the ECHP, total net monetary income of the household covers:

(+) Income from work, i.e., wages/salaries, self employed income

(+) non work private income, i.e., income from capital and property, and private transfers (for example from parents to their children)

(+) social transfers for retired and unemployed people, family sickness/invalidity, education, social assistance, housing and others.

(-) Social insurance contributions and income tax deducted at source.

This total income is estimated from detailed reporting by each household adult during 1994 for Wave 2. Most income components as obtained in the ECHP are collected net of income tax and social insurance payments. The main exceptions are incomes from self-employment and property, for which the reported gross amounts have been converted into net amounts using a simple statistical procedure.

- **Equivalence scales**

The aim of equivalence scales is to adjust incomes for the varying size and composition of household.

The equivalence scale used here is the *modified OECD scale*, i.e., 1.0 for the first adult, 0.5 for every other adult in the household and 0.3 for every child aged less than 14. This results in a number of *adult equivalents*.

- **Equivalised income**

The equivalised income is the income per adult equivalent. It is obtained by dividing total net monetary income of the household by the number of adult equivalents of the household. It follows that all members of the same household have the same equivalised income.

- **Income distribution measures**

The income distribution data refer to the distribution of *persons* arranged according to increasing level of their equivalised household income. Hence the median, deciles and quintiles of (equivalised) income distribution are defined in terms of number of persons rather than of households.

The decile ratio

Groups comprising 10% of units are known as "decile groups". The "bottom decile groups" (P10) is the 10% of individuals / households with the lowest income; the "top decile group" P90 is the 10% of individuals / households with the highest income. The decile ratio is P90/P10.

The share ratio

The share ratio, S 80/S20, is the ratio of the share of total income received by the top 20% of the population to that received by the bottom 20% of the population.

The Gini coefficient

The *Gini coefficient* is a summary measure of inequality in the income shares. It is defined in terms of the relationship of cumulative shares of the population arranged according to the level of equivalised income (bottom 10%, bottom 20% etc.), to cumulative share of the total income received by them.

The higher the level of the coefficient, the more unequal the income distribution.

Disparities in the income distribution

Whatever indicator is chosen (box p 175), income is always more unequally distributed in Portugal, Greece and Spain than in other countries. For certain indicators, Ireland and the United Kingdom join this group of countries. In contrast, income distribution seems to be more evenly distributed in all cases in Denmark.

On average, the 10% of the EU population that is least well-off received 2.5% of total income in 1994. By comparison, the 10% most well-off received 10 times more, i.e. 25%. If, instead of deciles (10%), we use quintiles (20%), the S80/S20 ratio is lower, less than 6. This ratio ranges from 3.2 in Denmark to 7.1 in Portugal. As a general rule, the ratios in Greece, Spain and Portugal are significantly above the average. Ireland and the United Kingdom are around or slightly above the average. Indicators for all the other Member States show relatively fewer disparities (Table 2).

Another way of analysing the differences in income distribution is to use the decile ratio (see box p. 175) comparing the top and bottom income groups. This ratio is less than 3 in Denmark and exceeds 5 in Greece and in Portugal. It is between 4 and 5 and, therefore, around the average in Spain, Ireland, Italy, Austria and the United Kingdom. In the other countries, the data reveal a more even distribution (Table 3).

Table 2 - Income distribution[1], 1994

(% share of total income)

	B	DK	D	EL	E	F*	IRL	I	L	NL*	A	P	UK	Weighted average
Share of bottom deciles														
10	2.9	4.4	2.7	2.2	2.5	3.3	3.0	2.4	3.1	4.1	2.7	2.2	3.0	2.6
20	7.8	10.7	7.7	6.4	6.7	8.4	7.2	7.1	8.1	9.0	7.7	6.1	7.4	7.1
50	29.5	34.8	29.9	26.3	26.4	30.2	25.3	28.2	29.3	32.8	29.8	25.3	26.3	27.9
Share of top deciles														
60	60.8	55.7	60.6	64.7	64.4	60.4	65.9	62.3	61.5	57.7	60.8	65.9	64.8	62.7
80	37.4	33.6	37.6	41.7	40.7	37.5	42.6	38.3	38.8	34.5	37.5	43.5	41.7	39.3
90	22.5	20.2	22.7	26.3	24.9	22.8	26.6	22.9	23.6	20.0	22.8	27.7	26.1	24.0
S80/S20	4.80	3.15	4.89	6.55	6.04	4.46	5.89	5.39	4.78	3.45	4.87	7.11	5.63	5.52

[1] This table shows how within each country, the total net monetary income is shared among different strata of the population formed according to the level of mean equivalised income

Source: Eurostat - European Community Household Panel - 2nd Wave

Table 3 - Indicators on income distribution, 1994

	B	DK	D	EL	E	F*	IRL	I	L	NL*	A	P	UK	Weighted average
P90/P10[1]	3.9	2.6	3.9	5.3	4.9	3.7	4.6	4.4	4.0	3.0	4.1	5.6	4.5	4.5
Gini coefficient[1]	0.296	0.227	0.296	0.351	0.340	0.290	0.357	0.314	0.304	0.247	0.297	0.368	0.345	0.322

[1] see box p. 175

Source: Eurostat - European Community Household Panel - 2nd Wave

The Gini coefficient is a useful summary tool for imparting a quick impression of the spread of incomes (see box p. 175). In 1994, the coefficient for the EU was 0.322 using a weighted average. Spain, United Kingdom, Ireland, Greece and, in particular, Portugal were significantly above the average, reflecting greater inequality in these countries (Table 3).

The higher the income, the lower the inequality

There is a relatively strong link between the standard of living, as measured by average equivalised net monetary income, and the degree of inequality in income distribution as measured by the Gini coefficient. In other words, the higher the income, the smaller the disparities tend to be. This holds for nearly all Member States, with the exception of the United Kingdom and Ireland (Figure 2).

Figure 2 - Income level and disparities in the distribution, 1994

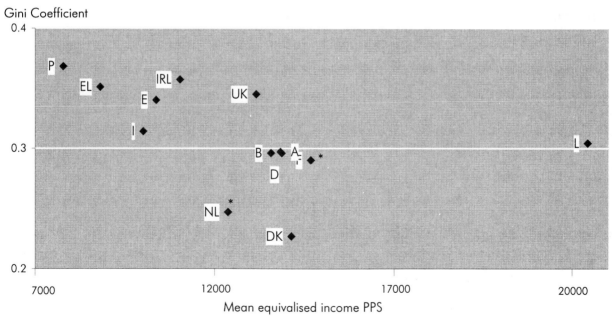

France, the Netherlands: provisional data

Source : Eurostat - European Community Household Panel, 2nd wave

Poverty : a variety of approaches and conventions

There is such a wide variety of approaches and conventions regarding poverty that it is important to clarify those used in this chapter.

Variety of approaches

Four approaches are generally distinguished.

• Monetary" poverty characterised by insufficient income. This is the most common approach for international comparisons. It can be further sub-divided :

- the "absolute" approach is based on the concept of a minimum level of subsistence.

- the "relative" approach is the most frequently used, above all in international comparisons. This consists of defining, for a given country, a standard of living considered to be normal; the "poor" are deemed to be those persons who cannot reach this standard. In this case, income disparities in relation to the average or affluent income groups are more significant than the level of poverty itself.

• Material" poverty results from the absence of basic consumer goods, e.g., not having a telephone in a country where the vast majority has one.

• "Perceived" poverty. A household may feel that it makes ends meet or, on the contrary, that it faces financial difficulties.

• Lastly, there is the administrative approach which counts all those receiving aid to combat poverty.

This chapter favours the relative monetary poverty concept. Non-monetary indicators are also used to take account of the multidimensional nature of poverty. Finally, in order to provide an idea of the dynamics of "exclusion", we look at some relevant indicators such as the long-term unemployment rate.

Variety of conventions

• The *choice of a "monetary" threshold:* what is the level of monetary income below which a person should be considered poor?

The thresholds most frequently used correspond to 50% or 60% of the median or mean equivalised net income. From a technical point of view, the median is the preferred choice (robustness of results in relation to the extreme values). The weakness of the arithmetic mean is that it may be skewed due to extreme values.

In this chapter, the threshold for poverty is set at 50% of median monetary income.

• The equivalence scale used here counts 1 for the first adult, 0.5 for every other adult in the household and 0.3 for every child aged less than 14.

• Income is calculated over the year. Imputed rent, public services provided to individuals and domestic production are excluded.

• Estimates relate to the population living in households and therefore exclude those living in institutions and the homeless, i.e., some of the most deprived people in the EU.

In conclusion, the results obtained depend largely on the conventions used. For this reason, a Eurostat Working Group made up of national representatives met for the third time (24-26 June 1998 in Luxembourg). Work has focussed on i) income definitions and concepts, ii) measures of monetary poverty, and iii) exclusion and measures of exclusion.

Poverty is multidimensional

Europe is rich but a significant minority of its citizens are poor[1]. However, there is still no widely accepted agreement on how best to measure poverty (see box opposite).

The definition (below) adopted by the Council of Ministers (19/12/1984) stresses the need for relative measures and refers to the multidimensional nature of the phenomenon but does not recommend a particular *measure* of poverty :

"Persons whose resources (material, cultural and social) are so limited as to exclude them from the minimum acceptable way of life in the Member State in which they live".

The high and low income recipients

In 1994, 4% of Danes had an income that was less than half the median income. In contrast, the proportion was around 15% in Greece, Spain and Portugal. Belgium, Germany, France and the United Kingdom were close to the EU average (11.3%). However, given the average living standards in each country, a poor person in Luxembourg could be among the relatively well-off in Portugal.

If, instead, 60% of median income is used, Ireland and the United Kingdom have similar figures to the three above-mentioned southern countries: slightly more than one person in five in these countries can be considered to have a "low" income (Table 4). Ireland and the United Kingdom appear to be most affected by a change of threshold due to the relatively large proportion of the population with a "low" as opposed to a "very low" income. Whatever threshold is used, Denmark, the Netherlands and Germany always record the lowest "poverty" rates and Greece, Spain and Portugal the highest ones.

Table 4 - Poverty rates based on different cut-off points, 1994

(% of the population)

	B	DK	D	EL	E	F*	IRL	I	L	NL*	A	P	UK	Weighted average
Cut-off point below														
60% of the median[1]	18.4	9.7	17.9	21.1	21.2	16.6	22.2	19.4	15.0	10.1	17.7	22.5	20.9	20.5
50% of the median[1]	11.4	4.4	10.9	14.9	14.7	9.9	9.4	12.5	9.5	5.2	12.1	15.9	11.6	13.6
50% of the mean[2]	15.7	6.3	14.7	21.1	20.7	14.0	24.8	17.2	14.7	7.6	15.0	24.0	22.6	18.5

[1] All figures are based on the distribution of persons by net equivalised income
[2] The equivalised mean is computed as the mean of individual equivalised incomes weighted by the number of persons (household size)
Source: Eurostat - European Community Household Panel - 2nd Wave

---

[1]   "Poverty and social exclusion in Europe". Tony Atkinson in "Poverty and exclusion" La Documentation Française 1998.

Key role of employment intensity
··

With few exceptions, the young (less than 16) and older (over 64) generations are more likely to be in a low income household than people of working age (16-64). Other groups that are particularly at risk include single parent families, couples with 4 or more children and persons aged 65 and over living on their own. However, these groups do not account for the majority of people in poverty – people of all ages and different family types are affected.

The position of individuals in the income distribution depends largely on the employment intensity (i.e. full time, full year) within their households. For the Europe of Twelve, 75% of individuals living in a household with at least one full time wage or salary earner have an income (per adult equivalent) in the three upper income quintiles. This figure is more than 80% in Belgium, Greece, Ireland and the United Kingdom. Individuals in working households where no-one is in full time employment are more likely to be found in the lowest income quintiles (Table 5).

Table 5 - Percentage of individuals in the income distribution by household "employment intensity"

(as a % of individuals in each household type)

	Full-time, full-year employed households			Other working households		
	1st quintile	2nd quintile	3rd to 5th quintile	1st quintile	2nd quintile	3rd to 5th quintile
B	4	14	81	28	22	49
DK	5	16	79	30	27	43
D	9	19	72	39	18	43
EL	4	15	81	27	24	49
E	6	16	78	35	23	42
F	9	18	73	34	22	44
IRL	2	12	86	20	24	56
I	8	18	74	33	19	48
L	15	18	67	32	13	55
NL	9	19	72	33	19	48
P	6	18	76	42	22	36
UK	5	14	81	28	23	50
EU-12	7	17	75	33	21	46

Source: "Low income and low pay in a household context" Statistics in Focus Population and social conditions - 1998/6

Making ends meet

In Portugal, 59% of households declared that they were unable to afford a week's holiday (1995). In Greece, Spain and the United Kingdom the proportion varied between 40% and 50%. In contrast, the figure was as low as 11% in Germany. As one might expect, the number of households reporting that they could not afford new clothes was much lower in nearly all countries. The highest proportions were found in Greece and Portugal (Table 6).

Around 60% of the households in Spain, Ireland the United Kingdom reported difficulties in making ends meet. In contrast, the proportion in Denmark, Germany and the Netherlands was around half this level (30%). More than three-quarters of Greek and Portuguese households claimed to have difficulties making ends meet (Table 7).

Replies to 'opinion' questions are subjective by nature and should therefore be treated with caution. Nevertheless, the conclusions reached on monetary poverty are consistent with those on non-monetary poverty.

Table 6 - Percentage of households declaring that they cannot afford certain items, 1995

(%)

	Cannot afford a week's annual holiday away from home	Cannot afford new clothes
B	28	12
DK	15	5
D	11	14
EL	50	32
E	46	8
F	32	9
IRL	38	8
I	38	15
L	13	5
NL	14	13
A	24	10
P	59	47
UK	42	16

Source: Eurostat - European Community Household Panel, 2nd wave

Table 7 - Thinking of your household's total income "Is your household able to make ends meet", 1995

(%)

	With great difficulty, difficulty, some difficulty	Fairly easily, easily, very easily
B	42	58
DK	31	69
D	30	70
EL	78	22
E	63	37
F	51	49
IRL	60	40
I	68	32
L	17	83
NL	31	69
A	54	46
P	78	22
UK	62	38

Source: Eurostat - European Community Household Panel, 2nd wave

Employability: a key factor for non-exclusion

P*eople are excluded not just because they are currently without a job or income but because they have little expectations for the future.* As a result, exclusion is more than a multidimensional phenomenon, it integrates dynamics and we need forward looking indicators to describe it.

Without claiming to measure exclusion, we have chosen to illustrate it with two indicators which according to much research impact significantly on exclusion in the long run: the first refers to the proportion of young people who leave school without qualifications beyond the level of compulsory education, the second looks at the number of adults who have been unemployed at least 12 months.

The first is often referred to as a proxy measure of "drop outs". The EU average (19%) conceals marked differences between countries. Between 9% and 11% of the young people aged 15 to 24 have left school with, at best, a lower secondary education in Belgium, Germany, France, Austria and Finland. The proportion is as high as 33% in Portugal and 28% in Italy and the United Kingdom. Women seem to be better qualified particularly in the southern countries (Table 8). These differences should be treated with caution as in certain countries such as the United Kingdom, many adults return to the education system at a later stage.

Table 8 - Proportion of young people aged 15-24 having left education with at best attaining level ISCED 2[1] 1996

(%)

	EU-15	B	DK	D	EL	E	F	IRL	I	L	NL	A	P	FIN	S	UK
TOTAL	19	9	14	9	17	25	11	15	28	27	15	11	33	10	13	28
Females	18	8	13	10	15	21	10	11	25	29	14	13	28	10	14	29
Males	21	11	14	9	19	30	12	18	30	25	15	9	38	11	13	27

[1] "left education" = not having participated in any education and training course in the 4 weeks preceding the interview.

For definition of ISCED 2, see chapter on Education and Training (p. 75).

Source: Eurostat - Labour Force Survey

In 1997, more than 7 million persons aged 25 and over in the EU were seeking employment for at least 12 months. This represents on average 53% of the total unemployed; in Belgium, Ireland and Italy it accounts for more than 60% (Table 9).

For those in long-term unemployment, there can be serious implications: they may not be entitled to any social benefits, their self-confidence and self-esteem may suffer and they can lose contact with the labour market. Research has shown that this can lead in the long run to exclusion.

Table 9 - Long term unemployment[1] of people aged 25 and over, 1997

	EU-15	B	DK	D	EL	E	F	IRL	I	L	NL	A	P	FIN	S	UK
Number of long term unemployed (1000)	7 048	193	38	1 779	147	1 308	1 091	68	1 192	(1)	159	49	137	103	141	643
As a % of total unemployed	53	66	34	53	58	56	44	62	68	(40)	54	32	63	39	40	45

[1] 12 months and over

Source: Eurostat - Labour Force survey

Consumption, Housing conditions

The decisive role of income

Throughout the Union, the standard of living in terms of consumption, housing conditions and consumer durables has improved considerably over the last thirty years.

Between 1985 and 1995, private consumption in the EU-15 continued to increase in spite of the economic difficulties at the beginning of the 1990s. For the Union as a whole, the relative shares of the main consumer expenditure categories have changed over this period: in 1985 "food, beverages and tobacco" accounted for the largest share of household consumption. Today, this category is in second position behind "gross rent, fuel and electricity" (see chapter 1 on Economic Background). However, there are significant variations between Member States and across various household types. The reason depends largely on economic resources although national habits and consumer preference can also be important factors. For instance, the decision to buy a car is not confined exclusively to affordability.

Some recent findings using data from the Household Budget Surveys (1994) and European Community Household Panel (first wave 1994, see p. 172) are:

— The consumption of the lowest income households rarely exceeds two-thirds of the consumption estimated for the average household.

— Households headed by manual workers, farmers or unemployed persons generally live below the national average standard of living.

— The level of income tends to influence the structure of consumer expenditure, e.g., the share of expenditure on "food, beverages and tobacco" within a total budget decreases considerably as the level of income rises. High-income households, on the other hand, devote a larger share of their budget to leisure, hotels and restaurants than low income ones. The share of a household's budget devoted to housing (gross rent, fuel and power) is similar across all income groups.

— Home ownership has increased significantly over the last three decades from 45% in 1970 to 59% in 1994. Around two-thirds of couples (married or not) tend to own their accommodation.

— One in ten households is living in "overcrowded" conditions (more than one person per room).

— Basic amenities such as hot running water are now available to the vast majority of the Union's citizens. However, Portugal and Greece seem to be lagging behind.

— 40% of homeowners are still paying off a loan or mortgage although the proportion varies significantly between countries. In 1994, 5% of homeowners and 8% of tenants were in arrears with their repayments during the previous 12 months.

— In most Member States there is a relatively strong correlation between household income and the quality of the housing conditions.

The Union's Consumers

Total disposable income impacts strongly on the level and structure of household consumption. Other factors such as consumer preference, age, family size, cultural traditions and place of residence (urban or rural) also play a role.

Consumption in low and high income households

Consumer expenditure per adult equivalent by income quartile provides clear evidence of the link between income and consumption and also of disparities between countries. For instance, in Italy the upper quartile (the 25% most well-off) consumed on average 21 700 PPS in 1994 compared with 6 200 PPS for the lowest quartile (the 25% least well-off). In Denmark, figures were 17 000 and 9 700 respectively.

Figure 1 - Consumer expenditure per adult equivalent in 1994 by income quartile[1]

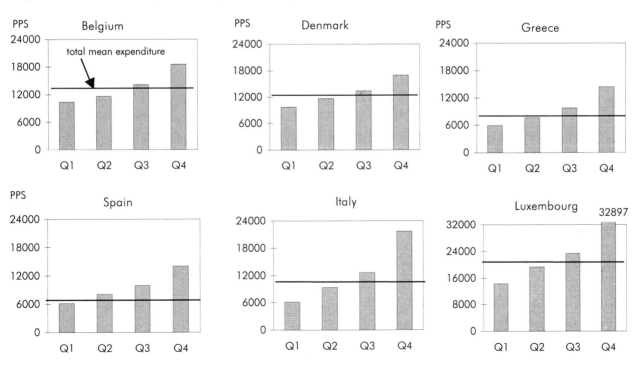

Figure 1 - Consumer expenditure per adult equivalent in 1994 by income quartile[1] (continued)

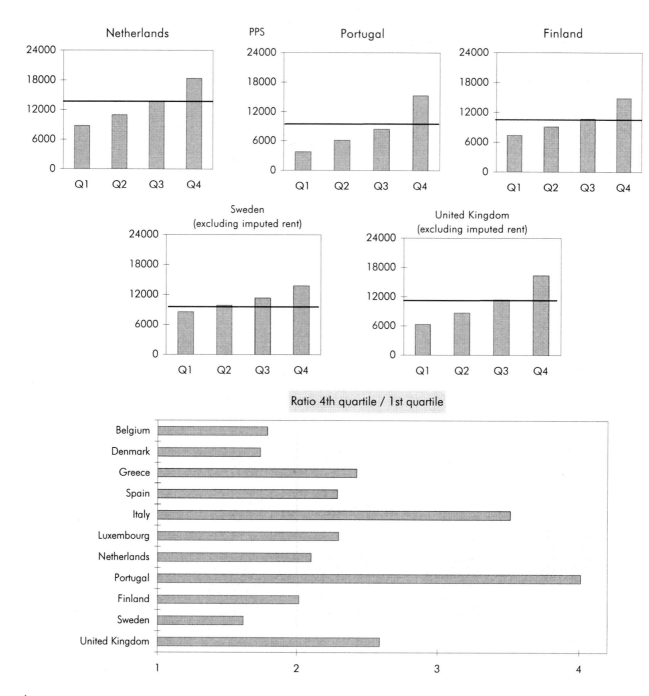

[1] For each country, classes Q1, Q2, Q3 and Q4 have been fixed by sorting the income per equivalent adult in ascending order so as to obtain an identical number of households in each class. Thus, of 4 million Belgium households, the 25% poorest (1 million households in the income class Q1) consume on average 10 300 PPS compared with 18 800 PPS for the 25% richest (1 million households in class Q4).

Source : Eurostat - Household Budget Surveys, 1994

Finally, the consumption (as defined in the Household Budget Surveys, see box p. 194) of the lowest quartile rarely exceeds two-thirds of the consumption estimated for the average household. At the other end of the distribution scale, e.g. in Italy and Portugal, the most well-off households consume up to 1.8 times the national average. Italy and Portugal also present the largest disparities between the households of the first and fourth quartiles: respectively 3.5 and 4. In the other countries, the inter-quartile ratio is smaller: less than 2 in Belgium and in Sweden, while it does not exceed 2.6 elsewhere (Figure 1 opposite).

The level of income tends to influence the structure of consumer expenditure. However, the share of a household's budget devoted to housing (gross rent, fuel and power) is similar across all income groups (Figure 2 which provides an average for 9 Member States is considered to be representative of the various national situations). The least well-off households (the first quartile) tend to rent and therefore apply a substantial share of their budget to paying their rents. The households at the top of the range tend to be owner-occupiers, which explains the high rates of imputed rent in their total consumption: from 13% in Greece and Italy to 20% in Finland and 21% in Luxembourg.

Figure 2 - Structure of consumer expenditure in some EU countries[1] in 1994 by income quartile

(As a % of total consumer expenditure)

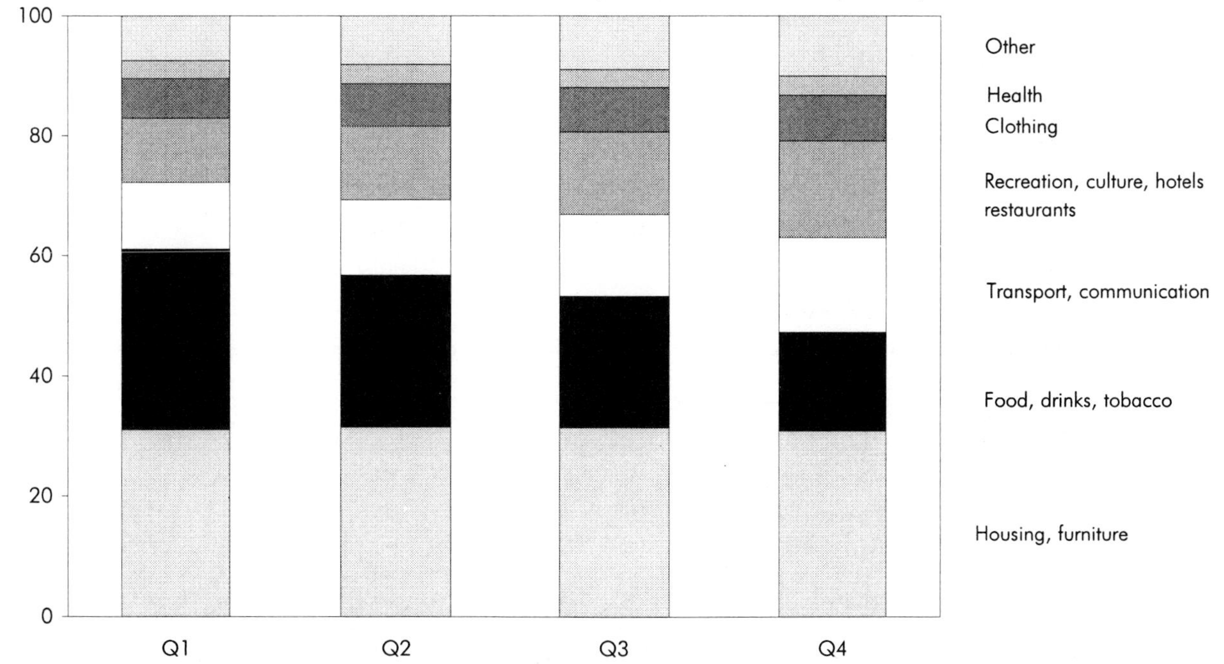

[1] Countries considered are Belgium, Denmark, Greece, Spain, Italy, Luxembourg, the Netherlands, Portugal and Finland. Sweden and the United Kingdom were excluded because of incomplete data on imputed rent.
Source : Eurostat - Household Budget Surveys, 1994

The share of expenditure applied to "food, beverages and tobacco" within a total budget decreases considerably as the level of income rises. These items account for over 30% of purchases by the least well-off households (first quartile) but only 16% of the budget of the last quartile.

High-income households, on the other hand, devote 16% of their budget to expenditure on leisure, hotels and restaurants as against 11% for the low income ones. The share of expenditure on transport also increases significantly as income levels rise (from 9 to 14%), mainly due to higher rates of vehicle ownership in well-off households (See p. 202, "Owning a car").

Diversity of budgets by socio-economic category

Households headed by a manual worker, farmer or unemployed person generally live below the national average standard of living. On the other hand, consumption in those headed by self-employed people and non-manual workers is equal to or above the average everywhere (Table 1).

Table 1 - Consumption per adult equivalent in 1994 by socio-economic category

(Index 100 = average consumption)

	B	DK	EL	E	I	L	NL	P	FIN	S[1]	UK[1]
Manual worker	90	99	88	87	90	83	98	86	99	94	103
Non-manual worker	109	112	126	118	113	116	113	156	115	108	133
Self-employed person	102	124	117	106	116	122	114	100	120	103	124
Farmer	98	100	86	81	81	81	90	67	94	72	102
Unemployed	78	80	82	75	.	76	77	91	78	.	66
Average consumption	100	100	100	100	100	100	100	100	100	100	100

[1] Excluding imputed rent

Source : Eurostat - Household Budget Surveys, 1994

In most countries, housing accounts for over 20% of total consumption irrespective of the socio-economic category of a household. Food generally takes second position. It does, however, represent as much as one-quarter of the consumer expenditure of farmers in the southern EU Member States, or even more if expenditure on alcohol and tobacco is included.

Part of the food consumption of households comes from domestic production (own consumption). The extent of this phenomenon varies considerably according to the product in question and socio-economic category. Own consumption may account for as much as 29% of the food consumption of Greek farmers whereas it is less than 10% for other household categories (Figure 3). Considering all social categories together, Greece still has the highest level of own consumption. Almost one in two Greek households reports consuming a food product from its own holding, private garden or business. Vegetables head the list of "non-purchased" products.

Figure 3 - Share of own consumption in food consumption by socio-economic category, 1994

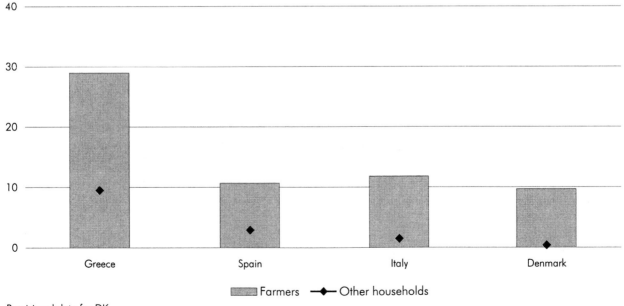

Provisional data for DK

Source : Eurostat - Household Budget Surveys, 1994

Consumption varies according to household size

As a general rule, the more numerous a household, the more modest its consumption per adult equivalent. This emerges in every household with more than two or three members, or more than four in Finland and Portugal (Figure 4).

Single-person households devote a substantial part of their budget to rent, close to 30% in Belgium, Spain and Finland. Other households spend much less by virtue of economies of scale (Figure 5). Expenditure on transport by single-person households is relatively low: rates of private vehicle ownership, for example, are lower for this category of households than for the rest of the population in Finland and the Netherlands. Closer analysis of the household consumption of this type reveals higher expenditure on public transport and package travel.

For couples with children, expenditure on food and clothing reflects the number of children in the household. In Finland and Greece, for example, consumption of 'milk, cheese and eggs' amounts to 2.7% and 3.5% of the budget of a childless couple, and 3.4% and 5.1%, respectively, of a couple with three children. On a more general level, the impact of the number of children on the food budget is very significant in Greece, Spain, Italy and Portugal (Figure 6).

The increase is particularly marked between the second and third child. In the northern EU Member States, the increase in the budget share devoted to food is more uniform, possibly because family allowances compensate supplementary household consumption.

Figure 4 - Consumer expenditure by adult equivalent in 1994 by household size

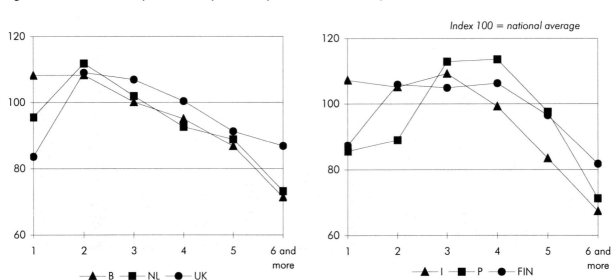

Source : Eurostat - Household Budget Surveys, 1994

Figure 5 - Expenditure on rent[1] by type of household, 1994

% of total expenditure

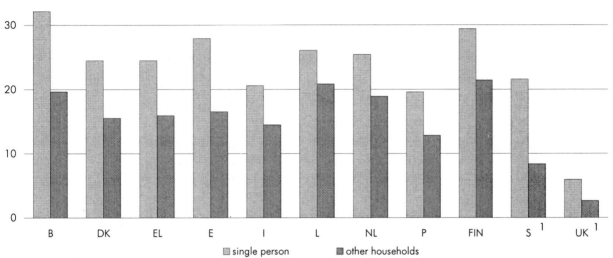

[1] Share of real and imputed rents (excluding imputed rent in Sweden and United Kingdom)
Source : Eurostat - Household Budget Surveys, 1994

Figure 6 - Budget share spent on food in 1994 by number of children

% of total expenditure

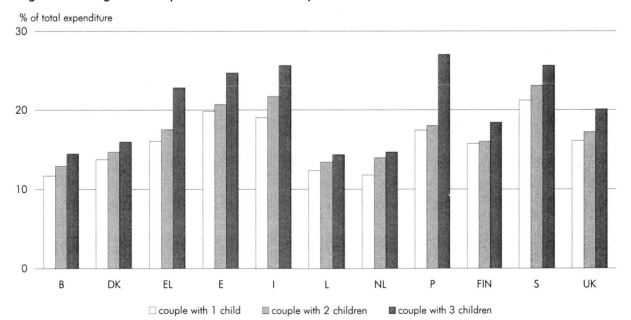

Source : Eurostat - Household Budget Surveys, 1994

Household Budget Surveys in the European Union

The section on European consumers draws on data from the Household Budget Surveys conducted in all the Member States of the European Union. In order to guarantee comparability, Eurostat harmonises the data in a process of converting national data files to a predefined Community format.

Unfortunately, the survey years do not always coincide with the reference year fixed by Eurostat. When this is the case, the data are deflated using the general consumer price index of the country concerned. The first reference year was set to 1988, the second to 1994. For 1994 data, 11 countries are now available: Belgium, Denmark, Greece, Spain, Italy, Luxembourg, the Netherlands, Portugal, Finland, Sweden, plus United Kingdom with provisional data.

The Household Budget Surveys collect micro-data concerning expenditure as well as income and general socio-economic characteristics (profession, age, etc.) of private households. The goods and services recorded are classified under the Classification Of Individual Consumption by Purpose - Household Budget Survey (COICOP-HBS) which covers 12 functions:

— Food and non-alcoholic drinks;
— Alcoholic drinks, tobacco;
— Clothing and footwear;
— Housing, water, electricity and other fuels;
— Furnishings, household equipment and routine maintenance of the house;
— Health (including out-patient and hospital services);
— Transport (including purchase of vehicles, petrol, transport services);
— Communications (including postal services, telephone);
— Leisure and culture (including television, photography, personal computers, games, toys, cinemas, museums, books, package
    tours);
— Education;
— Hotels, cafés and restaurants;
— Other goods and services (including personal care, personal effects such as jewellery and travel goods, day nurseries, insurance,
    financial services).

Own production - Imputed rents

In addition to households' traditional monetary expenditure, Household Budget Surveys also include own production (for example family vegetable gardens), benefits in kind received and imputed rents of owner-occupiers. The purpose of calculating the imputed rent of owners is to compare the levels of consumption of households with very different housing patterns. The monetary expenditure of tenants is taken into account, whereas the purchase of dwellings by owners is not (capital expenditure). The imputed rent of owner-occupiers is thus an evaluation based on the rent that would be paid for similar accommodation rented on the market.

Consumption in Household Budget Surveys and National Accounts

Although Household Budget Survey concepts are often based on National Accounts definitions, any comparison with National Accounts final household consumption should take into account that:

— Household Budget Surveys cover only national 'private households' excluding institutional households (hospitals, etc.) and foreign tourists consumption.

— Household Budget Surveys collect individual data on a representative sample through individual questionnaires. They do not have any accounting objective at national level. Thus National Accounts may use other statistical sources (retail sales for instance) to build the final consumption aggregates.

— Some data collection procedures may affect the comparability of data regarding the main consumption functions such as 'health' and 'housing'.

Further information: "Household Budget Surveys in the EU. Methods and Recommendations for Harmonization" — 1997 —

Housing conditions and equipment

Housing provides shelter, is the basic infrastructure underpinning people's social and community existence and directly affects the economic lives of those living in the household. As we have seen, it is also the most important item of household expenditure in nearly all countries.

Housing conditions are determined by a number of factors: a household's economic resources, its size and structure, consumer preferences, available building stock and national government policy. This analysis looks mainly at the influence of the first three factors with regard to home ownership, basic amenities, housing space and consumer durables. In general, there is a relatively strong correlation in most countries between household income and the quality of the housing conditions.

Large differences across the Union in the type of housing

For the European Union as a whole, there are marginally more households (53%) living in single-family houses (detached or terraced) than in apartments. This European average however masks markedly different national situations (Figure 7). The vast majority of the population in Ireland, the United Kingdom and Belgium live in single-family houses. In contrast, the majority of Germans, Spaniards, Italians and, to a lesser extent, Greeks reside in apartments.

> **Reference person**
>
> In this chapter, the household is the only statistical unit used. As a result, the term 'the unemployed" refers to a household where the reference person is unemployed as opposed to the total number of unemployed persons.
>
> The household interview of the ECHP is conducted with the reference person. see box p. 57.

Figure 7 - Single-family houses or apartments: where households live, 1994

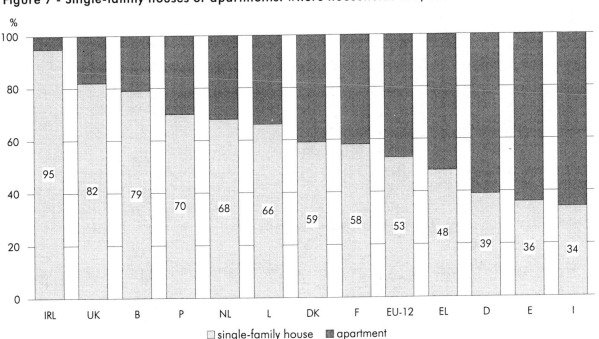

Source : Eurostat - ECHP, 1994

In addition to cultural traditions and the degree of urbanisation, the level of income of a household also impacts on the type of housing. In four countries, Denmark, Germany, Netherlands and the United Kingdom, affluent households have a greater tendency to live in single-family houses than low income ones (see box for definitions). By contrast, in Greece, Spain and Portugal the situation is completely reversed with considerably more affluent people living in apartments. For the other countries, the differences are minimal.

Significant increase in home ownership over the last twenty-five years

In 1970, the percentage of owner-occupiers was 45% for the Community as a whole ; in 1980 it had climbed to 54% and in 1994 it was estimated at 59%. Ireland, Italy, the Netherlands and the United Kingdom experienced the largest rises (around 30%) from 1970 to 1994. It is clear that national government policies can play a decisive role in the level of home ownership, c.f., the rise in the United Kingdom during the Eighties.

Today, around 80% of households in Ireland, Spain and Greece own the accommodation they live in. Only in Germany and the Netherlands do the majority rent (Table 2).

Table 2 - Trend in the percentage of owner-occupied dwellings, 1970-1994[1]

(%)

	1970/71	1981/82	1990/91	1994
EU-12	45*	54	59	59*
B	53	58	65	66
DK	49	55	54	53
D	36	40	39	41
EL	:	70	76	77
E	:	73	78	79
F	45	51	54	55
IRL	61	74	79	81
I	51	59	68	77
L	57	60	65	66
NL	35	42	45	48
A	41	48	50	53
P	:	57	65	61
FIN	58	61	67	62
S	:	:	56	:
UK	50	56	66	67

[1] Data for 1970-1991 are not directly comparable with 1994 data. The first set come from the Census and are based on dwellings while data for 1994 are taken from the first wave of the ECHP and are based on households.
Source : Eurostat - Censuses of population (1970/71-1990/91), ECHP 1994

In the Europe of Twelve, households living in single-family houses (77%) are twice as likely to be owner-occupiers as those living in apartments (38%). Single-family house ownership across countries ranges from 63% in the Netherlands to 91% in Greece. The spread of apartment ownership is decidedly greater, ranging from 76% in Spain to 15% and 17% respectively in the Netherlands and Germany (excluding Ireland where the proportion of people living in flats is very small) (Table 3).

Owner-occupying depends largely on household type and income level

The chances of owning one's own home increase with age (savings, inheritance, donations, etc.) (Figure 8). Young adults (under the age of 30) living alone are unlikely to have sufficient resources to become owners; consequently, more than 85% live in rented accommodation. In contrast, 47% of single persons over the age of 65 have bought their own home.

'Dependent' children

Dependent children are considered to be aged under 25, living in a household in which at least one of their parents is a member and whose main activity in 1993 was one of the following :

in education or training ; unemployed ; doing housework ; looking after children or other persons ; in community or military service ; otherwise economically inactive

Table 3 - Owner-occupiers by type of housing, 1994

(%)

	EU-12	B	DK	D	EL	E	F	IRL	I	L	NL	P	UK
All homes	59	66	53	41	78	79	55	81	70	66	47	61	67
Houses	77	78	78	79	91	85	77	85	83	85	63	67	75
Apartments	38	27	18	17	65	76	24	6	64	30	15	51	27

Reading note : In total, 59% of EU-12 households own their home. 77% of households living in a single family house own theirs while 38% of households living in an appartment own theirs.

Source : Eurostat - ECHP, 1994

Two-thirds of couples (married or cohabiting) own their accommodation. This applies to all couples regardless of whether they have children or not. In contrast, only one-third of single-parents (with one or more dependent children, see p. 197) own their home.

As one might expect, there is a strong correlation between income and ownership. On average, 51% of households with low income are home-owners compared with 77% of affluent households. In Denmark, Germany, France, the Netherlands and the United Kingdom, the differences between the low income and more affluent groups are particularly pronounced.

Figure 8 - Owner-occupiers by type of household, EU-12, 1994

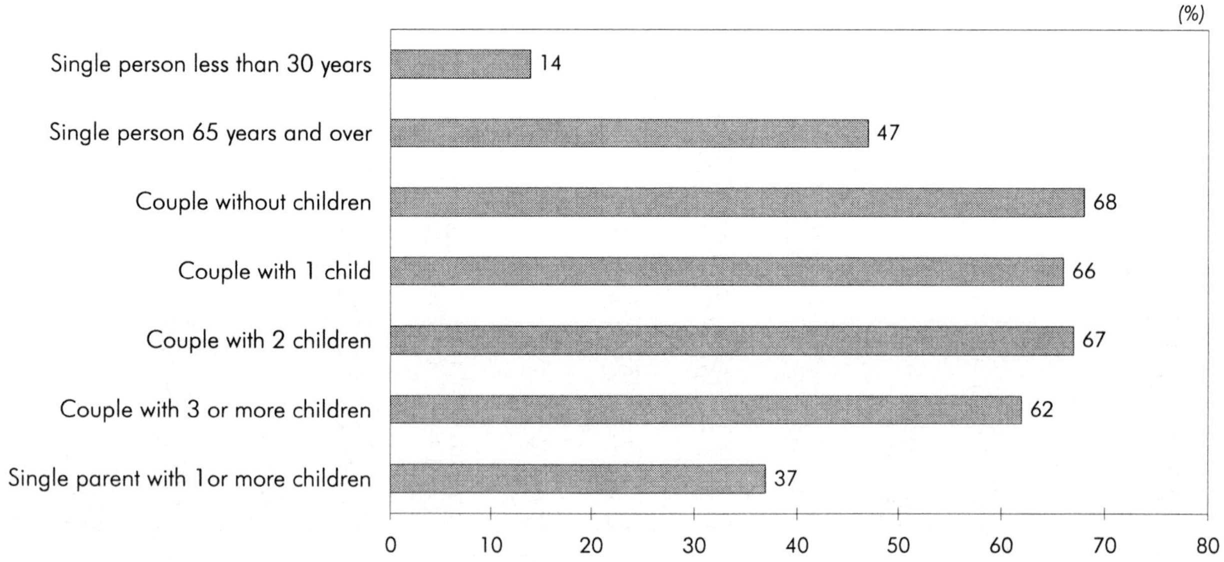

(%)

Type of household	Value
Single person less than 30 years	14
Single person 65 years and over	47
Couple without children	68
Couple with 1 child	66
Couple with 2 children	67
Couple with 3 or more children	62
Single parent with 1 or more children	37

Source : Eurostat - ECHP, 1994

A second home : more common in the southern EU countries, in Finland and Sweden

On average, 9% of households in the Europe of Twelve possess a second home. Greece, Spain, Italy and Luxembourg are well above the European average (Figure 9). The three former countries are among those with the largest disparities in income distribution in the Union while the latter has by far the highest net monetary income in the EU (see chapter on Income). Other research has shown that the proportion of households with second homes is very high (around 20%) in Sweden and Finland.

36% of European households indicated that they cannot afford a second home while the remaining 55% do not want one or do not have one for other reasons. There is a conclusive link with income levels - affluent households (25%) are five times more likely than those with low income (5%) to have a second home (1994).

Figure 9 - Percentage of households with a second home, 1994

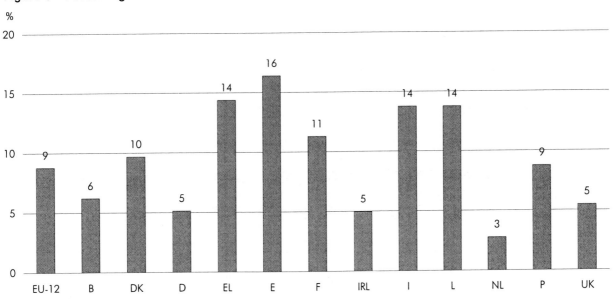

Source : Eurostat - ECHP, 1994

Around one in ten households live in overcrowded accommodation

The average number of rooms[1] per household stood at 4.8 for EU-12 in 1994. More significantly, this means an average of 1.9 rooms per person. Greece, Italy, Austria and Portugal lie below the EU average with around 1.5 rooms per person (Table 4). 11% of EU-12 households can be considered to be living in overcrowded conditions (more than one person per room). The phenomenon is particularly prevalent in Greece, Italy and Portugal (Figure 10). Low income groups are especially vulnerable: only 3% of affluent households are living in overcrowded conditions compared with 16% of low income ones. 21% of the unemployed are subject to overcrowding compared with 14% of those in employment. The retired (2%) are much less affected although this is to be expected given the fact that any children will have almost certainly left home and that a large number of retired people live on their own.

Table 4 - Average number of rooms per household member, 1994

EU-12	B	DK	D	EL	E	F	IRL	I	L	NL	A	P	FIN	S	UK
1.9	2.1	2.3	2.0	1.4	1.7	1.9	1.8	1.5	2.1	1.7	1.2	1.5	1.7	:	2.2

Source : Eurostat - ECHP, 1994. FIN - Housing statistics 1994. A - National source 1994.

Figure 10 - Percentage of households that are overcrowded - more than one person per room[1], 1994

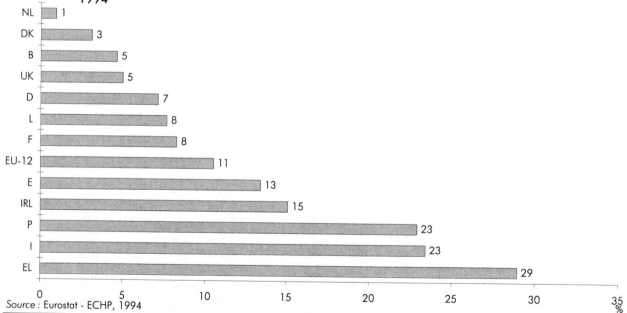

Source : Eurostat - ECHP, 1994

[1]   Kitchens, bathrooms, toilets, rooms used solely for business, hallways, landings, cloakrooms and storerooms are excluded.

The vast majority of European households are now equipped with basic amenities

More than 95% of European Union households have basic amenities in their accommodation: bathroom or shower, inside toilet and hot running water. In Portugal and Greece however these amenities are less common. While, for example, 3% of households across the Union declare that they do not have an indoor flushing toilet, the proportion rises to 10% in Greece and 16% in Portugal (Table 5).

Households with low income are more likely to be without these basic amenities, e.g., 8% are without a bath or shower compared with an overall average of 3%. The retired also seem to be more vulnerable - for EU-12 as a whole, 6% of retired households are without a bath or shower.

Table 5 - Percentage of households lacking basic amenities by income level - 1994

	A bath or shower		An indoor flushing toilet		Hot running water	
	All house-holds	Low[1] income house-holds	All households	Low[1] income house-holds	All households	Low[1] income house-holds
EU-12	3	8	3	6	4	9
B	5	12	4	7	5	9
DK	4	12	2	5	1	5
D	3	5	2	5	7	12
EL	9	25	10	28	18	41
E	2	5	2	3	4	8
F	5	13	3	9	3	7
IRL	5	9	4	6	6	11
I	3	6	1	3	3	5
L	2	3	1	2	4	9
NL	1	3	1	3	1	2
P	18	35	16	30	24	45
UK	1	1	0	1	0	0

[1] For definition of low-income households (see box p. 196)
Source: Eurostat - ECHP, 1994

Owning a car : not just a question of resources

The proportion of households with selected consumer durables varies between countries. The reason depends often as much on consumer preference and other factors as it does on affordability.

Across the Europe of Twelve, 72% of households have at least one car. 19% do not want one (or don't have one for other reasons) while the remaining 9% cannot afford one. More than one-third of Dutch households do not want a car (Figure 11). The highest rates of car ownership are found in Luxembourg, Italy and France. Couples with children are much more likely to have a car - around 90% for the Union as a whole.

In addition to consumer preferences, the size and terrain of the country, the extent of public transport and the general infrastructure are likely to impact on the decision to buy a car or not. In Ireland, Spain, Greece and Portugal, households unable to afford a car outnumber those that do not want one.

As one might expect, the level of income in the household is an important factor - 92% of affluent households have a car as against 52% of low income ones. However, only 19% of the low income group indicate that they cannot afford one, 29% not having one for other reasons. 27% of the unemployed feel unable to afford a car - only 60% have one.

Figure 11 - Percentage of households who possess a car, 1994

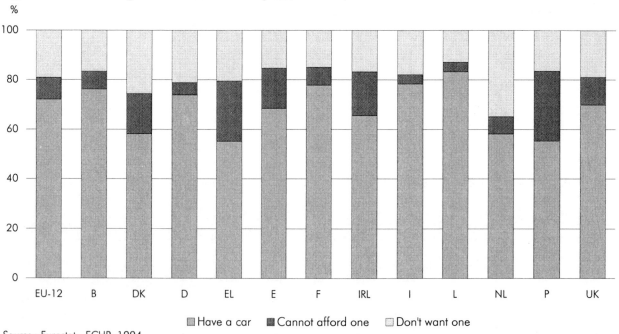

Source : Eurostat - ECHP, 1994

More than 90% of European households possess a telephone. Portugal (74%) and Ireland (78%) fall well below the EU average. 5% of households are unable to afford a telephone while the remaining 4% do not want one.

Young persons living alone are less likely to have a telephone (84%) with 10% indicating that they cannot afford one. There is a similar picture for the low income group (82%) and the unemployed (78%).

As a result of technological progress, the relative prices of equipment such as televisions, video recorders, etc have fallen considerably in recent years. There has been a remarkable rise in the acquisition of colour televisions over the last fifteen years. In 1980 just over 50% of households had one. In 1988, the proportion had risen to 85%. Today 95% of European households have their own colour television (Table 6).

Ownership of consumer durables such as video recorders (58%), microwave ovens (39%), dishwashers (27%) tends to depend on consumer preference rather than on affordability. Only 11% of households say that they cannot afford a video recorder while 31% do not want one. The corresponding figures for microwaves are 12% and 49%, and for dishwashers 16% and 57%.

The United Kingdom is by far the largest consumer of video recorders (75%) and microwaves (65%) while Luxembourg has the largest proportion of dishwashers (50%). The Greeks (5%), Italians (11%) and Portuguese (11%) are much less likely to have a microwave than other countries.

Table 6 - Percentage of households owning selected consumer durables, 1994

	EU-12	B	DK	D	EL	E	F	IRL	I	L	NL	P	UK
Car	72	76	58	74	55	68	78	66	78	83	58	55	70
Telephone	91	92	96	91	88	84	96	78	92	98	98	74	91
Colour TV	95	96	95	97	87	98	92	95	95	97	97	84	96
Video recorder	58	61	55	55	40	60	54	65	52	62	64	45	75

Source : Eurostat - ECHP, 1994

In arrears with mortgage payments, rent and utility bills

Just over 40% of European home owners are still paying off a loan or mortgage (1994). There are significant differences between Greece, Spain, Italy and Portugal where the percentages vary between 10-20 % and the other countries which are all above the European average. More than 80% of home owners in Denmark and the Netherlands continue to pay off a loan or mortgage. The decision to take out a loan or mortgage depends on several factors including national practices, interest rates, tax relief and incentives, etc.

Among this group of home owners (with an existing loan or mortgage), 5% were in arrears with their repayments during the previous 12 months (1994). In addition, 8% of those households renting their accommodation were in arrears with their rent payments (Table 7). The unemployed (21%), single-parents (15%) and couples with children were particularly affected. The problem increases with the number of children, e.g., 9% of couples with one dependent child, 13% with two and 21% with three or more dependent children.

Table 7 - Percentage of household with existing loans or mortgages and those in arrears with (re)payments during the past 12 months, 1994

(%)

	Percentage of home owners with an existing loan or mortgage	Mortgage payments (among home owners with an existing loan or mortgage)	Rent for accommodation (among households renting their accommodation)	Utility bills (electricity, water, gas)
EU-12	42	5	8	6
B	44	6	12	8
DK	86	2	4	3
D	46	1	2	2
EL	11	36	41	36
E	21	9	11	5
F	46	4	11	9
IRL	48	9	27	10
I	18	5	9	4
L	48	2	4	3
NL	83	1	4	2
P	19	3	3	4
UK	64	7	15	9

Source : Eurostat - ECHP, 1994

6% of European households found themselves in arrears with utility bills (electricity, water, gas). The picture is relatively homogeneous for all countries with one striking exception: 36% in Greece. Single-parents (18%) and couples with three or more dependent children (15%) seem to be particularly vulnerable when it comes to paying their utility bills on time (Figure 12). The unemployed also find themselves in a precarious position with 19% in arrears.

Respondents to the ECHP were asked to what extent[1] housing costs[2] represented a financial burden to them: 22% of European home owners with loans to repay opted for 'a heavy burden'. In Spain and Italy, this applies to almost half of all homeowners. Similarly, 23% of tenants in the European Union felt that housing costs made considerable inroads into their budgets. In the Netherlands, Denmark and Luxembourg, only 8 to 9% of tenants expressed this opinion. In Greece, the proportion rose to 73%.

Figure 12 - Percentage of households in arrears with utility bills during the past 12 months by household type, EU-12, 1994

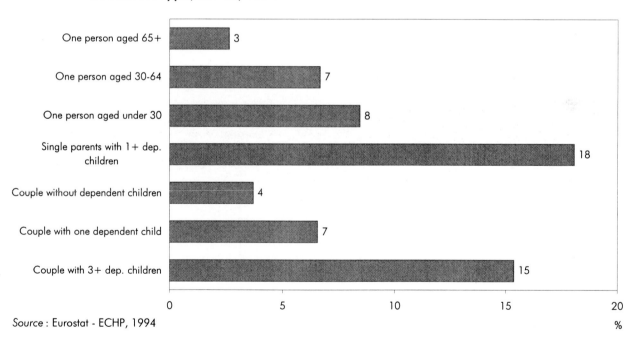

Source : Eurostat - ECHP, 1994

%

---

[1]   Respondents were asked to choose between "a heavy burden", "somewhat of a burden" or "not a problem".
[2]   Housing costs include loan or mortgage repayments, rent, rates, local taxes, heating, water, electricity, etc.

Housing complaints

From a list of potential problems, noise (from neighbours or outside) emerged as the most common complaint in the European Union (27%). Spaniards, Italians and Germans reported this nuisance in greatest numbers.

22% of households reported that they had either a leaky roof or damp or rot. This is particularly prevalent in Portugal (43%). Slightly fewer (20%) cited crime or vandalism in the area. The proportion is 32% in the United Kingdom, as against a mere 8% in Greece.

Just under one in five households (19%) found their home too small. The proportion is higher in Portugal and Greece. These two Member States have the lowest average number of available rooms per person. Pollution (17%) seems to concern Italians, Greeks and Spaniards above all. The Danes and the Irish raised this problem least.

Finally, 12% did not feel that their heating facilities were "adequate". The Greeks (38%) and Portuguese (41%) appear to be particularly affected by this problem. The above data are based on a self-assessment of the respondents situation and their interpretation should therefore be treated with caution (Table 8).

Table 8 - Percentage of households declaring that they experience specific problems with their accommodation, 1994

(%)

	Shortage of space	Lack of adequate heating facilities	Leaky roof or damp or rot	Noise from neighbours or outside	Pollution, grime or other environmental problems	Vandalism or crime in the area
EU-12	19	12	22	27	17	20
B	15	9	22	23	13	19
DK	16	5	13	15	7	14
D	15	6	14	29	14	11
EL	30	38	29	26	21	8
E	23	5	31	33	20	26
F	16	13	26	27	16	25
IRL	16	11	18	11	10	16
I	21	20	15	32	25	18
L	13	6	13	16	17	16
NL	10	7	21	24	16	17
P	35	41	43	18	19	19
UK	21	14	28	22	16	32

Note : Each household is asked "Do you have any of the following problems with your accommodation?" The categories 'leaky roof', damp walls, floors, foundations' and 'rot in window frames or floors' have been combined. A household is included in this group if it experiences at least one of the 3 problems.
Source : Eurostat - ECHP, 1994

Are Europeans satisfied with their housing situation ? Using a 6-point satisfaction scale where 6 indicates fully satisfied, the average score is 4.5 for the Union as a whole. The Greeks and Portuguese appear to be less satisfied with their housing situation. This seems to be in line with the general objective findings of this chapter, i.e., that these countries generally have poorer quality housing than the other Member States. At the other end of the scale, the inhabitants of Denmark, Luxembourg and the Netherlands have the highest levels of contentment. As one might expect, in all Member States low income groups are less satisfied than more affluent ones (Figure 13).

Homelessness: a growing problem

Due to the lack of comparable data, it is particularly difficult to determine the extent of homelessness affecting the EU Member States. However, research would seem to indicate that the homeless have grown in numbers across the Union during the 1980s and 1990s. A number of reasons have been put forward including family breakdown, rising unemployment and reductions in welfare benefits. In 1997, the European Parliament adopted a Resolution of 29 May 1997 on the social aspects of housing in which it insisted that "the fundamental right to decent and affordable housing for all be given operational reality by concrete policies and measures carried out at the appropriate level."

Figure 13 - Housing satisfaction of low income and affluent households, 1994

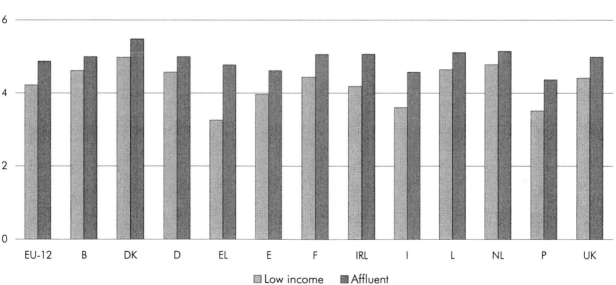

Source : Eurostat - ECHP, 1994

Life expectancy and Health

The role of lifestyle

Throughout the European Union, heart disease, cancers and accidents dominate mortality. Some specific causes of death are still on the increase but, overall, total mortality is decreasing. As a consequence people continue to live longer which is one of the major reasons for the ageing of populations; the other major reason being decreasing fertility rates. Living longer goes hand in hand with more persons having one or more disabilities or handicaps, and with an increased demand for health care services.

Some new health risks have emerged, such as AIDS and drug dependency. Lifestyles detrimental to health, such as smoking and excessive drinking, are having a negative effect on the further improvement of health and on the lowering of mortality.

These developments have brought Member States' health systems under increasing strain: expenditure on health is being constantly forced upwards while the pressure on public finances has led Member States to place constraints on public expenditure, including the area of health.

— Over the last five decades, the total increase in life expectancy is well over 10 years.
— Women are living, on average, about six years longer than men.
— Differences between Member States in life expectancy are narrowing.
— Two out of three Europeans claim to be in good health.
— One in three men and one in four women develop cancer before the age of 75.
— Breast cancer is the most prevalent cancer in women.
— Lung cancer in women is increasing. For men there is a decrease in some Member States.
— On average, 29 % of the population aged 15 and over is smoking every day; increased smoking in adolescents gives rise for concern.
— Newly reported AIDS cases in the EU are estimated to have decreased by 10 % in 1996.
— Between 1985 and 1995/1996, the proportion of GDP devoted to health care increased in all but four countries.

According to the Treaties, Community action in the area of public health focuses in particular on encouraging co-operation between Member States, lending support to their action, promoting co-ordination of their policies and programmes, and making better use of Community policies where these relate to public health.

The Community's public health strategy until around the turn of the century is centred on the development of eight action programmes, six of these focusing on specific disease areas, complemented by two further 'horizontal' programmes, which deal with general issues such as health monitoring and health promotion.

Community action in the field of public health

(Reference to official documents in brackets)	Date of adoption by Commission (EC), Council (C) and European Parliament (EP)
— Framework for action in the field of public health (COM(93)559 final)	EC - Nov 1993
— Programme of Community action on health promotion, information, education and training (1996-2000) - Decision N° 645/96/EC (OJ N° L 95 of 16.4.1996, p.1)	C/EP - March 1996
— Third action plan to combat cancer (1996-2000) Decision N° 646/96/EC (OJ N° L 95 of 16.4.1996, p.9)	C/EP - March 1996
— Programme of Community action on the prevention of AIDS and certain other communicable diseases (1996-2000) - Decision N° 647/96/EC (OJ N° L 95 of 16.4.1996, p.16)	C/EP - March 1996
— Proposal for creating a network for the epidemiological surveillance and control of communicable diseases in the European Community (COM(96)78 final) (OJ N° C123, 26.4 1996, p.10)	EC - March 1996
— Programme of Community action for the prevention of drug dependence (1996-2000) - Decision N° 102/97/EC (OJ N° L 19 of 22.1.1997, p.1)	C/EP - Dec 1996
— Programme of Community action on health monitoring (1997-2001) - Decision N° 1400/97/EC (OJ N° L 193 of 22.7.997, p1)	C/EP - June 1997
— Proposal for a programme of Community action on injury prevention (COM(97)178 final) (OJ N° C202, 2.7 1997, p.20)	EC - May 1997
— Proposal for a programme of Community action on rare diseases (COM(97)225 final) (OJ N° 203, 3.7 1997, p.6)	EC - May 1997
— Proposal for a programme of Community action on pollution-related diseases (COM(97)266 final) (OJ N° 214, 16.7 1997, p.7)	EC - June 1997

Europeans live longer...

According to mortality rates measured in 1996, baby girls in the European Union may expect to live on average 80.5 years and newly born boys 74 years. The USA has reported levels similar to those in the EU, while Japan has recorded higher levels (Figure 1).

Since 1945 the total rise in life expectancy amounts to well over 10 years. The average increase was almost 2 years every decade (Figure 2).

Figure 1 - Life expectancy at birth, EU-15 and selected countries, 1996

Source : Eurostat Demographic Statistics

Figure 2 - Life expectancy at birth, EU-15, 1960-1996

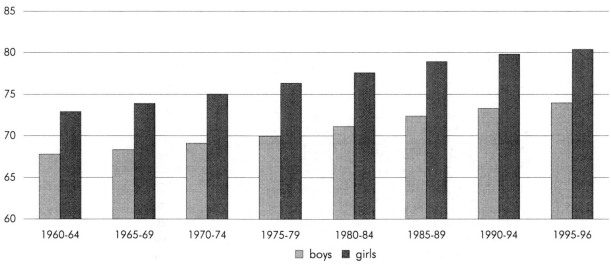

Source : Eurostat Demographic Statistics

Life expectancy

Life expectancy at birth is the average number of years a person would live if age-specific mortality rates observed for a certain calendar year or period were to continue.

The gender difference was and still is substantial: women live on average six years longer than men. But there are remarkable differences between the Member States (Figure 3).

According to Eurostat's population scenarios, life expectancy will continue to rise over the next 50 years (see chapter on Population).

Progress in medical research and care has led to a dramatic improvement in the infant mortality rate over the last 35 years. In 1960, an average of 35 infants per 1 000 live births died before they reached their first birthday. By 1995, the rate had fallen to 6 deaths per 1 000 live births. In 1960 and, to a lesser extent, 1980, there were appreciable differences between Member States. Today, however, the picture is homogeneous throughout the Union with the rate ranging from 4 to 8 deaths depending on the country.

Figure 3 - Life expectancy at birth: number of years women live longer than men, 1996, EU-15 and selected countries

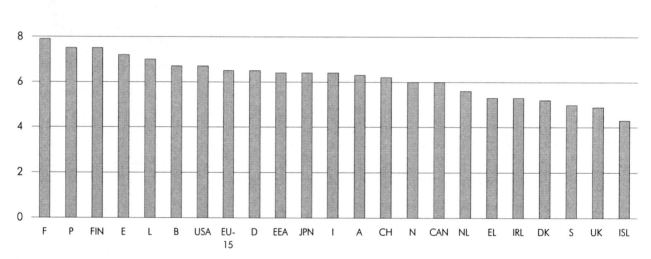

Source : Eurostat Demographic Statistics

Table 1 - Infant mortality rate, 1960-1995

(per 1 000 live births)

	EU-15	B	DK	D	EL	E	F	IRL	I	L	NL	A	P	FIN	S	UK
1960	35	31	22	35	40	44	28	29	44	32	18	38	78	21	17	22
1980	12	12	8	12	18	12	10	11	15	12	9	14	24	8	7	12
1995	6*	6	5	5	8	6*	5*	6	6*	6	6	5	8	4	4	6

The rate is defined as the number of infants who die within the first year of life divided by the number of live births (per 1 000 live births).
Source : Eurostat Demographic Statistics

Two thirds of Europeans claim to be in 'good' health...

Living longer does not necessarily mean living in better health. Therefore, information on the status of health is becoming much more important; such information is still scarce in the European Union and the data available at present are not easily comparable. From the European Community Household Panel (ECHP), it appears that two out of three Europeans of 16 years of age and over perceive their own health as 'very good' (22 %) or 'good' (43 %) One out of ten reports a 'bad' (7 %) or 'very bad' (3 %) health status; 25 % perceive their own health as 'fair' (Figure 4).

For the total population these percentages may become somewhat higher since a considerable number of Europeans live in homes or institutions for long-term nursing care because they cannot live independently, e.g. due to a physical handicap, mental deficiency or terminal disease.

Health questions in the ECHP used in this chapter

115. How is your health in general? (very good; good; fair; bad ; very bad)

116. Are you hampered in your daily activities by any chronic physical or mental problem, illness or disability? (yes, severely; yes to some extent; no)

Age standardisation

Because health is related to age, and the age distribution varies between Member States, it could be misleading to compare Member State totals on health variables without age standardisation. For that reason we computed age-standardised figures, meaning that in all Member States the age distribution according to the European standard population was used to recalculate the Member State totals.

Figure 4 - Percentage of population[1] with perceived health "bad" and "very bad", EU-12, 1994

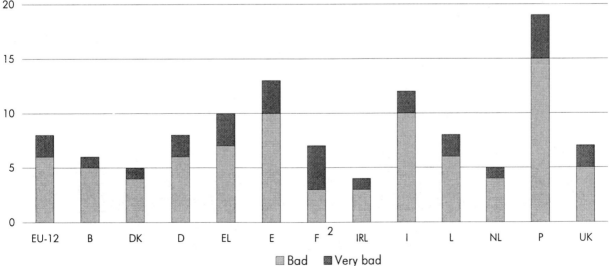

(as a % of the population aged 16 and over)

Bad   Very bad

[1] European standard population (see Box above)

[2] France: satisfaction with health is measured: "not at all satisfied" and "not satisfied" are shown in the graph

Source : Eurostat - European Community Household Panel (ECHP) ; first wave 1994

From the same survey we know that almost a quarter of persons living in house-holds report being hampered in their daily activities because of a 'chronic physical or mental health problem, illness or disability' (8 % are 'severely' hampered, 16 % 'to some extent') (Figure 5). These proportions are in line with estimates made by Euro-stat and Member States about persons with a physical disability.

In all Member States, the ECHP reveals that persons with a high level of education and/or income report better health than persons with a low level of education and/or income (Figure 6).

Figure 5 - Percentage of population[1] hampered in their daily activities because of chronic conditions, EU-12, 1994

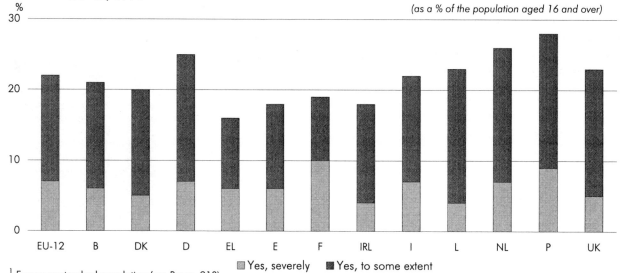

(as a % of the population aged 16 and over)

☐ Yes, severely ■ Yes, to some extent

[1] European standard population (see Box p. 213)
Source: Eurostat - European Community Household Panel (ECHP) ; first wave 1994

Figure 6 - Percentage of population[1] with perceived health "(very) bad" by level of education, EU-12, 1994

(as a % of the population aged 16 and over)

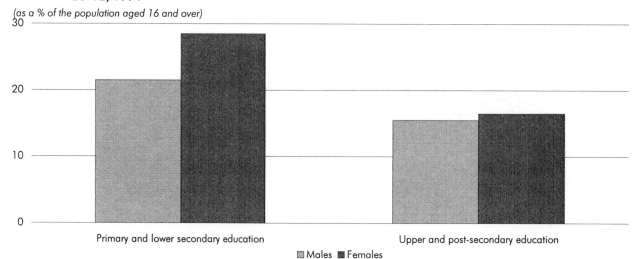

☐ Males ■ Females

[1] European standard population (see Box p. 213)
Source : Eurostat - European Community Household Panel (ECHP) ; first wave 1994

Cardio-vascular diseases and cancer remain the major causes of death

Mortality is dominated by four main groups of causes of death: cardio-vascular diseases (heart and blood vessels), cancer, respiratory diseases and external causes (including accidents and suicides), which together account for at about 75% of all deaths (Figure 7).

Many of these important causes of death are strongly related to lifestyles such as smoking and diet, which underline the importance of actions launched at Community level towards the prevention of diseases and on health information and education.

Mortality patterns differ significantly according to age and sex. As a general rule, mortality is higher among men than women in all age groups. There is a large variation between Member States in the standard death rates (SDR) for women (for the ages 25-74): in Denmark, United Kingdom and Ireland women have a significantly higher mortality rate than the EU average (see box p. 216).

Figure 7 - Groups of causes of death in the nineties, EU-15

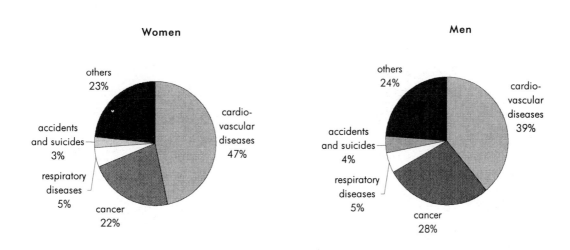

Note : E, IRL, I, S - 1993 data. DK, F, NL, UK - 1994 data. Other countries - 1995 data
Source : World Health Statistics Annual, WHO Geneva

After the first year of life, mortality reaches its lowest level within the 5-10 year old age-group, and increases thereafter with age. While cancers and heart diseases dominate total mortality, accidents and suicides represent more than half of the deaths in the younger age group (15-34) (Figure 8).

Causes of death statistics

In all EU Member States every death is registered: the cause of death, which is given on the death certificate, is coded according to the recommendations of the World Health Organisation (WHO) and following the rules of the International Classification of Diseases (ICD).

Standard death rates (SDR) by age

The mortality rate is affected by the age structure of the population. The age effect can be offset, in part at least, by the use of a standard population. The standardised rate is thus an adjusted gross rate that enables comparisons to be made between countries and between the two sexes. Here, the standard reference population is the 'standard European population', i.e. structured by age in the 'region of Europe' as defined by the WHO.

Cardio-vascular diseases include ischaemic heart diseases, dominated by acute myocardial infarct (heart attack), cerebrovascular diseases ('brain infarct' or stroke), arteriosclerosis and diseases of other parts of the circulatory system, such as trombophlebitis.

Respiratory diseases include inter alia respiratory infections, pneumonia, pleuritis and asthma.

Figure 8 - Distribution of total deaths by cause and sex for ages 15-34 years, EU-12, 1991

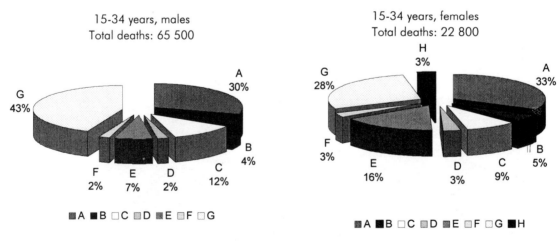

15-34 years, males
Total deaths: 65 500

15-34 years, females
Total deaths: 22 800

■A ■B □C ▨D ▨E □F □G

■A ■B □C ▨D ▨E □F □G ■H

A: other causes
B: other cardiovascular diseases
C: suicide
D: respiratory diseases

E: other cancers
F: cardiovascular diseases (mainly heart infarct for men and stroke for women)
G: accidents
H: breast cancer

Source : World Health Statistics Annual, WHO Geneva

Ischaemic heart diseases (predominantly acute heart infarct) account for nearly half of all deaths from cardio-vascular diseases. Acute heart infarct is the largest single cause of death in the European Union, representing around 20 % of all deaths. However, for more than ten years a decline in the number of deaths due to ischaemic heart diseases has been observed in some EU countries. More recently, this downward trend has become evident in the majority of countries although it is more striking in the northern EU Member States, in the younger age group and among men. It is important to note, however, that this cause of death is lower in the southern Member States than elsewhere in the EU (Table 2).

One-third of men and one-quarter of women develop cancer before the age of 75 ... and one-fifth of men and one in ten women will die from cancer before that age. In the EU, breast cancer and lung cancer are the most reported single causes of cancer death (Table 2).

Table 2 - Standardised death rates for ischaemic heart diseases by sex, 1985-1994

(per 100 000 population)

	1985		1990		1994	
	Men	Women	Men	Women	Men	Women
EU-15	215	96	186	86	171	81
B	172	75	129	55	:	:
DK	345	166	293	148	233	114
D	257	113	225	107	219	109
EL	130	53	137	59	123	56
E	114	50	106	48	105	47
F	112	48	91	40	81	34
IRL	399	182	339	157	319	149
I	151	70	135	63	128	60
L	223	95	163	68	150	67
NL	248	102	194	82	166	73
A	238	109	216	108	211	107
P	114	55	119	60	104	54
FIN	428	172	359	158	300	142
S	354	158	270	120	247	114
UK	367	168	306	145	266	126

E, IRL, I, S : 1993 instead of 1994

Source : World Health Statistics Annual, WHO Geneva

In contrast to stomach cancer, which shows a downward trend, most other important cancers are still increasing with the exception of lung cancer among middle-aged men, where the risk and mortality appears to have stabilised or in some countries even decreased (Table 4).

The most prevalent cancer amongst women is still breast cancer (Table 3). Breast cancer cannot be prevented but survival rates can be significantly increased if breast cancer is found and treated early enough.

Table 3 - Standardised death rates for total, all cancers, lung cancer and breast cancer, EU-15, 1994

(per 100 000 population)

	TOTAL SDR		ALL CANCERS		LUNG CANCER		BREAST CANCER
	Men	Women	Men	Women	Men	Women	Women
EU-15	955	563	266	148	73	15	31
B[1]	1030	586	303	156	108	13	35
DK	1063	689	280	207	74	40	37
D	1028	610	266	159	69	13	31
EL	842	578	219	116	75	10	23
E[2]	913	516	258	118	71	5	25
F	878	454	284	126	68	8	28
IRL[2]	1132	709	274	181	72	27	37
I[2]	906	535	276	144	82	11	29
L	998	563	268	154	78	16	34
NL	953	567	286	162	96	19	38
A	985	596	251	155	62	15	31
P	1114	662	229	123	42	7	25
FIN	1031	577	222	126	62	10	23
S[2]	876	546	195	144	33	15	25
UK	967	616	262	177	77	31	37

[1] 1992

[2] 1993

Source : World Health Statistics Annual, WHO Geneva

Cancer of the cervix is the third most common female cancer in the EU. Since 1970, mortality rates for cervix cancer have fallen significantly (Table 5), especially for women under 65 years, which may be partly attributable to effective screening programmes (Table 8 p. 221). Early detection and screening is one of the key actions in the third EC action plan against cancer (1996-2000).

Table 4 - Standardised death rates for cancer of the trachea, bronchus and lung, 1985-1994

(per 100 000 population)

	EU-15	B	DK	D	EL	E	F	IRL	I	L	NL	A	P	FIN	S	UK
1985																
Males	79	120	84	75	72	59	66	77	85	101	117	71	36	87	37	100
Females	12	10	28	10	10	5	6	25	10	15	12	12	6	10	12	30
1990																
Males	76	109	78	72	73	68	68	71	84	92	104	68	38	73	36	88
Females	14	12	34	11	11	5	7	27	11	13	15	13	6	10	14	31
1994																
Males	73	:	74	69	75	71	68	72	82	78	96	62	42	62	33	77
Females	15	:	40	13	10	5	8	27	11	16	19	15	7	10	15	31

Source : HFA database, WHO Geneva

Table 5 - Trend in the standardised death rate of cancer of the cervix, 1970-1992

(per 100 000 population)

	EU-15	B[2]	DK	D[4]	EL	E	FIN	IRL	I[3]	L[1]	NL	A	P[1]	FIN	S	UK
1992	3.28	3.36	7.13	4.62	1.86	2.24	2.23	4.43	1.11	3.50	2.98	3.82	3.42	1.88	2.98	5.26
% change since 1970	-41	-35	-41	-41	68	88	-34	-22	-50	-65	-60	-42	-69	-71	-62	-37

[1] 1971
[2] 1989
[3] 1991
[4] excluding new Länder to 1990

Source : HFA database, WHO Geneva

Changing diseases and lifestyles

So far, we have highlighted only a limited number of groups of diseases. But fatal sickness and death is dominated by hundreds and thousands of specific diseases and accidents; many of them are not (or are hardly) under control. This is the case for a range of cancers, heart diseases and many accidents on the road and at home, during leisure time or from violence. As a result, prevention and early detection require special attention.

Cancer screening as prevention

Although for young men the cancer incidence figures are decreasing in some countries, men are still mostly affected by lung cancer. But among women lung cancer is increasing. This different development is in line with smoking rates, which are rising among women, and falling among men (see p 223). For men and women, cancer of the colon and the rectum is the second most frequent cancer. (Table 6).

Table 6 - Estimated incidence of cancer in the European Union, 1990, ASR (W)[1]

(per 100 000 population)

	Males	Females
Lip, Oral Cavity, Pharynx	16.7	2.6
Oesophagus	6.1	1.2
Stomach	16.7	7.5
Colon/Rectum	33.8	23.7
Liver	5.8	2.0
Pancreas	6.1	3.9
Larynx	8.8	0.5
Lung	55.6	10.3
Melanoma of skin	4.6	6.5
Prostate	28.5	
Testis	4.8	
Breast		61.0
Cervix uteri		10.2
Corpus uteri		10.7
Ovary etc.		9.6
Bladder	18.8	3.4
Kidney etc.	8.6	3.9
Brain, nervous system	6.0	4.5
Thyroid	1.3	2.4
Non-Hodgkin lymphoma	9.5	5.9
Hodgkin's disease	2.7	1.7
Multiple myeloma	2.6	1.9
Leukaemias	8.3	5.5
All sites but skin	268.4	196.4

[1] ASR (W): Age-Standardised Rate using a standard world population

Source: EUCAN90 (IARC 1996)

For some cancers, screening programmes have proved effective in several Member States. Breast cancers detected through well-organised screening among 50-69 year-old women are, on average, identified four years earlier than clinical appearance: screening programmes in this age group have shown to be effective in reducing mortality. There appears to be a great difference between Member States in the proportion of women undergoing a screening test (Table 7). The highest percentages are recorded between 50 and 60 years of age. But in this age group, the percentages range from around 30% to around 70% depending on the country.

Early detection and screening of women for cervix cancer is one of the key actions in the third EC action plan against cancer (1996-2000). Women report more screening for cervix (Table 8) than for breast cancer.

Table 7 - Percentage of women reporting a mammography by age-group, EU-15, 1996

(%)

	EU-15	B	DK	D[1]	D[2]	EL	E	F	IRL	I	L	NL	A	P	FIN	S	UK
less than 40	8	11	11	15	14	3	13	6	3	3	14	6	19	11	2	2	3
40-49	25	31	34	30	26	19	33	24	10	27	47	17	41	22	12	30	11
50-59	38	32	51	37	31	31	32	34	2	36	64	51	57	36	58	71	40
60-69	28	17	57	26	23	15	24	33	7	19	36	56	27	23	34	57	33
70 and over	12	11	46	12	16	5	4	23	4	9	20	16	19	10	9	22	3
Total, 15 and over	18	17	31	22	21	12	19	18	5	15	28	18	29	18	18	28	13

[1] excluding new Länder

[2] new Länder

Source : European Commission DGX - Eurobarometer 44.3

Table 8 - Percentage of women reporting a cervical smear test, by age-group, EU-15, 1996

(%)

	EU-15	B	DK	D[1]	D[2]	EL	E	F	IRL	I	L	NL	A	P	FIN	S	UK
15-34	37	42	52	38	56	24	29	55	14	22	43	20	49	23	38	27	42
35-64	46	49	73	53	58	43	31	60	22	40	52	32	61	27	55	37	38
65 & over	17	20	58	18	27	16	13	21	1	16	18	15	22	7	13	11	9
Total, 15 & over	38	41	64	41	52	32	27	53	16	29	43	26	50	22	41	29	33

[1] Excluding new Länder

[2] New Länder

Source : European Commission DGX - Eurobarometer 44.3

Women account for an increasing proportion of AIDS cases

···

After a sudden and alarming rise in the eighties, which led the Commission to launch major HIV/AIDS prevention campaigns, annual newly reported AIDS cases are estimated to have decreased by 10 % in 1996 after reaching a plateau in 1994-1995. It appears that there are substantial differences between the countries: ranging from less than 10 cases per million inhabitants to well over 200 cases per million. High incidence rates are observed mainly in some southern EU countries (Table 9).

> Cases of *AIDS* notified for a given year may have been diagnosed in previous years. Consequently, the number of cases per year of diagnosis, adjusted to take account of notification delays, is more appropriate than the number of cases per year of notification for studying the epidemiological trends of AIDS.

Table 9 - AIDS incidence rates by year of diagnosis[1] and sex, 1985-1996

(per million population)

	1985		1990		1995		1996	
	M	F	M	F	M	F	M	F
EU-15	8	:	56	:	78	17	65	16
B	9	5	35	7	38	13	34	13
DK	14	1	71	7	72	11	50	10
D	9	0	35	4	36	5	27	5
F	19	2	130	24	147	36	109	26
EL	3	:	25	3	36	5	35	8
E	8	1	165	34	282	67	249	63
IRL	4	:	28	10	25	3	19	10
I	6	1	91	20	154	47	133	43
L	6	5	48	:	70	5	45	14
NL	9	0	52	5	55	10	43	8
A	7	1	36	7	38	13	28	6
P	6	0	47	5	124	22	136	25
FIN	2	:	6	0	15	1	8	1
S	8	:	28	3	36	7	25	5
UK	9	0	41	3	50	9	37	8

[1] Data adjusted for reporting delays (see box above)

Source : European Centre for Epidemiological Monitoring of AIDS, Paris

Among male adults and adolescents, injecting drug users (IDU) continue to account for the largest proportion of newly diagnosed cases (43%). According to mode of transmission, the second largest group is the homo/bisexual men (32%) followed by heterosexually active persons (14%). Women account for an increasing proportion of AIDS cases: 21% of adult/adolescent cases diagnosed in 1996 compared with 11% in 1986. Of these women, 46% had been heterosexually infected, a similar figure to the proportion of cases in the IDU group: 45% (Table 10).

Smoking, alcohol, drugs ... health threats to the young

It is widely recognised that smoking is a significant cause of heart diseases, cancers and respiratory diseases. While the general trend in smoking is downwards in most of the Member States, nearly one out of three Europeans (aged 15 and over) is smoking daily. In the younger age groups (15-34 years), 41 % of men and 34 % of women do so (Table 11).

Table 10 - Adult and adolescent new AIDS cases[1], according to mode of transmission, EU-15, 1996

Transmission group	Male		Female	
	N[1]	(%)[1]	N[1]	(%)[1]
Homo/bisexual	5448	32	.	.
Injecting drug user (IDU)	7266	43	1967	45
Homo/bisexual IDU	226	1	.	.
Haemophiliac/Coagulation disorder	183	1	8	0
Transfusion recipent	77	1	75	2
Heterosexual contact	2357	14	2005	46
Nosocomial infection	0	0	0	0
Other/Undetermined	1249	7	356	8
Male/Female total	16806	100	4411	100

[1] Data adjusted for reporting delays

Source : European Centre for Epidemiological Monitoring of AIDS, Paris

Table 11 - Percentage of population who are daily cigarette smokers, EU-15, 1995

(%)

	EU-15	B	DK	D	EL	E	F	IRL	I	L	NL	A	P	FIN	S	UK
Men and women																
Aged 15 and over	29	31	37	25	39	31	35	29	28	28	34	28	24	20	22	28
Aged 15-34	37	37	46	37	46	41	50	32	29	33	42	37	42	26	19	33
Men																
Aged 15 and over	34	34	39	32	49	39	39	31	33	28	37	35	37	22	18	30
Aged 15-34	41	39	53	43	51	41	54	34	29	32	49	49	54	32	16	32
Women																
Aged 15 and over	25	28	37	18	29	23	31	28	24	28	31	21	13	18	25	27
Aged 15-34	34	35	40	31	42	40	47	30	29	34	36	28	32	21	21	34

Source : European Commission DG X - Eurobarometer 43.0

The risk of a higher alcohol intake (more than one or two drinks per day) in relation to heart disease and mortality is relatively well-known. Consumption of alcohol is strongly associated with the risk of primary liver cancer, cancers of the upper digestive system and respiratory tract. There is some epidemiological evidence linking alcohol drinking to cancers of the colon and the female breast.

The average national figures on 'alcohol consumption', expressed as the average pure alcohol sold per capita (beverages calculated according to their alcohol volume) are presented in Figure 9. Sweden, Finland and UK have comparatively low figures with 7-9 litres per capita and year. France and Luxembourg lie at the other extreme (about 15 litres, per capita), with the remaining Member States averaging around 10-12 litres. However these data do not reflect entirely the alcohol 'consumption' of the inhabitants of each Member State, e.g. in Luxembourg, sales to non-residents are substantial and in all countries imports and any home production are concealed.

Figure 9 - Alcohol consumption: litres of pure alcohol sold per capita, EU-15, 1994

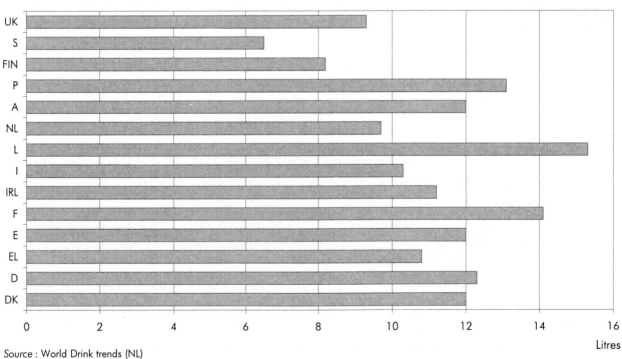

Source : World Drink trends (NL)

According to the WHO publication entitled "The Health of Youth", over 40% of 15-year-old boys in the United Kingdom, Belgium, Austria, France and Denmark say that they drink alcohol at least once a week (Figure 10). Girls of the same age appear to consume less alcohol. Many 15 year-olds admit to having been drunk at least twice (Table 12).

Drug use is primarily evident among younger adults. Throughout the Community cannabis is the most widely-used illegal drug (Table 13) while experience of heroine is much less common, except in major cities where heroin addiction can be much more prevalent than the national average.

Figure 10 - Percentage of boys and girls aged 15 admitting to drinking alcohol at least once a week, several Member States, 1993-1994

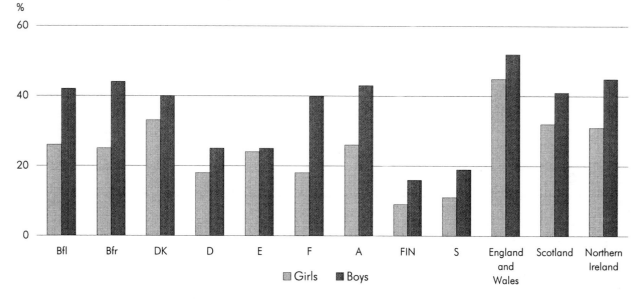

Source : The health of youth - a Cross-National Survey — WHO Regional Publications, European Series N° 69— 1996

Table 12 - Percentage of boys and girls (15 years of age) having been drunk at least twice, several Member States, 1993-1994

(%)

	Bfr	Bfl	DK	D	E	F	A	FIN	S	England and Wales	Scotland	Northern Ireland
Girls	20	16	67	26	19	13	30	50	22	59	51	36
Boys	27	31	65	34	23	24	46	52	27	61	53	44

Bfr : Belgium (french-speaking) Bfl : Belgium (flemish-speaking)

Source : The health of youth - a Cross-National Survey - WHO Regional Publications, European Series n° 69 - 1996

Table 13 - Lifetime prevalence of cannabis use in recent nation-wide surveys among general population in some EU countries

Country		Year	Method	All adults (age range)	(%)	Younger adults (age range)	(%)
Austria		1994	Interview	-		(15-40)	15
Belgium (Flemish Com.)		1995	Phone	(18-65)	5	(18-39)	9
Denmark	(1)	1994	Interview	-		(16-44)	37
	(2)	1994	Mail	(18-69)	31	(18-44)	43
Finland	(1)	1992	Mail	(18-74)	5	(18-34)	9
France	(1)	1992	Phone	(18-75)	11	(18-34)	22
		1995 (a)	Phone	(18-75)	15	(18-39)	26
Germany	(W)	1995	Phone	(18-59)	14	(18-39)	21
	(E)	1995	Phone	(18-59)	4	(18-39)	6
Spain		1995	Interview.	(15-70)	13	(15-39)	22
Sweden		1996	Interview	(15-75)	8	(16-39)	11
United Kingdom		1994	Interview	(16-59)	21	(16-39)	29

* Due to the differences in methodology among these surveys results cannot be directly compared. Some data are estimated.

Source : The 1997 annual report on the State of the drugs problem in the EU - EMCDDA - Lisbon

OECD "Ecosanté" database

The expenditure data are taken from the OECD 'Ecosanté' database. In its health accounts the OECD looks at the financing aspect of health care in its entirety.

Total health expenditure includes the medical care households receive (ranging from hospitals and physicians to ambulance services and pharmaceutical products), and their health expenses, including cost-sharing and the medicines they buy on their own initiative; government-supplied health services (e.g. schools, vaccination campaigns), investment in clinics, laboratories, etc.; administration costs; research and development; industrial medicine, outlays of voluntary organisations, caritative institutions and non-governmental health plans.

Public expenditure on health is the publicly financed share (i.e. by central and local authorities, public health centres and social insurance bodies) of total expenditure on health, namely: direct outlays; reimbursements to households (transfers); payments to producers to lower costs (subsidies); direct investments and capital transfers to private investors; the public sector also lowers the household burden through tax deductions and tax credits.

Rising health care expenditure

In 1995, Germany and Luxembourg spent twice as much per capita on health than Spain, Ireland and Portugal and three times more per capita than Greece. While the figure for Japan is close to that of most EU countries, health expenditure in the US is more than twice that of many EU countries (Table 14).

In 1995, France, the Netherlands and Portugal spent more than 8% of their GDP on health, which is still lower than the 14% in the US.

During the last decade (1985 to 1995/1996) all but four countries devoted an increased proportion of GDP to health care. In Sweden, Ireland and Germany the proportion decreased while it remained almost unchanged in Denmark. These variations over time are caused by the combined changes to Gross Domestic Product (GDP) and total health expenditure (Table 15).

Table 14 - Total health expenditure per head of population, 1985 - 1996

(PPS)

	B	DK	D	EL	E	F	IRL	I	L	NL	A	P	FIN	S	UK	USA	J
1985	890	816	1274	288	455	1088	586	834	895	932	815	387	852	1174	670	1733	823
1990	1247	1069	1642	389	813	1539	748	1322	1499	1325	1180	616	1292	1492	957	2689	1082
1995	1665	1368	2134	703	1075	1972	1106	1507	2206	1728	1634	1035	1373	1360	1246	3644	1581
1996	1693	1430	2222	748	1131	1978	923	1520	:	1756	1681	1077	1389	1405	1304	3708	:

PPS: purchasing power standards
Source : OECD Health Data, 1997

Table 15 - Total health expenditure as a percentage of GDP, 1985-1996

(%)

	B	DK	D	EL	E	F	IRL	I	L	NL	P	A	FIN	S	UK	USA	J
1985	7.4	6.3	8.5	4.0	5.7	8.5	7.8	7.1	6.1	7.9	6.3	6.7	7.3	9.0	5.9	10.7	6.7
1990	7.6	6.5	8.9	4.2	6.9	8.9	6.6	8.1	6.6	8.3	6.5	7.1	8.0	8.8	6.0	12.7	6.0
1995	8.0	6.4	7.7	5.8	7.6	9.9	:	7.7	7.0	8.8	8.2	7.9	7.7	7.2	6.9	14.2	7.2
1996	7.9	6.4	7.5	5.9	:	9.6	:	7.6	:	:	8.2	7.9	7.5	:	6.9	14.2	:

Source : OECD Health Data, 1997

Expenditure depends partly on the price of goods and services, and partly on the supply. Price inflation plays a part in the growth of nominal GDP and total health expenditure. The specific health care cost increases might be somewhat higher (or lower) than general inflation. However, it is particularly difficult to measure medical-specific inflation.

The general problem with the health sector is that 'health', as an output cannot be measured directly. While in most economic sectors goods and prices are readily available, these cannot be recorded directly for e.g. ambulatory and hospital services. Besides (medical) price inflation, various other factors have contributed to the increase in medical expenditure: in particular, the increased demand for health care by older populations with higher levels of disability and chronic diseases, the constant development of new and expensive medical techniques and the increased access to and utilisation of these techniques, together with increasing consumers' expectations of a healthier life.

In 1993, public expenditure (the proportion of total expenditure on health financed by the central and local authorities, public health centres and social insurance bodies) accounted on average for three quarters of total expenditure on health care. In the period 1985-1993 the increase in public expenditure on health care was generally lower than the increase in total health expenditure (Figure 11). These expenditure data have been calculated in constant 1990 prices, in order to remove the influence of the general inflation between 1985 and 1993. It should be borne in mind that the resulting expenditure changes may be attributable to 'price effects' of medical goods and services or to 'volume effects' or a combination of the two.

Figure 11 - Change (1980-1993) in total and public health expenditure, in constant prices, EU-15

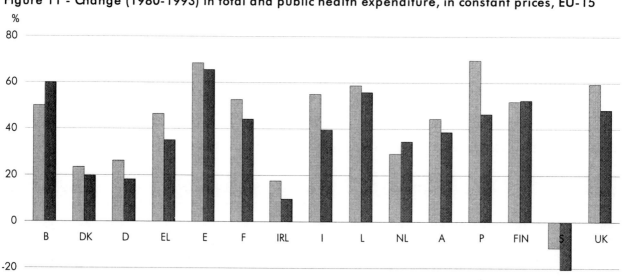

Source : OECD Health Data, 1997

BIBLIOGRAPHY

Bibliography

General

- European Commission, *Growth, Competitiveness, Employment – The challenges and Ways forward into the 21ˢᵗ Century, White Paper*, Brussels, 1993

- European Commission, *White Paper on European Social Policy*, Brussels, 1994

- Eurostat New Cronos database

- REGIO: Eurostat Regional database

- Eurostat *Yearbook 1997* – Annual publication

- Eurostat *Social Portrait of Europe*, Luxembourg, 1995

- Eurostat *Living conditions in Europe – Selected social indicators*, Luxembourg, 1998

- J. Vogel, *Social Report for the Nordic countries. Living Conditions and Inequality in the late 1980's*, Copenhagen, 1991

- INSEE, *Données sociales 1996 – La société française*, France, 1996

- Social and Cultural Planning Office, *Social and Cultural Report*, the Netherlands, 1996

- A. Barreto, *A situação Social em Portugal, 1960-1995*, Instituto de Ciências Sociais – Universidade de Lisboa, 1996

- Eurostat, *Youth in the European Union. From education to working life*, Luxembourg, 1997

- Eurostat, *Women and Men in the European Union – A statistical portrait*, Luxembourg, 1995

- UN-ECE, Statistics Sweden, Eurostat, UN International Research and Training Institute for the Advancement of Women, *Women and Men in Europe and North America*, Geneva, 1995

Economic Background — Chapter 1

- Communication from the Commission, *Social Action Programme 1998-2000*, Brussels 29/4/1998, Com-final

- European Commission, Directorate General for Economic and Financial Affairs, *Annual Economic Report*, Brussels, 1997

- European Commission, Eurostat, Statistics Europe, *The Economic Accounts of the European Union*, 1996

- European Commission, *First Report on Economic and Social Cohesion*, 1996

- Commission of the European Community, Directorate General for Regional Policy, *The Regions in the 90's*, Brussels, 1995

- Eurostat, *Social Protection expenditure and receipts, 1980-1995*, Doc. E2/Soc.Prot/98/3/EN

- European Commission, *Social Protection Report*, Preliminary 1998

- W. Adema, M. Einerhand, B. Eklind, J. Lotz and M. Pearson, *Net Public Social Expenditure*, Labour market and social policy, OECD Occasional papers No. 19, 1996

- NIDI, *Population, Labour and Social Protection in the European Union, Dilemnas and prospects*, Report No. 52, The Hague, 1998

- Eurostat, Statistics in Focus:

- EMU, *a Powerful Economic Entity*, General statistics, No. 1/1998

- *Almost one in four European regions below 75% of the 1995 EU average per capita GDP*, Regions No. 1/1998

Population — Chapter 2

- European Commission Directorate-General for Economic and Financial Affairs, *The Welfare State in Europe - challenges and reforms*, 1997, European Economy Reports and Studies, No. 4

- European Commission Directorate-General for Economic and Financial Affairs, D. Franco and T. Munzi, *Public pension expenditure prospects in the European Union: a survey of national projections*, 1996, European Economy Reports and Studies, No. 3

- European Commission Directorate-General for Employment, Industrial Relations and Social Affairs, *Demographic Report 1997*

- Eurostat, *Demographic Statistics 1998*

- Eurostat, *Migration Statistics 1996*

- Eurostat, *Population, households and dwellings in Europe: Main results of the 1990/91 censuses, 1996*

- Eurostat, Statistics in Focus - Population and Social Conditions:

  — *Slightly more births than deaths in 1997: the first set of demographic estimates for 1997*, No. 1/1998

  — Decline in births halted in 1996: principal demographic trends in the EU in 1996, No. 10/1997

  — Beyond the predictable: demographic changes in the EU up to 2050, No. 7/1997.

Households and Families — Chapter 3

- W.Dumon, DG V, European Observatory on National Family Policies, *Changing family policies in the Member States of the European Union*, 1994

- DG V, *Flexible working and the reconciliation of work and family life – or a new form of precariousness*, 1998

- Eurostat Statistics in Focus :

  — *About one marriage in four in the EU ends in divorce*, No. 14/1997

  — Family responsibilities and how they are shared in European households, No. 5/1997

Education and Training — Chapter 4

- European Commission, *Teaching and learning – Towards the learning society*, 1995

- Eurostat, *Education across the European Union – statistics and indicators, 1997*. Annual publication

- Eurydice/Cedefop/DG XXII, *Structures of the Education and Initial Training Systems in the European Union*, 1995

- Eurostat/Eurydice/DG XXII, *Key data on Education in the European Union, 1997*, joint publication

- Eurostat/Cedefop/DG XXII, *Key data on Vocational Training in the European Union 1997*, joint publication

- Eurostat, *Continuing Vocational Training Survey in Enterprises 1994 (CVTS) Main results*, 1997

- Eurostat Statistics in Focus – Population and Social Conditions:

- *Education and job prospects : what can we expect today*, No. 12/1995

- *Continuing Vocational Training Survey in enterprises : an essential part of lifelong learning*, No. 7/1996

- *Education in the European Union : Opportunities and choices*, No. 4/1997

- *Training after 30 years of age*, No. 11/1997

- *Transition from school to working life*, forthcoming

Labour Market — Chapter 5

- Council of the European Union, *Council Resolution of 15 December 1997 on the 1998 Employment Guidelines*, Official Journal No. C 030 28/01/1998, P. 1-5

- European Commission, *Employment in Europe 1997*, Luxembourg 1997, annual publication

- Eurostat, *Labour Force Survey – 1997 Results*, Luxembourg 1998, Annual publication

- Eurostat, *Labour Market Statistics 2/1998*, Luxembourg 1998, quarterly publication

- Eurostat Statistics in Focus – Population and Social Conditions:

- *Part-time work in the European Union*, No.13/1997

- *Labour Force Survey. Principal Results 1997*, No. 5/1998

- Eurostat Statistics in Focus – Regions

- *Unemployment in the regions of the European Union in 1997*, No. 3/1998

- OECD, *Employment Outlook 1997*, Paris 1997, Annual publication

- OECD, *The OECD Jobs Study: Facts, Analysis, Strategies*, Paris, 1994

- OECD, *The OECD Jobs Study: Evidence and Explanations*, Paris, 1994

- OECD, *Implementing the OECD Jobs Strategy: Lessons from Member Countries' Experience*, Paris, 1997

Working Environment — Chapter 6

- European Commission, *Communication on a Community programme concerning safety, hygiene and health at work (1996 - 2000)* - COM(95) 282 final.

- DG V, *Europe for safety and health at work* - Social Europe 3/1993.

- DG V, *Information notices on diagnosis of occupational diseases - 1994* (re-issue 1997).

- Eurostat, *Accidents at work in the European Union 1993-94-95* - CD-Rom (forthcoming).

- Lehner, Franz, *The European response to advanced manufacturing and globalisation*, Anthropocentric production systems (APS), Research Papers Series Vol. 4 (FAST programme), Brussels 1991.

- Phil, James, *Occupational Health and Safety, in*: Gold, Michael: "The Social dimension - Employment policy in the European Community", London, 1995.

- European Foundation for the improvement of living and Working Conditions, *Stress at work*, Euro-Review, Dublin 1997.

- Eurostat Statistics in Focus – Population and Social Conditions:

- *Accidents at work in the European Union in 1994*, No. 2/1998

Earnings — Chapter 7

- Eurostat, *Earnings, Industry and Services 1995*, Luxembourg 1996

- Eurostat, *Net earnings of employees in manufacturing industry in the European Union – Data 1980-1996*, Luxembourg, 1998

- Eurostat, *Minimum wages 1997 - A comparative study*, Luxembourg, 1998

- Bazen, S., and Benhayoun, G. (1996), *Les Bas salaires en Europe*, Presses Universitaires de France, collection "Que sais-je ?"

- Di Ruzza, R., and Pruvost, F. (1993), *Les salaires minima dans la Communauté Economique Européenne*, ISERES – Etudes et recherches

- Institute of Personnel Management (1991), *Minimum wage: An analysis of the issues*

- Centre d'Etude des Revenus et des Coûts (1991), *Les bas salaires dans les pays de la Communauté économique européenne*, La Documentation Française

- Eurostat Statistics in Focus – Population and Social Conditions:

- *How evenly are Earnings distributed ?*, No. 15/1997

- *Minimum wages in the European Union 1997*, No. 16/1997

- *The distribution of Earnings in the European Union*, No. 8/1998

Income — Chapter 8

- Institute of Social Studies Advisory Services, *Poverty in figures : Europe in the early 1980's*, Eurostat, 1990

- Aldi J.M. Hagenaars, Klaas de Vos, Asghas Zaidi, *Poverty statistics in the late 1980's : research based on micro data*, Eurostat, 1994

- Eurostat, Erasmus University, Economic Institute Tilburg, *Trend analysis of poverty in the European Community*, Final Report 1995, Doc. No. POV/72/95 EN

- T. Atkinson, M. Glaude, J. Freyssinet, C. Seibel, *Pauvreté et exclusion*, La Documentation Française, Paris, 1998

- WZB, J. O'Reilly, C. Spee, *Regulating work and Welfare of the future : Towards a new social contract or a new gender contract ?* Discussion paper, Berlin, 1997

- Conseil Supérieur de l'Emploi des Revenus et des Coûts, *Inégalités d'emploi et de revenu – les années 90*, La Documentation Française, Paris, 1996

- Statistics in Focus – Population and Social Conditions:

- Eurostat, *Income Distribution and poverty in EU12 – 1993*, No. 6/1997

- Eurostat, OECD, *Low income and low pay in a household context (EU12)*, No. 6/1998

- Vijay Verma, *Income Distribution and Poverty in EU13 – 1994*, Forthcoming

Consumption, Housing Conditions — Chapter 9

- Eurostat. Household budget Surveys: Comparative tables 1988-1994 (on CD-Rom – to be published in 1998).

- European Parliament Committee on Social Affairs and Employment. Report on the social aspects of housing. 15 April 1997.

- Eurostat Statistics in Focus – Population and Social Conditions:

  — *Housing conditions in the Europe of Twelve in 1994*, No.9/1997.

  — Household consumption in the European Union in 1994, No.4/1998.

Life Expectancy and Health — Chapter 10

- EC, *Communication of 24 November 1993 on the framework for action in the field of public health* - COM(93)559 final

- European Parliament and Council, Decision No. 1400/97/EC of the European Parliament and of the Council of 30 June 1997 adopting a programme of Community action on monitoring within the framework for action in the field of public health (1997 to 2001) – OJ No L 193, 22.7.97, p.1

- EC/DG V, *The state of health in the European Community*, annual health status report 1996

- EC/DG V, *The state of women's health in the European Community*, annual health status report 1997

- EC/DG V, *Public health in Europe,* 1997

- WHO, Geneva, *World Health Statistics Annual*, 1995

- WHO, Regional Office for Europe, Copenhagen, *Health for All (HFA) database* 1997

- WHO, Regional Office for Europe, Copenhagen, *The Health of Europe*, 1993

- WHO, Regional Office for Europe, Copenhagen, *Reform strategies*, 1996

- OECD, Paris, *ECO-Santé database*, 1997

- European Centre for Epidemiological Monitoring of AIDS, Paris, *HIV/AIDS Surveillance in Europe (quarterly reports)*, 1996, 1997

- Eurosurveillance team, Paris, *Eurosurveillance: European communicable diseases bulletin (monthly bulletins)*, 1996, 1997

- International Agency for Research on Cancer (IARC), Lyon, *Trends in cancer incidence and mortality*, 1993

- European Monitoring centre for Drugs and Drug Addiction (EMCDDA), Lisbon, *Annual Report on the state of the Drugs Problem in the EU*, reports of 1995 and of 1997

- Eurostat Statistics in Focus – Population and Social Conditions:

- *Self-reported health in the European Community*, No. 12/1997

ES — Clasificación de las publicaciones de Eurostat

TEMA

- 0 Diversos (rosa)
- 1 Estadísticas generales (azul oscuro)
- 2 Economía y finanzas (violeta)
- 3 Población y condiciones sociales (amarillo)
- 4 Energía e industria (azul claro)
- 5 Agricultura, silvicultura y pesca (verde)
- 6 Comercio exterior (rojo)
- 7 Comercio, servicios y transportes (naranja)
- 8 Medio ambiente (turquesa)
- 9 Investigación y desarrollo (marrón)

SERIE

- A Anuarios y estadísticas anuales
- B Estadísticas coyunturales
- C Cuentas y encuestas
- D Estudios e investigación
- E Métodos
- F Estadísticas breves

GR — Ταξινόμηση των δημοσιεύσεων της Eurostat

ΘΕΜΑ

- 0 Διάφορα (ροζ)
- 1 Γενικές στατιστικές (βαθύ μπλε)
- 2 Οικονομία και δημοσιονομικά (βιολετί)
- 3 Πληθυσμός και κοινωνικές συνθήκες (κίτρινο)
- 4 Ενέργεια και βιομηχανία (μπλε)
- 5 Γεωργία, δάση και αλιεία (πράσινο)
- 6 Εξωτερικό εμπόριο (κόκκινο)
- 7 Εμπόριο, υπηρεσίες και μεταφορές (πορτοκαλί)
- 8 Περιβάλλον (τουρκουάζ)
- 9 Έρευνα και ανάπτυξη (καφέ)

ΣΕΙΡΑ

- A Επετηρίδες και ετήσιες στατιστικές
- B Συγκυριακές στατιστικές
- C Λογαριασμοί και έρευνες
- D Μελέτες και έρευνα
- E Μέθοδοι
- F Στατιστικές εν συντομία

IT — Classificazione delle pubblicazioni dell'Eurostat

TEMA

- 0 Diverse (rosa)
- 1 Statistiche generali (blu)
- 2 Economia e finanze (viola)
- 3 Popolazione e condizioni sociali (giallo)
- 4 Energia e industria (azzurro)
- 5 Agricoltura, foreste e pesca (verde)
- 6 Commercio estero (rosso)
- 7 Commercio, servizi e trasporti (arancione)
- 8 Ambiente (turchese)
- 9 Ricerca e sviluppo (marrone)

SERIE

- A Annuari e statistiche annuali
- B Statistiche sulla congiuntura
- C Conti e indagini
- D Studi e ricerche
- E Metodi
- F Statistiche in breve

FI — Eurostatin julkaisuluokitus

AIHE

- 0 Sekalaista (vaaleanpunainen)
- 1 Yleiset tilastot (yönsininen)
- 2 Talous ja rahoitus (violetti)
- 3 Väestö- ja sosiaalitilastot (keltainen)
- 4 Energia ja teollisuus (sininen)
- 5 Maa- ja metsätalous, kalastus (vihreä)
- 6 Ulkomaankauppa (punainen)
- 7 Kauppa, palvelut ja liikenne (oranssi)
- 8 Ympäristö (turkoosi)
- 9 Tutkimus ja kehitys (ruskea)

SARJA

- A Vuosikirjat ja vuositilastot
- B Suhdannetilastot
- C Laskennat ja kyselytutkimukset
- D Tutkimukset
- E Menetelmät
- F Tilastokatsaukset

DA — Klassifikation af Eurostats publikationer

EMNE

- 0 Diverse (rosa)
- 1 Almene statistikker (mørkeblå)
- 2 Økonomi og finanser (violet)
- 3 Befolkning og sociale forhold (gul)
- 4 Energi og industri (blå)
- 5 Landbrug, skovbrug og fiskeri (grøn)
- 6 Udenrigshandel (rød)
- 7 Handel, tjenesteydelser og transport (orange)
- 8 Miljø (turkis)
- 9 Forskning og udvikling (brun)

SERIE

- A Årbøger og årlige statistikker
- B Konjunkturstatistikker
- C Tællinger og rundspørger
- D Undersøgelser og forskning
- E Metoder
- F Statistikoversigter

EN — Classification of Eurostat publications

THEME

- 0 Miscellaneous (pink)
- 1 General statistics (midnight blue)
- 2 Economy and finance (violet)
- 3 Population and social conditions (yellow)
- 4 Energy and industry (blue)
- 5 Agriculture, forestry and fisheries (green)
- 6 External trade (red)
- 7 Distributive trades, services and transport (orange)
- 8 Environment (turquoise)
- 9 Research and development (brown)

SERIES

- A Yearbooks and yearly statistics
- B Short-term statistics
- C Accounts and surveys
- D Studies and research
- E Methods
- F Statistics in focus

NL — Classificatie van de publikaties van Eurostat

ONDERWERP

- 0 Diverse (roze)
- 1 Algemene statistiek (donkerblauw)
- 2 Economie en financiën (paars)
- 3 Bevolking en sociale voorwaarden (geel)
- 4 Energie en industrie (blauw)
- 5 Landbouw, bosbouw en visserij (groen)
- 6 Buitenlandse handel (rood)
- 7 Handel, diensten en vervoer (oranje)
- 8 Milieu (turkoois)
- 9 Onderzoek en ontwikkeling (bruin)

SERIE

- A Jaarboeken en jaarstatistieken
- B Conjunctuurstatistieken
- C Rekeningen en enquêtes
- D Studies en onderzoeken
- E Methoden
- F Statistieken in het kort

SV — Klassifikation av Eurostats publikationer

ÄMNE

- 0 Diverse (rosa)
- 1 Allmän statistik (mörkblå)
- 2 Ekonomi och finans (lila)
- 3 Befolkning och sociala förhållanden (gul)
- 4 Energi och industri (blå)
- 5 Jordbruk, skogsbruk och fiske (grön)
- 6 Utrikeshandel (röd)
- 7 Handel, tjänster och transport (orange)
- 8 Miljö (turkos)
- 9 Forskning och utveckling (brun)

SERIE

- A Årsböcker och årlig statistik
- B Konjunkturstatistik
- C Redogörelser och enkäter
- D Undersökningar och forskning
- E Metoder
- F Statistiköversikter

DE — Gliederung der Veröffentlichungen von Eurostat

THEMENKREIS

- 0 Verschiedenes (rosa)
- 1 Allgemeine Statistik (dunkelblau)
- 2 Wirtschaft und Finanzen (violett)
- 3 Bevölkerung und soziale Bedingungen (gelb)
- 4 Energie und Industrie (blau)
- 5 Land- und Forstwirtschaft, Fischerei (grün)
- 6 Außenhandel (rot)
- 7 Handel, Dienstleistungen und Verkehr (orange)
- 8 Umwelt (türkis)
- 9 Forschung und Entwicklung (braun)

REIHE

- A Jahrbücher und jährliche Statistiken
- B Konjunkturstatistiken
- C Konten und Erhebungen
- D Studien und Forschungsergebnisse
- E Methoden
- F Statistik kurzgefaßt

FR — Classification des publications d'Eurostat

THÈME

- 0 Divers (rose)
- 1 Statistiques générales (bleu nuit)
- 2 Économie et finances (violet)
- 3 Population et conditions sociales (jaune)
- 4 Énergie et industrie (bleu)
- 5 Agriculture, sylviculture et pêche (vert)
- 6 Commerce extérieur (rouge)
- 7 Commerce, services et transports (orange)
- 8 Environnement (turquoise)
- 9 Recherche et développement (brun)

SÉRIE

- A Annuaires et statistiques annuelles
- B Statistiques conjoncturelles
- C Comptes et enquêtes
- D Études et recherche
- E Méthodes
- F Statistiques en bref

PT — Classificação das publicações do Eurostat

TEMA

- 0 Diversos (rosa)
- 1 Estatísticas gerais (azul-escuro)
- 2 Economia e finanças (violeta)
- 3 População e condições sociais (amarelo)
- 4 Energia e indústria (azul)
- 5 Agricultura, silvicultura e pesca (verde)
- 6 Comércio externo (vermelho)
- 7 Comércio, serviços e transportes (laranja)
- 8 Ambiente (turquesa)
- 9 Investigação e desenvolvimento (castanho)

SÉRIE

- A Anuários e estatísticas anuais
- B Estatísticas conjunturais
- C Contas e inquéritos
- D Estudos e investigação
- E Métodos
- F Estatísticas breves

European Commission

Social portrait of Europe

Luxembourg: Office for Official Publications of the European Communities

1998 — V, 236 pp. — 21 x 29.7 cm

ISBN 92-827-9093-2

Price (excluding VAT) in Luxembourg: ECU 21

This third edition of the *Social portrait of Europe* provides a review of the current social trends in the 15 Member States of the European Union. The data used come mainly from the national statistical institutes and are based largely on harmonised sources available in Eurostat, such as the European labour force survey (LFS) and the European Community Household Panel (ECHP). The 10 chapters each focus on a different area of social policy: Economic background (Chapter 1), Population (Chapter 2), Households and families (Chapter 3), Education and training (Chapter 4), Labour market (Chapter 5), Working environment (Chapter 6), Earnings (Chapter 7), Income (Chapter 8), Consumption and housing conditions (Chapter 9), Life expectancy and health (Chapter 10).